HEARN'S JAPAN

Published by TOYO PRess:

TOYO REFERENCE SERIES

Alice Mabel Bacon, *Japanese Women*
Isabella Lucy Bird, *Traveling Japan's Deep Interior*
Frank Brinkley and Dairoku Kikuchi, *A History of the Japanese People*
John la Farge, *An Artist's Letters from Japan*
William Elliot Griffis, *The Religions of Japan*
Lafcadio Hearn, *Hearn's Japan. Vols. I-XIV*
Lucian Swift Kirtland, *Samurai Trails*
Inazo Nitobe, *Bushidō*
Kakuzo Okakura, *The Book of Tea*
Edward Sylvester Morse, *Japanese Homes and Their Surroundings*
Ernest Satow: *Japan's Critical Years*

TOYO ILLUSTRATED EDITIONS

Eiko Ozaki, *Warriors of Old Japan*
Eiko Ozaki, *Japanese Fairy Tales*
Lafcadio Hearn, *Hearn's Japan*

HEARN'S JAPAN

Writings from a Mystical Country

VOLUME I

LAFCADIO HEARN

EDITED BY WILLIAM DE LANGE

TOYO REFERENCE SERIES

First edition, 2018

Originally published as *Glimpses of Unfamiliar Japan I*

Published by TOYO PRess
Visit us at: **www.toyopress.com**

Copyright © 2018 TOYO PRess

ISBN 978-94-92722-08-9

Contents

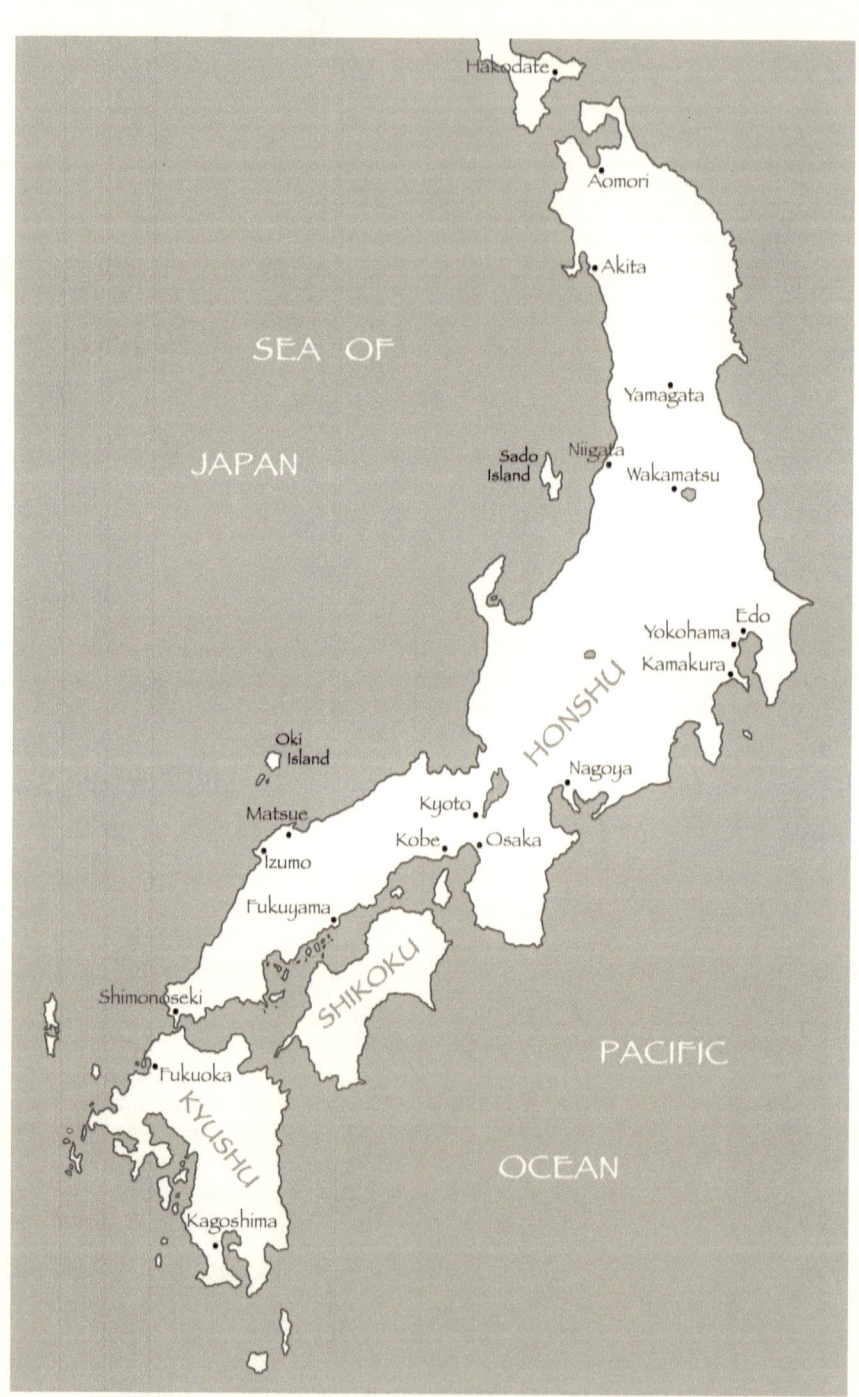

Hakodate

Aomori

Akita

SEA OF

Yamagata

JAPAN

Sado
Island

Niigata

Wakamatsu

HONSHU

Yokohama

Edo

Kamakura

Oki
Island

Nagoya

Matsue

Kyoto

Izumo

Kobe

Osaka

Fukuyama

SHIKOKU

Shimonoseki

PACIFIC

Fukuoka

KYUSHU

OCEAN

Kagoshima

First Impressions

'Do not fail to write down your first impressions as soon as possible,' said a kind English professor whom I had the pleasure of meeting soon after my arrival in Japan, 'they are evanescent, you know; they will never come to you again, once they have faded out. And yet of all the strange sensations you may receive in this country you will feel none so charming as these.' I am trying now to reproduce them from the hasty notes of the time, and find that they were even more fugitive than charming; something has evaporated from all my recollections of them—something impossible to recall. I neglected the friendly advice, in spite of all resolves to obey it: I could not, in those first weeks, resign myself to remain indoors and write, while there was yet so much to see and hear and feel in the sun-steeped ways of the wonderful Japanese city. Still, even if I could revive all the lost sensations of those first experiences, I doubt if I could express and fix them in words. The first charm of Japan is intangible and volatile as a perfume.

It began for me with my first *kuruma*-ride out of the European quarter of Yokohama into the Japanese town; and so much as I can recall of it is hereafter set down.

Kuruma
It is with the delicious surprise of the first journey through Japanese streets—unable to make one's *kuruma* runner understand anything but gestures, frantic gestures to roll on anywhere, everywhere, since all is unspeakably pleasurable and new—that one first receives the real sensation of being in the Orient, in this Far East so much read of, so long dreamed

of, yet, as the eyes bear witness, heretofore all unknown. There is a romance even in the first full consciousness of this rather commonplace fact; but for me this consciousness is transfigured inexpressibly by the divine beauty of the day. There is some charm unutterable in the morning air, cool with the coolness of Japanese spring and wind-waves from the snowy cone of Mount Fuji; a charm perhaps due rather to softest lucidity than to any positive tone—an atmospheric limpidity extraordinary, with only a suggestion of blue in it, through which the most distant objects appear focused with amazing sharpness. The sun is only pleasantly warm; the *jinrikisha*, or *kuruma*, is the most cosy little vehicle imaginable; and the street-vistas, as seen above the dancing white mushroom-shaped hat of my sandalled runner, have an allurement of which I fancy that I could never weary.

Elfish everything seems; for everything as well as everybody is small, and queer, and mysterious: the little houses under their blue roofs, the little shopfronts hung with blue, and the smiling little people in their blue costumes. The illusion is only broken by the occasional passing of a tall foreigner, and by divers shop signs bearing announcements in absurd attempts at English. Nevertheless such discords only serve to emphasise reality; they never materially lessen the fascination of the funny little streets.

It is at first a delightfully odd confusion only, as you look down one of them, through an interminable flutter of flags and swaying of dark blue drapery, all made beautiful and mysterious with Japanese or Chinese lettering. For there are no immediately discernible laws of construction or decoration: each building seems to have a fantastic prettiness of its own; nothing is exactly like anything else, and all is bewilderingly novel.

But gradually, after an hour passed in the quarter, the eye begins to recognise in a vague way some general plan in the construction of these low, light, queerly-gabled wooden houses, mostly unpainted, with their first stories all open to the street, and thin strips of roofing sloping above each shop-front, like awnings, back to the miniature balconies of paper-screened second stories. You begin to understand the common plan of the tiny shops, with their matted floors well raised above the street level, and the general perpendicular arrangement of sign-lettering, whether undulating on drapery or glimmering on gilded and lacquered signboards. You observe that the same rich dark blue which dominates in popular costume rules also in shop draperies, though there is a sprinkling of other tints—bright blue and white and red (no greens or yellows). And then you note also that the dresses of the labourers are lettered with the same wonderful lettering as the shop draperies. No arabesques could produce such an effect. As modified for decorative purposes these ideographs have a speaking symmetry which no design without a meaning could possess. As they appear on the back of a workman's frock—pure white on dark blue—and large enough to be easily read at a great distance (indicating some guild or company of which the wearer is a member or employee), they give to the poor cheap garment a fictitious appearance of splendour.

And finally, while you are still puzzling over the mystery of things, there will come to you like a revelation the knowledge that most of the amazing picturesqueness of these streets is simply due to the profusion of Chinese and Japanese characters in white, black, blue, or gold, decorating every-thing—even surfaces of doorposts and paper screens. Perhaps, then, for one moment, you will imagine the effect of English lettering substituted for those magical characters; and the mere idea will give to whatever aesthetic sentiment you may possess a brutal shock, and you will become, as I have become, an enemy of the Romaji-kai—that society founded for the ugly utilitarian purpose of introducing the use of English letters in writing Japanese.

The Art of the Strokes

An ideograph does not make on the Japanese brain any impression similar to that created in the Occidental brain by a letter or combination of let-ters—dull, inanimate symbols of vocal sounds. To the Japanese brain an ideograph is a vivid picture: it lives; it speaks; it gesticulates. And the whole space of a Japanese street is full of such living characters—figures that cry out to the eyes, words that smile or grimace like faces.

What such lettering is, compared with our own lifeless types, can be understood only by those who have lived in the farther East. For even the printed characters of Japanese or Chinese imported texts give no suggestion of the possible beauty of the same characters as modified for decorative inscriptions, for sculptural use, or for the commonest advertising purposes. No rigid convention fetters the fancy of the calligrapher or designer: each strives to make his characters more beautiful than any others; and generations upon generations of artists have been toiling from time immemorial with like emulation, so that through centuries and centuries of tireless effort and study, the primitive hieroglyph or ideograph has been evolved into a thing of beauty. It consists only of a certain number of brush-strokes; but in each stroke there is an undiscoverable secret art of grace, proportion, imperceptible curve, which actually makes it seem alive, and bears witness that even during the lightning-moment of its creation the artist felt with his brush for the ideal shape of the stroke equally along its entire length, from head to tail. But the art of the strokes is not all; the art of their combination is that which produces the enchantment, often so as to astonish the Japanese themselves. It is not surprising, indeed, considering the strangely personal, animate, esoteric aspect of Japanese lettering, that there should be wonderful legends of calligraphy relating how words written by holy experts became incarnate, and descended from their tablets to hold converse with mankind.

A World of Elves

My *kurumaya* calls himself 'Cha.' He has a white hat which looks like the top of an enormous mushroom; a short blue wide-sleeved jacket; blue drawers, close-fitting as 'tights,' and reaching to his ankles; and light straw sandals bound on his bare feet with cords of palmetto-fibre. Doubtless he typifies all the patience, endurance, and insidious coaxing powers of his class. He has already manifested his power to make me give him more than the law allows; and I have been warned against him in vain. For the first sensation of having a human being for a horse, trotting between shafts, unwearyingly bobbing up and down before you for hours, is alone enough to evoke a feeling of compassion. And when this human being, thus trotting between shafts, with all his hopes, memories, sentiments, and comprehensions, happens to have the gentlest smile, and the power to return the least favour by an apparent display of infinite gratitude, this com-passion becomes sympathy, and provokes unreasoning impulses to self-sacrifice. I think the sight of the profuse perspiration has also something to do with the feeling, for it makes one think of the cost of heart-beats and muscle-contractions, likewise of chills, congestions, and pleurisy. Cha's clothing is drenched; and he mops his face with a small sky-blue towel, with figures of bamboo-sprays and sparrows in white on it, which towel he carries wrapped about his wrist as he runs.

That which attracts me in Cha—Cha considered not as a motive power at all, but as a personality—I am rapidly learning to discern in the multitudes of faces turned toward us as we roll through these miniature streets. And perhaps the supremely pleasurable impression of this morning is that produced by the singular gentleness of popular scrutiny. Everybody looks at you curiously; but there is never anything disagreeable, much less hostile in the gaze: most commonly it is accompanied by a smile or half smile. And the ultimate consequence of all these kindly curious looks and smiles is that the stranger finds himself thinking of fairyland. Hackneyed to the degree of provocation this statement no doubt is: everybody describing the sensations of his first Japanese day talks of the land as fairyland, and of its people as fairy folk. Yet there is a natural reason for this unanimity in choice of terms to describe what is almost impossible to describe more accurately at the first essay. To find oneself suddenly in a world where everything is on a smaller and daintier scale than with us—a world of lesser and seemingly kindlier beings, all smiling at you as if to wish you well—a world where all movement is slow and soft, and voices are hushed—a world where land, life, and sky are unlike all that one has known elsewhere—this is surely the realisation, for imaginations nourished with English folklore, of the old dream of a world of elves.

Curiosities

The traveller who enters suddenly into a period of social change—especially change from a feudal past to a democratic present—is likely to regret the decay of things beautiful and the ugliness of things new. What of both I may yet discover in Japan I know not, but today, in these exotic streets, the old and the new mingle so well that one seems to set off the other. The line of tiny white telegraph poles carrying the world's news to papers printed in a mixture of Chinese and Japanese characters; an electric bell in some teahouse with an Oriental riddle of text pasted beside the ivory button, a shop of American sewing machines next to the shop of a maker of Buddhist images; the establishment of a photographer beside the establishment of a manufacturer of straw sandals: all these present no striking incongruities, for each sample of Occidental innovation is set into an Oriental frame that seems adaptable to any picture. But on the first day, at least, the old alone is new for the stranger, and suffices to absorb his attention. It then appears to him that everything Japanese is delicate, exquisite, admirable—even a pair of common wooden chopsticks in a paper bag with a little drawing on it; even a package of toothpicks of cherry-wood, bound with a paper wrapper wonderfully lettered in three different colours; even the little sky-blue towel, with designs of flying sparrows on it, which the *jinrikisha* man uses to wipe his face. The bank bills, the commonest copper coins, are things of beauty. Even the piece of plaited coloured string used by the shopkeeper in tying up your last purchase is a pretty curiosity. Curiosities and dainty objects bewilder you by their very multitude: on either side of you, wherever you turn your eyes, are countless wonderful things as yet incomprehensible.

But it is perilous to look at them. Every time you dare to look, something obliges you to buy it—unless, as may often happen, the smiling vendor invites your inspection of so many varieties of one article, each specially and all desirable, that you flee away out of mere terror at your own impulses. The shopkeeper never asks you to buy, but his wares are enchanted, and if you once begin buying you are lost. Cheapness means only a temptation to commit bankruptcy; for the resources of irresistible artistic cheapness are inexhaustible. The largest steamer that crosses the Pacific could not contain what you wish to purchase. For, although you may not confess the fact to yourself, what you really want to buy is not the contents of a shop; you want the shop and the shopkeeper, and streets of shops with their draperies and their inhabitants, the whole city and the bay and the mountains begirdling it, and Fuji-*yama*'s white witchery overhanging it in the speckless sky, all Japan, in fact, with its magical trees and luminous atmosphere, with all its cities and towns and temples, and forty millions of the most lovable people in the universe.

Now there comes to my mind something I once heard said by a practical American on hearing of a great fire in Japan, 'Oh! those people can afford fires; their houses are so cheaply built.' It is true that the frail wooden houses of the common people can be cheaply and quickly replaced; but that which was within them to make them beautiful cannot—and every fire is an art tragedy. For this is the land of infinite hand-made variety; machinery has not yet been able to introduce sameness and utilitarian ugliness in cheap production (except in response to foreign demand for bad taste to suit vulgar markets), and each object made by the artist or artisan differs still from all others, even of his own making. And each time something beautiful perishes by fire, it is a something representing an individual idea.

Happily the art impulse itself, in this country of conflagrations, has a vitality that survives each generation of artists, and defies the flame that changes their labour to ashes or melts it to shapelessness. The idea whose symbol has perished will reappear again in other creations—perhaps after the passing of a century—modified yet recognisably of kin to the thought of the past. And every artist is a ghostly worker. Not by years of groping and sacrifice does he find his highest expression; the sacrificial past is within him; his art is an inheritance; his fingers are guided by the dead in the delineation of a flying bird, of the vapours of mountains, of the colours of the morning and the evening, of the shape of branches and the spring burst of flowers: generations of skilled workmen have given him their cunning, and revive in the wonder of his drawing. What was conscious effort in the beginning became unconscious in later centuries—becomes almost automatic in the living man—becomes the art instinctive. One coloured print by Hokusai or Hiroshige, originally sold for less than a cent, may have more real art in it than many a Western painting valued at more than the worth of a whole Japanese street.

Tabi

Here are Hokusai's own figures walking about in straw raincoats, and immense mushroom-shaped hats of straw, and straw sandals—bare-limbed peasants, deeply tanned by wind and sun; and patient-faced mothers with smiling bald babies on their backs, toddling by on their *geta* (high, noisy, wooden clogs), and robed merchants squatting and smoking their little brass pipes among the countless riddles of their shops.

Then I notice how small and shapely the feet of the people are—whether bare brown feet of peasants, or beautiful feet of children wearing tiny, tiny *geta*, or feet of young girls in snowy *tabi*. The *tabi*, the white digitated stocking, gives to a small light foot a mythological aspect—the white cleft grace of the foot of a fauness. Clad or bare, the Japanese foot has the antique symmetry: it has not yet been distorted by the infamous foot-gear which has deformed the feet of Occidentals. Of every pair of Japanese wooden clogs, one makes in walking a slightly different sound from the other, as kring to krang; so that the echo of the walker's steps has an alternate rhythm of tones. On a pavement, such as that of a railway station, the sound obtains immense sonority; and a crowd will sometimes intentionally fall into step, with the drollest conceivable result of drawling wooden noise.

Delusion

'*Tera e yuke!*'

I have been obliged to return to the European hotel—not because of the noon-meal, as I really begrudge myself the time necessary to eat it, but because I cannot make Cha understand that I want to visit a Buddhist temple. Now Cha understands; my landlord has uttered the mystical words, '*Tera e yuke!*'

A few minutes of running along broad thoroughfares lined with gardens and costly ugly European buildings. Then, passing the bridge of a canal stocked with unpainted sharp-prowed craft of extraordinary construction, we again plunge into narrow, low, bright pretty streets—into another part of the Japanese city. And Cha runs at the top of his speed between more rows of little ark-shaped houses, narrower above than below, between other unfamiliar lines of little open shops. And always over the shops little strips of blue-tiled roof slope back to the paper-screened chamber of upper floors. And from all the facades hang draperies dark blue, or white, or crimson— foot-breadths of texture covered with beautiful Japanese lettering, white on blue, red on black, black on white. But all this flies by swiftly as a dream. Once more we cross a canal. We rush up a narrow street rising to meet a hill. Cha, halting suddenly before an immense flight of broad stone steps, sets the shafts of his vehicle on the ground that I may dismount, and, pointing to the steps, exclaims, '*Tera!*'

I dismount, and ascend them, and, reaching a broad terrace, find myself face to face with a wonderful gate, topped by a tilted, peaked, many-cornered Chinese roof. It is all strangely carven, this gate. Dragons are intertwined in a frieze above its open doors. The panels of the doors themselves are similarly sculptured. There are gargoyles—grotesque lion heads—protruding from the eaves. The whole is grey, stone-coloured. To me, nevertheless, the carvings do not seem to have the fixity of sculpture; all the snakeries and dragonries appear to undulate with a swarming motion, elusively, in eddyings as of water.

I turn a moment to look back through the glorious light. Sea and sky mingle in the same beautiful pale clear blue. Below me the billowing of bluish roofs reaches to the verge of the unruffled bay on the right, and to the feet of the green wooded hills flanking the city on two sides. Beyond that semicircle of green hills rises a lofty range of serrated mountains, indigo silhouettes. And enormously high above the line of them towers an apparition indescribably lovely—one solitary snowy cone, so filmily exquisite, so spiritually white, that but for its immemorially familiar outline, one would surely deem it a shape of cloud. Invisible its base remains, being the same delicious tint as the sky: only above the eternal snow line its dreamy cone appears, seeming to hang, the ghost of a peak, between the luminous land and the luminous heaven—the sacred and matchless mountain, Fuji-*yama*.

And suddenly, a singular sensation comes upon me as I stand before this weirdly sculptured portal—a sensation of dream and doubt. It seems to me that the steps, and the dragon-swarming gate, and the blue sky arching over the roofs of the town, and the ghostly beauty of Fuji, and the shadow of myself there stretching on the grey masonry, must all vanish presently. Why such a feeling? Doubtless because the forms before me—the curved roofs, the coiling dragons, the Chinese grotesqueries of carving—do not really appear to me as things new, but as things dreamed: the sight of them must have stirred to life forgotten memories of picture books. A moment, and the delusion vanishes; the romance of reality returns, with freshened consciousness of all that which is truly and deliciously new; the magical transparencies of distance, the wondrous delicacy of the tones of the living picture, the enormous height of the summer blue, and the white soft witchery of the Japanese sun.

Akira

I pass on and climb more steps to a second gate with similar gargoyles and swarming of dragons, and enter a court where graceful votive lanterns of stone stand like monuments. On my right and left two great grotesque stone lions are sitting—the lions of Buddha, male and female. Beyond is a long low light building, with curved and gabled roof of blue tiles, and three wooden steps before its entrance. Its sides are simple wooden screens covered with thin white paper. This is the temple.

On the steps I take off my shoes. A young man slides aside the screens closing the entrance, and bows me a gracious welcome. And I go in, feeling under my feet a softness of matting thick as bedding. An immense square apartment is before me, full of an unfamiliar sweet smell—the scent of Japanese incense. After the full blaze of the sun, the paper-filtered light here is dim as moonshine; for a minute or two I can see nothing but gleams of gilding in a soft gloom. Then, my eyes becoming accustomed to the obscurity, I perceive against the paper-paned screens surrounding the sanctuary on three sides shapes of enormous flowers cutting like silhouettes against the vague white light. I approach and find them to be paper flowers—symbolic lotus blossoms beautifully coloured, with curling leaves gilded on the upper surface and bright green beneath, At the dark end of the apartment, facing the entrance, is the altar of Buddha, a rich and lofty altar, covered with bronzes and gilded utensils clustered to right and left of a shrine like a tiny gold temple. But I see no statue; only a mystery of unfamiliar shapes of burnished metal, relieved against darkness, a darkness behind the shrine and altar—whether recess or inner sanctuary I cannot distinguish.

The young attendant who ushered me into the temple now approaches, and, to my great surprise, exclaims in excellent English, pointing to a richly decorated gilded object between groups of candelabra on the altar:

'That is the shrine of Buddha.'

'And I would like to make an offering to Buddha,' I respond.

'It is not necessary,' he says, with a polite smile.

But I insist; and he places the little offering for me on the altar. Then he invites me to his own room, in a wing of the building—a large luminous room, without furniture, beautifully matted. And we sit down on the floor and chat. He tells me he is a student in the temple. He learned English in Tokyo and speaks it with a curious accent, but a fine choice of words. Finally he asks me:

'Are you a Christian?'

I answer truthfully, 'No.' 'Are you a Buddhist?'

'Not exactly.' 'Why do you make offerings if you do not believe in Buddha?'

'I revere the beauty of his teaching, and the faith of those who follow it.'

'Are there Buddhists in England and America?'

'There are, at least, a great many interested in Buddhist philosophy.'

And he takes from an alcove a little book, and gives it to me to examine. It is an English copy of Henry Steel Olcott's *Buddhist Catechism*.

'Why is there no image of Buddha in your temple?' I ask.

'There is a small one in the shrine on the altar,' the student answers, 'but the shrine is closed. And we have several large ones. But the image of Buddha is not exposed here every day—only on festal days. And some images are exposed only once or twice a year.'

From my place, I can see, between the open paper screens, men and women ascending the steps, to kneel and pray before the entrance of the temple. They kneel with such naive reverence, so gracefully and so naturally, that the kneeling of our Occidental devotees seems a clumsy stumbling by comparison. Some only join their hands; others clap them three times loudly and slowly; then they bow their heads, pray silently for a moment, and rise and depart. The shortness of the prayers impresses me as something novel and interesting. From time to time I hear the clink and rattle of brazen coin cast into the great wooden money-box at the entrance.

I turn to the young student, and ask him, 'Why do they clap their hands three times before they pray?'

'Three times for the Sansai, the Three Powers: Heaven, Earth, Man.'

'But do they clap their hands to call the Gods, as Japanese clap their hands to summon their attendants?'

'Oh, no!' he replied. 'The clapping of hands represents only the awakening from the dream of the long night.'

'What night? what dream?'

He hesitates some moments before making answer, 'The Buddha said: All beings are only dreaming in this fleeting world of unhappiness.'

'Then the clapping of hands signifies that in prayer the soul awakens from such dreaming?'

'Yes.'

'You understand what I mean by the word "soul"?'

'Oh, yes! Buddhists believe the soul always was—always will be.'

'Even in Nirvana?'

'Yes.'

While we are thus chatting the chief priest of the temple enters—a very aged man—accompanied by two young priests, and I am presented to them. The three bow very low, showing me the glossy crowns of their smoothly-shaven heads, before seating themselves in the fashion of gods on the floor. I observe they do not smile. These are the first Japanese I have seen who do not smile: their faces are impassive as the faces of images. But their long eyes observe me very closely, while the student interprets their questions, and while I attempt to tell them something about the translations of the *sūtras* in our sacred books of the East, and about the labours of Samual Beal, Eugène Burnouf, Thomas William Rhys Davids and Johan Hendrik Caspar Kern, and others. They listen without change of countenance, and utter no word in response to the young student's translation of my remarks.

Tea is brought in and set before me in a tiny cup, placed in a little brazen saucer, shaped like a lotus leaf. I am invited to partake of some little sugar cakes (*kashi*), stamped with a figure which I recognise as the swastika, the ancient Indian symbol of the wheel of the law.

As I rise to go, all rise with me, and at the steps the student asks for my name and address. 'For,' he adds, 'you will not see me here again, as I am going to leave the temple. But I will visit you.'

'And your name?' I ask.

'Call me Akira,' he answers.

At the threshold I bow my good-bye; and they all bow very, very low, one blue-black head, three glossy heads like balls of ivory. And as I go, only Akira smiles.

Trees

'*Tera?*' queries Cha, with his immense white hat in his hand, as I resume my seat in the *jinrikisha* at the foot of the steps. Which no doubt means, do I want to see any more temples? Most certainly I do: I have not yet seen Buddha.

'Yes, *tera*, Cha.'

And again begins the long panorama of mysterious shops and tilted eaves, and fantastic riddles written over everything. I have no idea in what direction Cha is running. I only know that the streets seem to become always narrower as we go, and that some of the houses look like great wickerwork pigeon-cages only, and that we pass over several bridges before we halt again at the foot of another hill. There is a lofty flight of steps here also, and before them a structure which I know is both a gate and a symbol, imposing, yet in no manner resembling the great Buddhist gateway seen before. Astonishingly simple all the lines of it are: it has no carving, no colouring, no lettering on it; yet it has a weird solemnity, an enigmatic beauty. It is a *torii*.

'*Miya*,' observes Cha. Not a *tera* this time, but a shrine of the gods of the more ancient faith of the land—a *miya*.

I am standing before a Shintō symbol; I see for the first time, out of a picture at least, a *torii*. How describe a *torii* to those who have never looked at one even in a photograph or engraving? Two lofty columns, like gate-pillars, supporting horizontally two cross-beams, the lower and lighter beam having its ends fitted into the columns a little distance below their summits; the uppermost and larger beam supported on the tops of the columns, and projecting well beyond them to right and left. That is a *torii*: the construction varying little in design, whether made of stone, wood, or metal. But this description can give no correct idea of the appearance of a *torii*, of its majestic aspect, of its mystical suggestiveness as a gateway. The first time you see a noble one, you will imagine, perhaps, that you see the colossal model of some beautiful Chinese letter towering against the sky; for all the lines of the thing have the grace of an animated ideo-graph—have the bold angles and curves of characters made with four sweeps of a master-brush.

Passing the *torii* I ascend a flight of perhaps one hundred stone steps, and find at their summit a second *torii*, from whose lower cross-beam hangs festooned the mystic *shimenawa*. It is in this case a hempen rope of perhaps two inches in diameter through its greater length, but tapering off at either end like a snake. Sometimes the *shimenawa* is made of bronze, when the *torii* itself is of bronze; but according to tradition it should be made of straw, and most commonly is. For it represents the straw rope that the deity Futotama no Mikoto stretched behind the Sun-goddess, Amaterasu Ōmikami, after Ame no Tajikarao no Kami, the Heavenly Hand-strength God, had pulled her out, as is told in that ancient myth of Shintō professor Chamberlain has translated. And the *shimenawa*, in its commoner and simpler form, has pendent tufts of straw along its entire length, at regular intervals, because originally made, tradition declares, of grass pulled up by the roots which protruded from the twist of it.

Advancing beyond this *torii*, I find myself in a sort of park or pleasure-ground on the summit of the hill. There is a small temple on the right. It is all closed up, and I have read so much about the disappointing vacuity of Shintō temples that I do not regret the absence of its guardian. I see before me what is infinitely more interesting—a grove of cherry trees covered with something unutterably beautiful—a dazzling mist of snowy blossoms clinging like summer cloud-fleece about every branch and twig; and the ground beneath them, and the path before me, is white with the soft, thick, odorous snow of fallen petals.

Beyond this loveliness are flower plots surrounding tiny shrines; and mar-vellous grotto-work, full of monsters—dragons and mythologic beings chiselled in the rock; and miniature landscape work with tiny groves of dwarf trees, and Lilliputian lakes, and microscopic brooks and bridges and cascades. Here, also, are swings for children. And here are belvederes, perched on the verge of the hill, wherefrom the whole fair city, and the whole smooth bay speckled with fishing sails no bigger than pinheads, and the far, faint, high promontories reaching into the sea, are all visible in one delicious view—blue-pencilled in a beauty of ghostly haze indescribable.

Why should the trees be so lovely in Japan? With us, a plum or cherry tree in flower is not an astonishing sight; but here it is a miracle of beauty so bewildering that, however much you may have previously read about it, the real spectacle strikes you dumb. You see no leaves—only one great filmy mist of petals. Is it that the trees have been so long domesticated and caressed by man in this land of the gods, that they have acquired souls, and strive to show their gratitude, like women loved, by making themselves more beautiful for man's sake? Assuredly they have mastered men's hearts by their loveliness, like beautiful slaves. That is to say, Japanese hearts. Apparently there have been some foreign tourists of the brutal class in this place, since it has been deemed necessary to set up inscriptions in English announcing that 'IT IS FORBIDDEN TO INJURE THE TREES.'

Mirror
'*Tera?*'

'Yes, Cha, *tera*.'

But only for a brief while do I traverse Japanese streets. The houses separate, become scattered along the feet of the hills: the city thins away through little valleys, and vanishes at last behind. And we follow a curving road overlooking the sea. Green hills slope steeply down to the edge of the way on the right; on the left, far below, spreads a vast stretch of dun sand and salty pools to a line of surf so distant that it is discernible only as a moving white thread. The tide is out; and thousands of cockle gatherers are scattered over the sands, at such distances that their stooping figures, dotting the glimmering seabed, appear no larger than gnats. Some are coming along the road before us, returning from their search with well-filled baskets— girls with faces almost as rosy as the faces of English girls.

As the *jinrikisha* rattles on, the hills dominating the road grow higher. All at once Cha halts again before the steepest and loftiest flight of temple steps I have yet seen.

I climb and climb and climb, halting perforce betimes, to ease the violent aching of my quadriceps muscles. I reach the top completely out of breath and find myself between two lions of stone, one showing his fangs, the other with jaws closed. Before me stands the temple, at the farther end of a small bare plateau surrounded on three sides by low cliffs—a small temple, looking very old and grey. From a rocky height to the left of the building, a little cataract rumbles down into a pool, ringed in by a palisade. The voice of the water drowns all other sounds. A sharp wind is blowing from the ocean: the place is chill even in the sun, and bleak, and desolate, as if no prayer had been uttered in it for a hundred years.

Cha taps and calls, while I take off my shoes on the worn wooden steps of the temple; and after a minute of waiting, we hear a muffled step approaching and a hollow cough behind the paper screens. They slide open; and an old white-robed priest appears, and motions me, with a low bow, to enter. He has a kindly face; and his smile of welcome seems to me one of the most exquisite I have ever been greeted with. Then he coughs again, so badly that I think if I ever come here another time, I shall ask for him in vain.

I go in, feeling that soft, spotless, cushioned matting beneath my feet with which the floors of all Japanese buildings are covered. I pass the indispensable bell and lacquered reading desk and before me I see other screens only, stretching from floor to ceiling. The old man, still coughing, slides back one of these on the right, and waves me into the dimness of an inner sanctuary, haunted by faint odours of incense. A colossal bronze lamp, with snarling gilded dragons coiled about its columnar stem, is the first object I discern. In passing it, my shoulder sets ringing a festoon of little bells suspended from the lotus-shaped summit of it. Then I reach the altar, gropingly, unable yet to distinguish forms clearly. But the priest, sliding back screen after screen, pours in light on the gilded brasses and the inscriptions. I look for the image of the deity or presiding spirit between the altar-groups of convoluted candelabra. And I see—only a mirror, a round, pale disk of polished metal, and my own face therein, and behind this mockery of me a phantom of the far sea.

Only a mirror! Symbolising what? Illusion? Or that the universe exists for us solely as the reflection of our own souls? Or the old Chinese teaching that we must seek the Buddha only in our own hearts? Perhaps some day I shall be able to find out all these things.

As I sit on the temple steps, putting on my shoes to go, the kind old priest approaches me again, and, bowing, presents a bowl. I hastily drop some coins in it, imagining it to be a Buddhist alms bowl, before discovering it to be full of hot water. But the old man's beautiful courtesy saves me from feeling the grossness of my mistake. Without a word, and still preserving his kindly smile, he takes the bowl away. Returning presently with another bowl, empty, he fills it with hot water from a little kettle, and makes a sign to me to drink.

Tea is most usually offered to visitors at temples, but this little shrine is very, very poor. I have a suspicion that the old priest suffers betimes for want of what no fellow creature should be permitted to need. As I descend the windy steps to the roadway, I see him still looking after me, and I hear once more his hollow cough.

Then the mockery of the mirror recurs to me. I am beginning to wonder whether I shall ever be able to discover that which I seek—outside of myself! That is, outside of my own imagination.

Tera

'*Tera?*' once more queries Cha.

'*Tera*, no—it is getting late. Hotel, Cha.'

But Cha, turning the corner of a narrow street, on our homeward route, halts the *jinrikisha* before a shrine or tiny temple scarcely larger than the smallest of Japanese shops, yet more of a surprise to me than any of the larger sacred edifices already visited. On either side of the entrance stand two monster figures, nude, blood-red, demoniac, fearfully muscled, with feet like lions, and hands brandishing gilded thunderbolts, and eyes of delirious fury; the guardians of holy things, the *niō*, or "two kings."

These *niō* the first I saw in Japan, were very clumsy figures. There are magnificent *niō* to be seen in some of the great temple gateways in Tokyo, Kyoto, and elsewhere. The grandest of all are those in the Niō Mon, or 'Two Kings' Gate,' of the huge Todai-*ji* temple at Nara. They are eight hundred years old. It is impossible not to admire the conception of stormy dignity and hurricane-force embodied in those colossal figures. Prayers are addressed to the *niō*, especially by pilgrims. Most of their statues are disfigured by little pellets of white paper, which people chew into a pulp and then spit at them. There is a curious superstition that if the pellet sticks to the statue the prayer is heard. If, on the other hand, it falls to the ground, the prayer will not be answered.

Right between these crimson monsters a young girl stands looking at us; her slight figure, in robe of silver grey and girdle of iris-violet, relieved deliciously against the twilight darkness of the interior. Her face, impassive and curiously delicate, would charm wherever seen. But here, by strange contrast with the frightful grotesqueries on either side of her, it produces an effect unimaginable. Then I find myself wondering whether my feeling of repulsion toward those twin monstrosities be altogether lust, seeing that so charming a maiden deems them worthy of veneration. And they even cease to seem ugly as I watch her standing there between them, dainty and slender as some splendid moth, and always naively gazing at the foreigner, utterly unconscious that they might have seemed to him both unholy and uncomely.

What are they? Artistically they are Buddhist transformations of Brahma and of Indra. Enveloped by the absorbing, all-transforming magical atmosphere of Buddhism, Indra can now wield his thunderbolts only in defence of the faith that has dethroned him: he has become a keeper of the temple gates; nay, has even become a servant of *bosatsu* (bodhisattva), for this is only a shrine of Kannon, Goddess of Mercy, not yet a Buddha.

'Hotel, Cha, hotel!' I cry out again, for the way is long, and the sun sinking—sinking in the softest imaginable glow of topazine light. I have not seen Shaka (so the Japanese have transformed the name Sakya-Muni); I have not looked upon the face of the Buddha. Perhaps I may be able to find his image tomorrow, somewhere in this wilderness of wooden streets, or upon the summit of some yet unvisited hill.

The sun is gone; the topaz light is gone; and Cha stops to light his lantern of paper. We hurry on again, between two long lines of painted paper lanterns suspended before the shops: so closely set, so level those lines are, that they seem two interminable strings of pearls of fire. And suddenly a sound—solemn, profound, mighty—peals to my ears over the roofs of the town, the voice of the tsurigane, the great temple bell of Nogiyama.

All too short the day seemed. Yet my eyes have been so long dazzled by the great white light, and so confused by the sorcery of that interminable maze of mysterious signs that made each street vista seem a glimpse into some enormous grimoire, that they are now weary even of the soft glowing of all these paper lanterns, likewise covered with characters that look like texts from a book of magic. And I feel at last the coming of that drowsiness that always follows enchantment.

Anma

'Anma kamishimo gohyak mon!'

A woman's voice ringing through the night, chanting in a tone of singular sweetness words of which each syllable comes through my open window like a wavelet of flute-sound. My Japanese servant, who speaks a little English, has told me what they mean, those words:

'Anma kamishimo gohyak mon!'

And always between these long, sweet calls I hear a plaintive whistle, one long note first, then two short ones in another key. It is the whistle of the *anma*, the poor blind woman who earns her living by shampooing the sick or the weary, and whose whistle warns pedestrians and drivers of vehicles to take heed for her sake, as she cannot see. And she sings also that the weary and the sick may call her in.

' *Anma kamishimo gohyak mon!*'

The saddest melody, but the sweetest voice. Her cry signifies that for the sum of 'five hundred *mon*' she will come and rub your weary body 'above and below,' and make the weariness or the pain go away. Five hundred *mon* are the equivalent of five *sen* (Japanese cents); there are ten *rin* to a *sen*, and ten *mon* to one *rin*. The strange sweetness of the voice is haunting—makes me even wish to have some pains, that I might pay five hundred mon to have them driven away.

I lie down to sleep, and I dream. I see Chinese texts—multitudinous, weird, mysterious—fleeing by me, all in one direction; ideographs white and dark, on signboards, on paper screens, on backs of sandalled men. They seem to live, these ideographs, with conscious life; they are moving their parts, moving with a movement as of insects, monstrously, like phasmidae. I am rolling always through low, narrow, luminous streets in a phantom *jinrikisha*, whose wheels make no sound. And always, always, I see the huge white mushroom-shaped hat of Cha dancing up and down before me as he runs.

Kōbō Daishi

The Tablet

Kōbō Daishi, most holy of Buddhist priests, and founder of the Shingon-sho—which is the sect of Akira—first taught the men of Japan to write the writing called *hiragana* and the syllabary *I-ro-ha*; and Kōbō Daishi was himself the most wonderful of all writers, and the most skilful wizard among scribes.

And in the book, *Kōbō Daishi Ichihidai-ki*, it is related that when he was in China, the name of a certain room in the palace of the emperor having become effaced by time, the Emperor sent for him and bade him write the name anew. Thereupon Kōbō Daishi took a brush in his right hand, and a brush in his left, and one brush between the toes of his left foot, and another between the toes of his right, and one in his mouth also. And with those five brushes, so holding them, he limned the characters on the wall. And the characters were beautiful beyond any that had ever been seen in China—smooth-flowing as the ripples in the current of a river. Then Kōbō Daishi took a brush, and with it from a distance spattered drops of ink on the wall. And the drops as they fell became transformed and turned into beautiful characters. And the Emperor gave to Kōbō Daishi the name Gohitsu Osho, The Priest who writes with Five Brushes.

At another time, while the saint was dwelling in Takawasan, near Kyoto, the emperor, being desirous that Kōbō Daishi should write the tablet for the great temple called Kongojō-*ji*, gave the tablet to a messenger and bade him carry it to Kōbō Daishi, that Kōbō Daishi might letter it. But when the emperor's messenger, bearing the tablet, came near the place where Kōbō Daishi dwelt, he found a river before him so much swollen by rain

20

that no man might cross it. In a little while Kōbō Daishi appeared on the farther bank and, hearing from the messenger what the Emperor desired, called to him to hold up the tablet. The messenger did so, and Kōbō Daishi, from his place on the farther bank, made the movements of the letters with his brush. And as fast as he made them they appeared on the tablet which the messenger was holding up.

Monju Bosatsu

Now in that time Kōbō Daishi was wont to meditate alone by the river-side. One day, while so meditating, he was aware of a boy standing before him, gazing at him curiously. The garments of the boy were as the garments worn by the needy, but his face was beautiful. While Kōbō Daishi wondered, the boy asked him, 'Are you Kōbō Daishi, whom men call "Gohitsu Oshō"—the priest who writes with five brushes at once?'

Kōbō Daishi answered, 'I am he.'

Then said the boy, 'If you be he, write, I pray you, on the sky.'

Rising, Kōbō Daishi, took his brush, and made with it movements toward the sky as if writing. And presently on the face of the sky the letters appeared, most beautifully wrought.

Then the boy said, 'Now I shall try;' and he wrote also on the sky as Kōbō Daishi had done.

And he said again to Kōbō Daishi, 'I pray you, write for me—write on the surface of the river.'

Then Kōbō Daishi wrote on the water a poem in praise of the water. For a moment the characters remained, all beautiful, on the face of the stream, as if they had fallen on it like leaves. But presently they moved with the current and floated away.

'Now I will try,' said the boy, and he wrote on the water the dragon character—the character *ryū* in the writing which is called *sōsho*, the 'grass script.' And the character remained on the flowing surface and moved not.

But Kōbō Daishi saw that the boy had not placed the *ten*, the little dot belonging to the character, beside it. And he asked the boy, 'Why did you not put the ten?'

'Oh, I forgot!' answered the boy; 'please put it there for me,' and Kōbō Daishi then made the dot.

And lo! the dragon character became a dragon, and the dragon moved terribly in the waters. The sky darkened with thunder clouds, and blazed with lightnings, and the dragon ascended in a whirl of tempest to heaven.

Then Kōbō Daishi asked the boy, 'Who are you?'

And the boy said, 'I am he whom men worship on the mountain Gotai; I am the Lord of Wisdom—Monju Bosatsu!' And even as he spoke the boy changed; his beauty became luminous like the beauty of gods, and his limbs radiant, shedding soft light about. Smiling, he rose to heaven and vanished beyond the clouds.

Onomo Toku

Once, Kōbō Daishi himself forgot to put the *ten* beside the character *o* on the tablet he painted with the name of the Ōtemon gate of the emperor's palace. The emperor at Kyoto having asked him why he had not put the ten beside the character, Kōbō Daishi answered, 'I forgot, but I will put it on now.' Then the emperor bade ladders be brought, for the tablet was already in place, high above the gate. But Kōbō Daishi, standing on the pavement before the gate, simply threw his brush at the tablet, and the brush, so thrown, made the *ten* there most admirably and fell back into his hand.

Kōbō Daishi also painted the tablet of the gate called Kokamon of the emperor's palace at Kyoto. Now there was a man, dwelling near that gate, whose name was Kino Momoye. He ridiculed the characters which Kōbō Daishi had made, and pointed to one of them, saying, 'Why, it looks like a swaggering wrestler!' But the same night Momoye dreamed that a wrestler had come to his bedside and leaped on him, and was beating him with his fists. And, crying out with the pain of the blows, he awoke, and saw the wrestler rise in air, and change into the written character he had laughed at, and go back to the tablet over the gate.

There was another writer, famed greatly for his skill, named Onomo Toku, who laughed at some characters on the tablet of the Shukakumon gate, written by Kōbō Daishi. He said, pointing to the character *shu*, 'Verily *shu* looks like the character "rice".' And that night he dreamed that the character he had mocked at became a man, and that the man fell on him and beat him, and jumped up and down on his face many times—even as a *kometsuki*, a rice cleaner, leaps up and down to move the hammers that beat the rice—saying the while, 'Lo! I am the messenger of Kōbō Daishi!' And, waking, he found himself bruised and bleeding as one that had been grievously trampled.

And long after Kōbō Daishi's death it was found that the names written by him on the two gates of the emperor's palace--Bifukumon, the Gate of Beautiful Fortune, and Kokamon, the Gate of Excellent Greatness—were well-nigh effaced by time. And the emperor ordered a *dainagon* (high officer in the ancient imperial court), whose name was Yukinari, to restore the tablets. But Yukinari was afraid to perform the command of the emperor, by reason of what had befallen other men. Fearing the divine anger of Kōbō Daishi, he made offerings, and prayed for some token of permission. And the same night, in a dream, Kōbō Daishi appeared to him, smiling gently, and said, 'Do the work as the emperor desires and have no fear.' So he restored the tablets in the first month of the fourth year of Kankō, as is recorded in the book, *Honchō bunsui*.

And all these things have been related to me by my friend Akira.

Jizō

No Fear of Gods

I have passed another day in wandering among the temples, both Shintō and Buddhist. I have seen many curious things, but not yet the face of Buddha.

Repeatedly, after long wearisome climbing of stone steps, passing under gates full of gargoyles—heads of elephants and heads of lions—and entering shoeless into scented twilight, into enchanted gardens of golden lotus flowers of paper, and there waiting for my eyes to become habituated to the dimness, I have looked in vain for images. Only an opulent glimmering confusion of things half seen—vague altar splendours created by gilded bronzes twisted into riddles, by vessels of indescribable shape, by enigmatic texts of gold, by mysterious glittering pendent things—all framing in only a shrine with doors fast closed.

What has most impressed me is the seeming joyousness of popular faith. I have seen nothing grim, austere, or self-repressive. I have not even noted anything approaching the solemn. The bright temple courts and even the temple steps are thronged with laughing children, playing curious games. Mothers, entering the sanctuary to pray, suffer their little ones to creep about the matting and crow. The people take their religion lightly and cheerfully: they drop their cash in the great alms box, clap their hands, murmur a very brief prayer, then turn to laugh and talk and smoke their little pipes before the temple entrance. Into some shrines, I have noticed the worshippers do not enter at all; they merely stand before the doors and pray for a few seconds, and make their small offerings. Blessed are they who do not too much fear the gods which they have made!

Curious Things

Akira is bowing and smiling at the door. He slips off his sandals, enters in his white digitated stockings and, with another smile and bow, sinks gently into the proffered chair. Akira is an interesting boy. With his smooth beardless face and clear bronze skin and blue-black hair trimmed into a shock that shadows his forehead to the eyes, he has almost the appearance, in his long wide-sleeved robe and snowy stockings, of a young Japanese girl.

I clap my hands for tea, hotel tea, which he calls 'Chinese tea.' I offer him a cigar, which he declines, but with my permission, he will smoke his pipe. Thereupon he draws from his girdle a Japanese pipe case and tobacco pouch combined; pulls out of the pipe-case a little brass pipe with a bowl scarcely large enough to hold a pea; pulls out of the pouch some tobacco so finely cut that it looks like hair, stuffs a tiny pellet of this preparation in the pipe, and begins to smoke. He draws the smoke into his lungs, and blows it out again through his nostrils. Three little whiffs, at intervals of about half a minute, and the pipe, emptied, is replaced in its case.

Meanwhile I have related to Akira the story of my disappointments.

'Oh, you can see him today,' responds Akira, 'if you will take a walk with me to the monastery of Zōtoku-in. For this is the Busshoe, the festival of the birthday of Buddha. But he is very small, only a few inches high. If you want to see a great Buddha, you must go to Kamakura. There is a Buddha in that place, sitting on a lotus, and he is fifty feet high.'

So I go forth under the guidance of Akira. He says he may be able to show me 'some curious things.'

Daikichi

There is a sound of happy voices from the temple, and the steps are crowded with smiling mothers and laughing children. Entering, I find women and babies pressing about a lacquered table in front of the doorway. Upon it is a little tub-shaped vessel of sweet tea—*amacha*. Standing in the tea is a tiny figure of Buddha, one hand pointing upward and one downward. The women, having made the customary offering, take up some of the tea with a wooden ladle of curious shape, and pour it over the statue, and then, filling the ladle a second time, drink a little, and give a sip to their babies. This is the ceremony of washing the statue of Buddha.

Near the lacquered stand on which the vessel of sweet tea rests is another and lower stand supporting a temple bell shaped like a great bowl. A priest approaches with a padded mallet in his hand and strikes the bell. But the bell does not sound properly: he starts, looks into it, and stoops to lift out of it a smiling Japanese baby. The mother, laughing, runs to relieve him of his burden; and priest, mother, and baby all look at us with a frankness of mirth in which we join.

Akira leaves me a moment to speak with one of the temple attendants, and presently returns with a curious lacquered box, about a foot in length, and four inches wide on each of its four sides. There is only a small hole in one end of it; no appearance of a lid of any sort.

'Now,' says Akira, 'if you wish to pay two *sen*, we shall learn our future lot according to the will of the gods.'

I pay the two *sen*, and Akira shakes the box. Out comes a narrow slip of bamboo, with Chinese characters written thereon.

'*Kitsu!*' cries Akira. 'Good fortune. The number is fifty-one.'

Again he shakes the box. A second bamboo slip issues from the slit.

'*Daikichi!* Great good-fortune. The number is ninety-nine.

Once more the box is shaken; once more the oracular bamboo protrudes.

'*Kyō!*' laughs Akira. 'Evil will befall us. The number is sixty-four.'

He returns the box to a priest, and receives three mysterious papers, numbered with numbers corresponding to the numbers of the bamboo slips. These little bamboo slips, or divining sticks, are called *mikuji*.

This, as translated by Akira, is the substance of the text of the paper numbered fifty-one:

> He who draweth forth this *mikuji*, let him live according to the heavenly law and worship Kannon. If his trouble be a sickness, it shall pass from him. If he have lost aught, it shall be found. If he have a suit at law, he shall gain. If he love a woman, he shall surely win her, though he should have to wait. And many happinesses will come to him.

The *daikichi mikuji* reads almost similarly, with the sole differences that, instead of Kannon, the deities of wealth and prosperity—Daikoku,

Bishamon, and Benten—are to be worshipped, and that the fortunate man will not have to wait at all for the woman loved. But the *kyō mikuji* reads:

> He who draweth forth this *mikuji*, it will be well for him to obey the heavenly law and to worship Kannon the Merciful. If he have any sickness, even much more sick he shall become. If he have lost aught, it shall never be found. If he have a suit at law, he shall never gain it. If he love a woman, let him have no more expectation of winning her. Only by the most diligent piety can he hope to escape the most frightful calamities. And there shall be no felicity in his portion.

'All the same, we are fortunate,' declares Akira. 'Twice out of three times we have found luck. Now we will go to see another statue of Buddha.' And he guides me, through many curious streets, to the southern verge of the city.

Hakaba

Before us rises a hill, with a broad flight of stone steps sloping to its summit, between foliage of cedars and maples. We climb; and I see above me the Lions of Buddha waiting—the male yawning menace, the female with mouth closed. Passing between them, we enter a large temple court, at whose farther end rises another wooded eminence.

And here is the temple, with roof of blue-painted copper tiles, and tilted eaves and gargoyles and dragons, all weather-stained to one neutral tone. The paper screens are open, but a melancholy rhythmic chant from within tells us that the noonday service is being held: the priests are chanting the syllables of Sanscrit texts transliterated into Chinese—intoning the *sūtra* called the Sutra of the Lotus of the Good Law. One of those who chant keeps time by tapping with a mallet, cotton-wrapped, some grotesque object shaped like a dolphin's head, all lacquered in scarlet and gold, which gives forth a dull, booming tone—a *mokugyo*.

To the right of the temple is a little shrine, filling the air with fragrance of incense-burning. I peer in through the blue smoke that curls up from half a dozen tiny rods planted in a small brazier full of ashes; and far back in the shadow I see a swarthy Buddha, tiara-coiffed, with head bowed and hands joined, just as I see the Japanese praying, erect in the sun, before the thresholds of temples. The figure is of wood, rudely wrought and rudely coloured: still the placid face has beauty of suggestion.

Crossing the court to the left of the building, I find another flight of steps before me, leading up a slope to something mysterious still higher, among enormous trees. I ascend these steps also, reach the top, guarded by two small symbolic lions, and suddenly find myself in cool shadow, and startled by a spectacle totally unfamiliar.

Dark—almost black—soil and the shadowing of trees immemorially old, through whose vaulted foliage the sunlight leaks thinly down in rare flecks; a crepuscular light, tender and solemn, revealing the weirdest host of unfamiliar shapes—a vast congregation of grey, columnar, mossy things, stony, monumental, sculptured with Chinese ideographs. And about them, behind them, rising high above them, thickly set as rushes in a marsh verge, tall slender wooden tablets, like laths, covered with similar fantastic lettering, pierce the green gloom by thousands, by tens of thousands.

And before I can note other details, I know that I am in a *hakaba*, a cemetery—a very ancient Buddhist cemetery.

These laths are called *sotoba* (derived from the Sanscrit *stūpa*). All have notches cut on their edges on both sides near the top-five notches, and all are painted with Chinese characters on both faces. One inscription is always the phrase 'To promote Buddhahood,' painted immediately below the dead man's name; the inscription on the other surface is always a sentence in Sanscrit whose meaning has been forgotten even by those priests who perform the funeral rites. One such lath is planted behind the tomb as soon as the monument (*haka*) is set up; then another every seven days for forty-nine days, then one after the lapse of a hundred days; then one at the end of a year; then one after the passing of three years; and at successively longer periods others are erected during one hundred years.

And in almost every group I notice some quite new, or freshly planed unpainted white wood, standing beside others grey or even black with age. There are many, still older from whose surface all the characters have disappeared. Others are lying on the sombre clay. Hundreds stand so loose in the soil that the least breeze jostles and clatters them together.

Not less unfamiliar in their forms, but far more interesting, are the monuments of stone. One shape I know represents five of the Buddhist elements:

a cube supporting a sphere that upholds a pyramid on which rests a shallow square cup with four crescent edges and tilted corners, and in the cup a pyriform body poised with the point upwards. These successively typify Earth, Water, Fire, Wind, Ether, the five substances wherefrom the body is shapen, and into which it is resolved by death. The absence of any emblem for the Sixth element, Knowledge, touches more than any imagery conceivable could do. And still, in the purpose of the symbolism, this omission was never planned with the same idea that it suggests to the Occidental mind.

Very numerous also among the monuments are low, square, flat-topped shafts, with a Japanese inscription in black or gold, or merely cut into the stone itself. Then there are upright slabs of various shapes and heights, mostly rounded at the top, usually bearing sculptures in relief. Finally, there are many curiously angled stones, or natural rocks, dressed on one side only, with designs etched on the smoothed surface. There would appear to be some meaning even in the irregularity of the shape of these slabs; the rock always seems to have been broken out of its bed at five angles, and the manner in which it remains balanced perpendicularly on its pedestal is a secret that the first hasty examination fails to reveal.

The pedestals vary in construction; most have three orifices in the projecting surface in front of the monument supported by them, usually one large oval cavity, with two small round holes flanking it. These smaller holes serve for the burning of incense rods; the larger cavity is filled with water. I do not know exactly why. Only my Japanese companion tells me 'it is an ancient custom in Japan thus to pour out water for the dead.' There are also bamboo cups on either side of the monument in which to place flowers.

Many of the sculptures represent Buddha in meditation, or in the attitude of exhorting. A few represent him asleep, with the placid, dreaming face of a child, a Japanese child; this means Nirvana. A common design on many tombs also seems to be two lotus-blossoms with stalks intertwined.

In one place I see a stone with an English name on it, and above that name a rudely chiselled cross. Verily the priests of Buddha have blessed tolerance, for this is a Christian tomb!

All is chipped and mouldered and mossed. The grey stones stand closely in hosts of ranks, only one or two inches apart, ranks of thousands upon thousands, always in the shadow of the great trees. Overhead innumerable birds sweeten the air with their trilling; and far below, down the steps behind us, I still hear the melancholy chant of the priests, faintly, like a humming of bees.

Akira leads the way in silence to where other steps descend into a darker and older part of the cemetery. At the head of the steps, to the right, I see a group of colossal monuments, very tall, massive, mossed by time, with characters cut more than two inches deep into the grey rock. Behind them, in lieu of laths, are planted large *sotoba*, twelve to fourteen feet high, and thick as the beams of a temple roof. These are graves of priests.

Jizo-gao

Descending the shadowed steps, I find myself face to face with six little statues about three feet high, standing in a row on one long pedestal. The first holds a Buddhist incense box; the second, a lotus; the third, a pilgrim's staff (*tsue*); the fourth is telling the beads of a Buddhist rosary; the fifth stands in the attitude of prayer, with hands joined; the sixth bears in one hand the *shakujō* or mendicant priest's staff, having six rings attached to the top of it and in the other hand the mystic jewel, *nyo-i hōju*, by virtue of which all desires may be accomplished. But the faces of the six are the same: each figure differs from the other by the attitude only and emblematic attribute, and all are smiling the like faint smile. About the neck of each figure a white cotton bag is suspended, and all the bags are filled with pebbles. Pebbles have been piled high also about the feet of the statues, and on their knees, and on their shoulders. Even on their aureoles of stone, little pebbles are balanced. Archaic, mysterious, but inexplicably touching, all these soft childish faces are.

Roku Jizō—'The Six Jizō'—these images are called in the speech of the people, and such groups may be seen in many a Japanese cemetery. They are representations of the most beautiful and tender figure in Japanese popular faith, that charming divinity who cares for the souls of little children, and consoles them in the place of unrest, and saves them from the demons. 'But why are those little stones piled about the statues?' I ask.

Well, it is because some say the child ghosts must build little towers of stones for penance in the Sai no Kawara, the dry riverbed of the Sanzu river, which is the place to which all children after death must go. The *oni*, who are demons, come to throw down the little stone piles as fast as the children build. These demons frighten the children, and torment them. But the little souls run to Jizō, who hides them in his great sleeves, and comforts them, and makes the demons go away. Every stone one lays on the knees or at the feet of Jizō, with a prayer from the heart, helps some child soul in the Sai no Kawara to perform its long penance.

'All little children,' says the young Buddhist student who tells all this, with a smile as gentle as Jizō's own, 'must go to the Sai no Kawara when they die. And there they play with Jizō. The Sai no Kawara is beneath us, below the ground.

'Jizō has long sleeves to his robe; and they pull him by the sleeves in their play; and they pile up little stones before him to amuse themselves. Those stones you see heaped about the statues are put there by people for the sake of the little ones, most often by mothers of dead children who pray to Jizō. But grown people do not go to the Sai no Kawara when they die.'

And the young student, leaving the Roku Jizō, leads the way to other strange surprises, guiding me among the tombs, showing me the sculptured divinities.

Some of them are quaintly touching; all are interesting; a few are positively beautiful.

The greater number have halo. Many are represented kneeling, with hands joined exactly like the figures of saints in old Christian art. Others, holding lotus flowers, appear to dream the dreams that are meditations. One figure reposes on the coils of a great serpent. Another, coiffed with something resembling a tiara, has six hands, one pair joined in prayer, the rest, extended, holding out various objects. This figure stands on a prostrate demon, crouching face downwards. Yet another image, cut in low relief, has arms innumerable. The first pair of hands are joined, with the palms together. From behind the line of the shoulders, as if shadowily emanating therefrom, multitudinous arms reach out in all directions, vapoury, spiritual, holding forth all kinds of objects as in answer to supplication, and symbolising, perhaps, the omnipotence of love. This is but one of the many forms of Kannon, the goddess of mercy, the gentle divinity who refused the rest of Nirvana to save the souls of men, and who is most frequently pictured as a beautiful Japanese girl. But here she appears as Senjū Kannon (Kannon of the Thousand Hands). Close by stands a great slab bearing on the upper portion of its chiselled surface an image in relief of Buddha, meditating on a lotus. Below are carven three weird little figures, one with hands on its eyes, one with hands on its ears, one with hands on its mouth. They are Apes.

'What do they signify?' I inquire.

My friend answers vaguely, mimicking each gesture of the three sculptured shapes, 'I see no bad thing; I hear no bad thing; I speak no bad thing.'

Gradually, by dint of reiterated explanations, I learn to recognise some of the gods at sight. The figure seated on a lotus, holding a sword in its hand, and surrounded by bickering fire, is Fudo-*sama*——Buddha as the Unmoved, the Immutable: the sword signifies intellect; the fire, power. Here is a meditating divinity, holding in one hand a coil of ropes: the divinity is Buddha; those are the ropes which bind the passions and desires. Here also is Buddha slumbering, with the gentlest, softest Japanese face—a child face—and eyes closed, and hand pillowing the cheek, in Nirvana. Here is a beautiful virgin figure, standing on a lily: Kannon-*sama*, the Japanese Madonna. Here is a solemn seated figure, holding in one hand a vase, and lifting the other with the gesture of a teacher: Yakushi-*sama*, Buddha the All-Healer, Physician of Souls.

Also, I see figures of animals. The deer of Buddhist birth-stories stands, all grace, in snowy stone, on the summit of *toro*, or votive lamps. On one tomb I see, superbly chiselled, the image of a fish, or rather the idea of a fish, made beautifully grotesque for sculptural purposes, like the dolphin of Greek art. It crowns the top of a memorial column. The broad open jaws, showing serrated teeth, rest on the summit of the block bearing the dead man's name; the dorsal fin and elevated tail are elaborated into decorative impossibilities.

'*Mokugyo*,' says Akira. It is the same Buddhist emblem as that hollow wooden object, lacquered scarlet-and-gold, on which the priests beat with a padded mallet while chanting the *sūtra*.

Fnally, in one place I perceive a pair of sitting animals, of some mythological species, supple of figure as greyhounds.

'Kitsune,' says Akira—'foxes.'

So they are, now that I look on them with knowledge of their purpose; idealised foxes, foxes spiritualised, impossibly graceful foxes. They are chiselled in grey stone. They have long, narrow, sinister, glittering eyes; they seem to snarl. They are weird, very weird creatures, the servants of the rice god, retainers of Inari-*sama*, and properly belong, not to Buddhist iconography, but the imagery of Shintō.

No inscriptions on these tombs correspond to our epitaphs. Only family names—the names of the dead and their relatives and a sculptured crest, usually a flower. On the *sotoba*, only Sanscrit words.

Farther on, I find other figures of Jizō, single reliefs, sculptured on tombs. But one of these is a work of art so charming that I feel a pain at being obliged to pass it by. More sweet, assuredly, than any imaged Christ, this dream in white stone of the playfellow of dead children, like a beautiful young boy, with gracious eyelids half closed, and face made heavenly by such a smile as only Buddhist art could have imagined, the smile of infinite lovingness and supremest gentleness. Indeed, so charming the ideal of Jizō is that in the speech of the people a beautiful face is always likened to his—'Jizō-gao,' as the face of Jizō.

Flower-blue Eyes

We come to the end of the cemetery, to the verge of the great grove. Beyond the trees, what caressing sun, what spiritual loveliness in the tender day! A tropic sky always seemed to me to hang so low that one could almost bathe one's fingers in its lukewarm liquid blue by reaching upward from any dwelling roof. This sky, softer, fainter, arches so vastly as to suggest the heaven of a larger planet. The clouds are not clouds, but only dreams of clouds, so filmy they are—ghosts of clouds, diaphanous spectres, illusions!

All at once I become aware of a child standing before me, a very young girl who looks up wonderingly at my face; so light her approach that the joy of the birds and whispering of the leaves quite drowned the soft sound of her feet. Her ragged garb is Japanese, but her gaze, her loose fair hair, are not of Japan only. The ghost of another race—perhaps my own—watches me through her flower-blue eyes.

A strange playground surely is this for you, my child. I wonder if all these shapes about you do not seem very weird, very strange, to that little soul

33

of yours. But no, it is only I who seem strange to you. You have forgotten the other birth, and your father's world.

Half-caste and poor and pretty, in this foreign port! Better you were with the dead about you, child! Better than the splendour of this soft blue light the unknown darkness for you. There the gentle Jizō would care for you, and hide you in his great sleeves, and keep all evil from you, and play shadowy play with you. And this your forsaken mother, who now comes to ask an alms for your sake, dumbly pointing to your strange beauty with her patient Japanese smile, would put little stones on the knees of the dear god that you might find rest.

Sozu Baba

'Oh, Akira! you must tell me something more about Jizō, and the ghosts of the children in the Sai no Kawara.'

'I cannot tell you much more,' answers Akira, smiling at my interest in this charming divinity; 'but if you will come with me now to Kuboyama, I will show you, in one of the temples there, pictures of the Sai no Kawara and of Jizō, and the judgment of souls.'

So we take our way in two *jinrikisha* to the Temple Rinko-*ji*, on Kuboyama. We roll swiftly through a mile of many-coloured narrow Japanese streets. Then through a half-mile of pretty suburban ways, lined with gardens, behind whose clipped hedges are homes light and dainty as cages of wicker work. Leaving our vehicles, we ascend green hills on foot by winding paths and traverse a region of fields and farms. After a long walk in the hot sun we reach a village almost wholly composed of shrines and temples.

The outlying sacred place—three buildings in one enclosure of bamboo fences—belongs to the Shingon sect. A small open shrine, to the left of the entrance, first attracts us. It is a dead house: a Japanese bier is there. But almost opposite the doorway is an altar covered with startling images.

What immediately rivets the attention is a terrible figure, all vermilion red, towering above many smaller images—a goblin shape with immense cavernous eyes. His mouth is widely opened as if speaking in wrath, and his brows frown terribly. A long red beard descends on his red breast. And on his head is a strangely shaped crown, a crown of black and gold, having three singular lobes: the left lobe bearing an image of the moon; the right, an image of the sun; the central lobe is all black. But below it, on the deep gold-rimmed black band, flames the mystic character signifying King. Also, from the same crown-band protrude at descending angles, to left and right, two gilded sceptre-shaped objects. In one hand the King holds an object similar of form, but larger, his *shaku* or regal wand. And Akira explains.

This is Enma-ō, Lord of Shadows, Judge of Souls, King of the Dead. Of any man having a terrible countenance the Japanese are wont to say, 'His face is the face of Enma.'

At his right hand white Jizō-*sama* stands on a many-petalled rosy lotus.

At his left is the image of an aged woman—weird *sozu baba*, she who takes the garments of the dead away by the banks of the River of the Three Roads, which flows through the phantom world. Pale blue her robe is; her hair and skin are white; her face is strangely wrinkled; her small, keen eyes are hard. The statue is very old, and the paint is scaling from it in places, so as to lend it a ghastly leprous aspect.

There are also images of the Sea-goddess Benten and of Kannon-*sama*, seated on summits of mountains forming the upper part of miniature landscapes made of some unfamiliar composition, and beautifully coloured; the whole being protected from careless fingering by strong wire nettings stretched across the front of the little shrines containing the panorama. Benten has eight arms: two of her hands are joined in prayer; the others, extended above her, hold different objects: a sword, a wheel, a bow, an arrow, a key, and a magical gem. Below her, standing on the slopes of her mountain throne, are her ten robed attendants, all in the attitude of prayer. Still farther down appears the body of a great white serpent, with its tail hanging from one orifice in the rocks, and its head emerging from another. At the very bottom of the hill lies a patient cow. Kannon appears as Senjū Kannon, offering gifts to men with all the multitude of her arms of mercy.

But this is not what we came to see. The pictures of heaven and hell await us in the Zen-*shū* temple close by, where we turn our steps.

On the way my guide tells me this:

'When one dies the body is washed and shaven, and attired in white, in the garments of a pilgrim. And a wallet (*sanya-bukuro*), like the wallet of a Buddhist pilgrim, is hung about the neck of the dead. In this wallet are placed three *rin*. And these coin are buried with the dead.

'For all who die must, except children, pay three *rin* at the Sanzu no Kawa, rhe River of the Three Roads. When souls have reached that river, they find there the old woman of the three roads, Sodzu-*baba*, waiting for them: she lives on the banks of that river, with her husband, Tendatsu-*ba*. And if the old woman is not paid the sum of three *rin*, she takes away the clothes of the dead, and hangs them on the trees.'

Kakemono

The temple is small, neat, luminous with the sun pouring into its widely opened *shōji*. Akira must know the priests well, so affable their greeting is. I make a little offering, and Akira explains the purpose of our visit.

We are invited into a large bright apartment in a wing of the building, overlooking a lovely garden. Little cushions are placed on the floor for us to sit on, and a smoking box is brought in, and a tiny lacquered table about eight inches high. And while one of the priests opens a cupboard, or alcove with doors, to find the *kakemono*, another brings us tea, and a plate of curious confectionery consisting of various pretty objects made of a paste of sugar and rice flour. One is a perfect model of a chrysanthemum blossom; another is a lotus; others are simply large, thin, crimson lozenges bearing admirable designs—flying birds, wading storks, fish, even miniature landscapes. Akira picks out the chrysanthemum, and insists I eat it. I begin to demolish the sugary blossom, petal by petal, feeling all the while an acute remorse for spoiling so beautiful a thing.

Meanwhile four *kakemono* have been brought in, unrolled, and suspended from pegs on the wall, and we rise to examine them.

They are very, very beautiful *kakemono*, miracles of drawing and of colour-subdued colour, the colour of the best period of Japanese art. They are very large, fully five feet long and more than three broad, mounted on silk.

And these are the legends of them:

First *kakemono*

In the upper part of the painting is a scene from the Shaba, the world of men which we are wont to call the real—a cemetery with trees in blossom, and mourners kneeling before tombs. All under the soft blue light of Japanese day.

Underneath is the world of ghosts. Down through the earth crust souls are descending. Here they are flitting all white through inky darknesses. Farther on, through weird twilight, they are wading the flood of the phantom River of the Three Roads, the Sanzu no Kawa. And here on the right is waiting for them Sodzu-*baba*, the old woman of the Three Roads, ghastly and grey, and tall as a nightmare. From some she is taking their garments—the trees about her are heavily hung with the garments of others gone before.

Farther down I see fleeing souls overtaken by demons—hideous blood-red demons, with feet like lions, with faces half human, half bovine, the physiognomy of minotaurs in fury. One is rending a soul asunder. Another demon is forcing souls to reincarnate themselves in bodies of horses, of dogs, of swine. And as they are thus reincarnated they flee away into shadow.

Second kakemono

Such a gloom as the diver sees in deep-sea water, a lurid twilight. In the midst a throne, ebony-coloured, and on it an awful figure seated—Enma Dai-O, Lord of Death and Judge of Souls, unpitying, tremendous. Frightful guardian spirits hover about him—armed goblins. On the left, in the foreground below the throne, stands the Wondrous Mirror, Tabari no Kagami, reflecting the state of souls and all the happenings of the world. A landscape now shadows its surface—a landscape of cliffs and sand and sea, with ships in the offing. Upon the sand lies a dead man, slain by a sword slash; the murderer is running away. Before this mirror stands a terrified soul, in the grasp of a demon, who compels him to look, and to recognise in the murderer's features his own face. To the right of the throne, on a tall-stemmed flat stand, like the ones on which offerings to the gods are placed in temples, a monstrous shape appears, like a double-faced head freshly cut off, and set upright on the stump of the neck. The two faces are the Witnesses: the face of the woman, Mirume, sees all that goes on in the Shaba. The other face is that of a bearded man, the face of Kaguhana, who smells all odours, and by them is aware of all that human beings do. Close to them, on a reading stand, a great book is open, the record book of deeds. And between the mirror and the witnesses white shuddering souls await judgment.

Farther down I see the sufferings of souls already sentenced. One, in lifetime a liar, is having his tongue torn out by a demon armed with heated pincers. Other souls, flung by scores into fiery carts, are being dragged away to torment. The carts are of iron, but resemble in form certain hand-wagons one sees every day being pulled and pushed through the streets by bare-limbed Japanese labourers, chanting always the same melancholy alternating chorus, *Haidak! hei! haidak hei!* But these demon-wagoners—naked, blood-coloured, having the feet of lions and the heads of bulls—move with their flaming wagons at a run, like *jinrikisha*-men.

All the souls so far represented are souls of adults.

Third kakemono

A furnace, with souls for fuel, blazing up into darkness. Demons stir the fire with poles of iron. Down through the upper blackness other souls are falling head downward into the flames.

Below this scene opens a shadowy landscape—a faint-blue and faint-grey world of hills and vales, through which a river serpentines—the Sai no Kawara. Thronging the banks of the pale river are ghosts of little children, trying to pile up stones. They are very, very pretty, the child souls, pretty as real Japanese children are (it is astonishing how well infant beauty is felt and expressed by the artists of Japan). Each child has one little short white dress.

In the foreground a horrible devil with an iron club has just dashed down and scattered a pile of stones built by one of the children. The little ghost, seated by the ruin of its work, is crying, with both pretty hands to its eyes. The devil appears to sneer. Other children also are weeping nearby. But, lo! Jizō comes, all light and sweetness, with a glory moving behind him like a great full moon. He holds out his *shakujō*, his strong and holy staff, and the little ghosts catch it and cling to it, and are drawn into the circle of his protection. And other infants have caught his great sleeves, and one has been lifted to the bosom of the god.

Below this Sai no Kawara scene appears yet another shadow world, a wilderness of bamboos! Only white-robed shapes of women appear in it. They are weeping; the fingers of all are bleeding. With fingernails plucked out they must continue through centuries to pick the sharp-edged bamboo grass.

Fourth kakemono

Floating in glory, Dainichi Nyorai, Kannon-*sama*, Amida Buddha. Far below them as hell from heaven surges a lake of blood, in which souls float. The shores of this lake are precipices studded with sword blades thickly set as teeth in the jaws of a shark, and demons are driving naked ghosts up the frightful slopes. Out of the crimson lake something crystalline rises, like a beautiful, clear waterspout. It is the stem of a flower—a miraculous lotus, bearing up a soul to the feet of a priest standing above the verge of the abyss. By virtue of his prayer was shaped the lotus which thus lifted up and saved a sufferer.

Alas! there are no other *kakemono*. There were several others: they have been lost!

Fifth kakemono

No: I am happily mistaken; the priest has found, in some mysterious recess, one more *kakemono*, a very large one, which he unrolls and suspends beside the others. A vision of beauty, indeed! But what has this to do with faith or ghosts? In the foreground a garden by the waters of the sea, of some vast blue lake—a garden like that at Kanagawa, full of exquisite miniature landscape work: cascades, grottoes, lily ponds, carved bridges, and trees snowy with blossom, and dainty pavilions out-jutting over the placid azure water. Long, bright, soft bands of clouds swim athwart the background. Beyond and above them rises a fairy magnificence of palatial structures, roof above roof, through an aureate haze like summer vapour: creations aerial, blue, light as dreams. And there are guests in these gardens, lovely beings, Japanese maidens. But they wear aureoles, star-shining: they are spirits!

This is Paradise, the Gokuraku; and all those divine shapes are *bosatsu*. And now, looking closer, I perceive beautiful weird things which at first escaped my notice.

They are gardening, these charming beings!—they are caressing the lotus-buds, sprinkling their petals with something celestial, helping them to blossom. And what lotus buds with colours not of this world. Some have burst open. And in their luminous hearts, in a radiance like that of dawn, tiny naked infants are seated, each with a tiny halo. These are souls, new

Buddhas, *hotoke* born into bliss. Some are very, very small; others larger. All seem to be growing visibly, for their lovely nurses are feeding them with something ambrosial. I see one that has left its lotus cradle, being conducted by a celestial Jizō toward the higher splendours far away.

Above, in the loftiest blue, are floating *tennin*, angels of the Buddhist heaven, maidens with phoenix wings. One is playing with an ivory plectrum on some stringed instrument, just as a dancing girl plays her *shamisen*. Others are sounding those curious Chinese flutes, composed of seventeen tubes, which are still used in sacred concerts at the great temples.

Akira says this heaven is too much like earth. The gardens, he declares, are like the gardens of temples, in spite of the celestial lotus flowers, and in the blue roofs of the celestial mansions he discovers memories of the teahouses of the city of Kyoto.

Well, what after all is the heaven of any faith but ideal reiteration and prolongation of happy experiences remembered—the dream of dead days resurrected for us, and made eternal? And if you think this Japanese ideal too simple, too naive, if you say there are experiences of the material life more worthy of portrayal in a picture of heaven than any memory of days passed in Japanese gardens and temples and teahouses, it is perhaps because you do not know Japan, the soft, sweet blue of its sky, the tender colour of its waters, the gentle splendour of its sunny days, the exquisite charm of its interiors, where the least object appeals to one's sense of beauty with the air of something not made, but caressed, into existence.

The Hymn of Jizō

'Now there is a *wasan* of Jizō,' says Akira, taking from a shelf in the temple alcove some much-worn, blue-covered Japanese book. 'A *wasan* is what you would call a hymn or psalm. This book is two hundred years old: it is called *Sai no Kawara kuchizusami no den*, which is, literally, *The Legend of the Humming of the Sai no Kawara*. And this is the *wasan*'; and he reads me the hymn of Jizō—the legend of the murmur of the little ghosts, the legend of the humming of the Sai no Kawara rhythmically, like a song:

'Not of this world is the story of sorrow.
The story of the Sai no Kawara,

At the roots of the Mount Shide;
Not of this world is the tale.
Yet it is most pitiful to hear.
For together in the Sai no Kawara are assembled
children of tender age in multitude,
Infants but two or three years old,
Infants of four or five, infants of less than ten:

In the Sai no Kawara they are gathered together.
And the voice of their longing for their parents,
The voice of their crying for their mothers and their fathers
—"Chichi koishi! haha koishi!"—
Is never as the voice of the crying of children in this world,
But a crying so pitiful to hear
That the sound of it would pierce through flesh and bone.
And sorrowful indeed the task they perform—
Gathering the stones of the bed of the river,
Therewith to heap the tower of prayers.
Saying prayers for the happiness of father,
they heap the first tower;
Saying prayers for the happiness of mother,
they heap the second tower;
Saying prayers for their brothers, their sisters,
and all whom they loved at home,
they heap the third tower.
Such, by day, are their pitiful diversions.
But ever as the sun begins to sink below the horizon,
Then do the oni, the demons of the hells, appear,
And say to them—"What is this that you do here?"
Lo! your parents still living in the Shaba world
"Take no thought of pious offering or holy work
"They do nought but mourn for you,
from morning till evening.
"Oh, how pitiful! alas! how unmerciful!
"Verily the cause of the pains that you suffer

"Is only the mourning, the lamentation of your parents."
And saying also, "Blame never us!"
The demons cast down the heaped-up towers,
They dash the stones down with their clubs of iron.
But lo! The teacher Jizō appears.
All gently he comes, and says to the weeping infants:—
"Be not afraid, dears! be never fearful!
"Poor little souls, your lives were brief indeed!
"Too soon you were forced to make
the weary journey to the Meido,
"The long journey to the region of the dead!
"Trust to me! I am your father and mother in the Meido,
"Father of all children in the region of the dead."
And he folds the skirt of his shining robe about them;
So graciously takes he pity on the infants.
To those who cannot walk he stretches forth his strong *shakujō*;
And he pets the little ones, caresses them,
takes them to his loving bosom
So graciously he takes pity on the infants.
Namu Amida Butsu!

Enoshima

Kamakura

A long, straggling country village, between low wooded hills, with a canal passing through it. Old Japanese cottages, dingy, neutral-tinted, with roofs of thatch, very steeply sloping, above their wooden walls and paper *shōji*. Green patches on all the roof slopes, some sort of grass; and on the very summits, on the ridges, luxurious growths of *yaneshōbu*, the roof plant, bearing pretty purple flowers. In the lukewarm air a mingling of Japanese odours, smells of *sake*, smells of seaweed soup, smells of *daikon*, the strong native radish; and dominating all, a sweet, thick, heavy scent of incense— incense from the shrines of gods.

Akira has hired two *jinrikisha* for our pilgrimage. A speckless azure sky arches the world, and the land lies glorified in a joy of sunshine. And yet a sense of melancholy, of desolation unspeakable, weighs on me as we roll along the bank of the tiny stream, between the mouldering lines of wretched little homes with grass growing on their roofs. For this mouldering hamlet represents all that remains of the million-peopled streets of Minamoto Yoritomo's capital, the mighty city of the Shogunate, the ancient seat of feudal power, whither came the envoys of Kublai Khan demanding tribute, to lose their heads for their temerity. And only some of the countless temples of the once magnificent city now remain, saved from the conflagrations of the fifteenth and sixteenth centuries, doubtless because built in high places, or because isolated from the maze of burning streets by vast courts and groves. Here still dwell the ancient gods in the great silence of their decaying temples, without worshippers, without revenues, surrounded by desolations of rice fields, where the chanting of frogs replaces the sea-like murmur of the city that was and is not.

Engaku-ji

The first great temple—Engaku-*ji*—invites us to cross the canal by a little bridge facing its outward gate—a roofed gate with fine Chinese lines, but without carving. Passing it, we ascend a long, imposing succession of broad steps, leading up through a magnificent grove to a terrace, where we reach the second gate. This gate is a surprise; a stupendous structure of two stories—with huge sweeping curves of roof and enormous gables—antique, Chinese, magnificent. It is more than four hundred years old, but seems scarcely affected by the wearing of the centuries. The whole of the ponderous and complicated upper structure is sustained upon an open-work of round, plain pillars and cross-beams. The vast eaves are full of bird-nests, and the storm of twittering from the roofs is like a rushing of water. Immense the work is, and imposing in its aspect of settled power. In its way, it has great severity: there are no carvings, no gargoyles, no dragons. And yet the maze of projecting timbers below the eaves will both excite and delude expectation, so strangely does it suggest the grotesqueries and fantasticalities of another art. You look everywhere for the heads of lions, elephants, dragons, and see only the four-angled ends of beams, and feel rather astonished than disappointed. The majesty of the edifice could not have been strengthened by any such carving.

After the gate another long series of wide steps, and more trees, millennial, thick-shadowing, and then the terrace of the temple itself, with two beautiful stone lanterns (*tōrō*) at its entrance. The architecture of the temple resembles that of the gate, although on a lesser scale. Over the doors is a tablet with Chinese characters, reading, 'Great, Pure, Clear, Shining Treasure.' But a heavy framework of wooden bars closes the sanctuary, and there is no one to let us in. Peering between the bars I see, in a sort of twilight, first a pavement of squares of marble, then an aisle of massive wooden pillars upholding the dim lofty roof, and at the farther end, between the pillars, Shaka, colossal, black-visaged, gold-robed, enthroned on a giant lotus fully forty feet in circumference. At his right hand some white mysterious figure stands, holding an incense box; at his left, another white figure is praying with clasped hands. Both are of superhuman stature. But it is too dark within the edifice to discern who they may be—whether disciples of the Buddha, or divinities, or figures of saints.

Beyond this temple extends an immense grove of trees—ancient cedars and pines—with splendid bamboos thickly planted between them, rising perpendicularly as masts to mix their plumes with the foliage of the giants: the effect is tropical, magnificent. Through this shadowing, a flight of broad stone steps slant up gently to some yet older shrine. And ascending them we reach another portal, smaller than the imposing Chinese structure through which we already passed, but wonderful, weird, full of dragons, dragons of a form sculptors no longer carve, which they have even forgotten how to make, winged dragons rising from a storm-whirl of waters or thereinto descending. The dragon on the panel of the left gate has her mouth closed; the jaws of the dragon on the panel of the right gate are open and menacing. Female and male they are, like the lions of Buddha. And the whirls of the eddying water, and the crests of the billowing, stand out from the panel in astonishing boldness of relief, in loops and curlings of grey wood time-seasoned to the hardness of stone.

The little temple beyond contains no celebrated image, but a *shari* only, or relic of Buddha, brought from India. And I cannot see it, having no time to wait until the absent keeper of the shari can be found.

Ōgane

'Now we shall go and look at the big bell,' says Akira.

We turn to the left as we descend along a path cut between hills faced for the height of seven or eight feet with protection walls made green by moss; and reach a flight of extraordinarily dilapidated steps, with grass springing between their every joint and break—steps so worn down and displaced by countless feet that they have become ruins, painful and even dangerous to mount. We reach the summit without mishap and find ourselves before a little temple, on the steps of which an old priest awaits us, with a smiling bow of welcome. We return his salutation, but before we enter, turn to look at the Ōgane on the right—the famous Great Bell.

Under a lofty open shed, with a tilted Chinese roof, the Great Bell is hung. I should judge it to be fully nine feet high, and about five feet in diameter, with lips about eight inches thick. The shape of it is not like that of our bells, which broaden toward the lips; this has the same diameter through all its height and is covered with Buddhist texts cut into the smooth metal. It is rung by means of a heavy swinging beam, suspended from the roof by chains, and moved like a battering-ram. There are loops of palm-fibre rope attached to the beam to pull it by. When you pull hard enough, so as to give it a good swing, it strikes a moulding like a lotus flower on the side of the bell. This it must have done many hundred times, for the square, flat end of it, though showing the grain of a very dense wood, has been battered into a convex disk with ragged protruding edges, like the surface of a long-used printer's mallet.

A priest makes a sign to me to ring the bell. I first touch the great lips with my hand very lightly, and a musical murmur comes from them. Then I set the beam swinging strongly, and a sound deep as thunder, rich as the bass of a mighty organ—a sound enormous, extraordinary, yet beautiful—rolls over the hills and away. Then swiftly follows another and lesser and sweeter billowing of tone. Then another. Then an eddying of waves of echoes. Only once was it struck, the astounding bell, yet it continues to sob and moan for at least ten minutes!

The age of this bell is six hundred and fifty years.

In the little temple nearby, the priest shows us a series of curious paintings, representing the six hundredth anniversary of the casting of the bell (for this is a sacred bell, and the spirit of a god is believed to dwell within it). Otherwise the temple has little of interest. There are some *kakemono* representing Iyeyasu and his retainers; and on either side of the door, separating the inner from the outward sanctuary, there are life-size images of Japanese warriors in antique costume. On the altars of the inner shrine are small images, grouped on a miniature landscape-work of painted wood—the Jūgo-Dōji, or Fifteen Youths—the sons of the goddess Benten. There are *shide* before the shrine, and a mirror on it, emblems of Shintō. The sanctuary has changed hands in the great transfer of Buddhist temples to the state religion.

In nearly every celebrated temple little Japanese prints are sold, containing the history of the shrine, and its miraculous legends. I find several such things on sale at the door of the temple, and in one of them,

ornamented with a curious engraving of the bell, I discover, with Akira's
aid, the following traditions:

Ono no Kimi

In the twelfth year of Bummei, this bell rang itself. And one who laughed
on being told of the miracle, met with misfortune. Another, who believed,
thereafter prospered, and obtained all his desires.

Now, in that time there died in the village of Tamanawa a sick man whose
name was Ono no Kimi. He descended to the region of the dead, and went
before the judgment seat of Enma ō. And Enma, Judge of Souls, said to
him, 'You come too soon! The measure of life allotted you in the Shaba
world has not yet been exhausted. Go back at once.' But Ono no Kimi
pleaded, saying, 'How may I go back, not knowing my way through the
darkness?' And Enma answered him, 'You can find your way back by listening
to the sound of the bell of Engaku-*ji*, which is heard in the Nanen-budi
world, going south.' And Ono no Kimi went south, and heard the bell, and
found his way through the darknesses, and revived in the Shaba-world.

Also in those days there appeared in many provinces a Buddhist priest
of giant stature, whom none remembered to have seen before, and whose
name no man knew, travelling through the land, and everywhere exhorting
the people to pray before the bell of Engaku-*ji*. At last it was discovered
that the giant pilgrim was the holy bell itself, transformed by supernatural
power into the form of a priest. And after these things had happened, many
prayed before the bell, and obtained their wishes.

Grotto-Work

'Oh! there is something still to see,' my guide exclaims as we reach the
great Chinese gate again. He leads the way across the grounds by another
path to a little hill, previously hidden from view by trees. The face of the
hill, a mass of soft stone perhaps one hundred feet high, is hollowed out
into chambers, full of images. These look like burial caves, and the images
seem funereal monuments. There are two stories of chambers—three above,
two below, and the former are connected with the latter by a narrow interior
stairway cut through the living rock. And all around the dripping walls of
these chambers on pedestals are grey slabs, shaped exactly like the *haka* in

Buddhist cemeteries, and chiselled with figures of divinities in high relief. All have glory-disks: some are naive and sincere like the work of our own mediaeval image makers. Several are not unfamiliar. I have seen before, in the cemetery of Kuboyama, this kneeling woman with countless shadowy hands; and this figure tiara-coiffed, slumbering with one knee raised, and cheek pillowed on the left hand—the placid and pathetic symbol of the perpetual rest. Others, like Madonnas, hold lotus flowers, their feet resting on the coils of a serpent. I cannot see them all, for the rock roof of one chamber has fallen in; and a sunbeam entering the ruin reveals a host of inaccessible sculptures half buried in rubbish.

But no!—this grotto-work is not for the dead, and these are not *haka*, as I imagined, but only images of the Goddess of Mercy. These chambers are chapels, and these sculptures are the Engaku-*ji* no Hyaku Kannon, 'the Hundred Kannon of Engaku-*ji*.' And I see in the upper chamber above the stairs a granite tablet in a rock-niche, chiselled with an inscription in Sanscrit transliterated into Chinese characters, 'Adoration to the great merciful Kanzeon, who looketh down above the sound of prayer.'

Kenchō-ji

Entering the grounds of the next temple, the Temple of Kenchō-*ji*, through the Gate of the Forest of Contemplative Words, and the Gate of the Great Mountain of Wealth, one might almost fancy one's self reentering, by some queer mistake, the grounds of Engaku-*ji*. For the third gate before us, and the imposing temple beyond it, constructed on the same models as those of the structures previously visited, were also the work of the same architect.[1] Passing this third gate—colossal, severe, superb—we come to a fountain of bronze before the temple doors, an immense and beautiful lotus-leaf of metal, forming a broad shallow basin kept full to the brim by a jet in its midst.

This temple also is paved with black and white square slabs, and we can enter it with our shoes. Outside it is plain and solemn as that of Engaku-*ji*, but the interior offers a more extraordinary spectacle of faded splendour. In lieu of the black Shaka throned against a background of flamelets, is a

---

1 In fact, both temples were designed by different architects, though they were completed shortly after each other, the Kenchō-*ji* in 1253, the Engaku-*ji* in 1282.

colossal Jizō-*sama*, with a nimbus of fire—a single gilded circle large as a wagon wheel, breaking into fire-tongues at three points. He is seated on an enormous lotus of tarnished gold—over the lofty edge of which the skirt of his robe trails down. Behind him, standing on ascending tiers of golden steps, are glimmering hosts of miniature figures of him, reflections, multiplications of him, ranged there by ranks of hundreds—the Thousand Jizō. From the ceiling above him droop the dingy splendours of a sort of dais-work, a streaming circle of pendants like a fringe, shimmering faintly through the webbed dust of centuries. And the ceiling itself must once have been a marvel, all beamed in caissons, each caisson containing, on a gold ground, the painted figure of a flying bird. Formerly the eight great pillars supporting the roof were also covered with gilding, but only a few traces of it still linger on their worm pierced surfaces, and about the bases of their capitals. There are wonderful friezes above the doors, from which all colour has long since faded away, marvellous grey old carvings in relief; floating figures of *tennin*, or heavenly spirits playing on flutes and *biwa*.

There is a chamber separated by a heavy wooden screen from the aisle on the right. The priest in charge of the building slides the screen aside, and bids us to enter. In this chamber is a drum elevated on a brazen stand— the hugest I ever saw, fully eighteen feet in circumference. Beside it hangs a big bell, covered with Buddhist texts. I am sorry to learn that it is prohibited to sound the great drum. There is nothing else to see except some dingy paper lanterns figured with the *svastika*—the sacred Buddhist symbol called by the Japanese *manji*.

Silk

Akira tells me that the book *Jizōkyō kosui* relates the legend of the great statue of Jizō in this same ancient temple of Kenchō-*ji*.

Formerly there lived at Kamakura the wife of a *rōnin* named Soga Sadayoshi. She lived by feeding silkworms and gathering the silk. She used often to visit the temple of Kenchō-*ji*, and one very cold day that she went there, she thought that the image of Jizō looked like one suffering from cold. She resolved to make a cap to keep the god's head warm—such a cap as the people of the country wear in cold weather. And she went home and made the cap and covered the god's head with it, saying, 'Would I were rich enough

49

to give you a warm covering for all your august body. But, alas! I am poor, and even this which I offer you is unworthy of your divine acceptance.'

Now this woman very suddenly died in the fiftieth year of her age, in the twelfth month of the fifth year of the period called Chisho. But her body remained warm for three days, so that her relatives would not suffer her to be taken to the burning ground. And on the evening of the third day she came to life again.

Then she related that on the day of her death she had gone before the judgment seat of Enma, king and judge of the dead. And Enma, seeing her, became angry, and said to her, 'You have been a wicked woman, and have scorned the teaching of the Buddha. All your life you have passed in destroying the lives of silkworms by putting them into heated water. Now you shall go to hell and there burn until your sins shall be expiated.' Forthwith she was seized and dragged by demons to a great pot filled with molten metal, and thrown into the pot, and she cried out horribly. And suddenly Jizō-*sama* descended into the molten metal beside her, and the metal became like a flowing of oil and ceased to burn. And Jizō put his arms about her and lifted her out. And he went with her before King Enma, and asked that she should be pardoned for his sake, forasmuch as she had become related to him by one act of goodness. So she found pardon, and returned to the Shaba world.

'Akira,' I ask, 'it cannot then be lawful, according to Buddhism, for anyone to wear silk?'

'Assuredly not,' replies Akira; 'and by the law of Buddha priests are expressly forbidden to wear silk. Nevertheless,' he adds with that quiet smile of his, in which I am beginning to discern suggestions of sarcasm, 'nearly all the priests wear silk.'

Hakada Jizō

Akira also tells me this:

It is related in the seventh volume of the book *Kamakura-shi* that there was formerly at Kamakura a temple called Enmei-*ji*, in which there was enshrined a famous statue of Jizō, called Hadaka Jizō, or Naked Jizō. The statue was indeed naked, but clothes were put on it, and it stood upright with its feet on a chessboard. Now, when pilgrims came to the temple and paid a certain fee, the priest of the temple would remove the clothes of the statue. And then all could see that, though the face was the face of Jizō, the body was the body of a woman.

Now this was the origin of the famous image of Hadaka Jizō standing on the chessboard. On one occasion the great prince Taira no Tokyori was playing chess with his wife in the presence of many guests. And he made her agree, after they had played several games, that whosoever should lose the next game would have to stand naked on the chessboard. And in the next game they played his wife lost. And she prayed to Jizō to save her from the shame of appearing naked. And Jizō came in answer to her prayer and stood on the chessboard, and disrobed himself, and changed his body suddenly into the body of a woman.

Eyes of Nightmare

As we travel on, the road curves and narrows between higher elevations, and becomes more sombre. '*Oi! matte!*' my Buddhist guide calls softly to the runners, and our two vehicles halt in a band of sunshine, descending, through an opening in the foliage of immense trees, over a flight of ancient mossy steps. 'Here,' says my friend, 'is the temple of the King of Death. It is called Ennō-*ji* and is a temple of the Zen sect. It is more than seven hundred years old, and there is a famous statue in it.'

We ascend to a small, narrow court in which the edifice stands. At the head of the steps, to the right, is a stone tablet, very old, with characters cut at least an inch deep into the granite of it, Chinese characters signifying, 'This is the Temple of Enma, King.'

The temple resembles outwardly and inwardly the others we have visited, and, like those of Shaka and of the colossal Jizō of Kamakura, has a paved floor, so that we are not obliged to remove our shoes on entering. Everything is worn, dim, vaguely grey. There is a pungent scent of mouldiness; the paint has long ago peeled away from the naked wood of the pillars. Throned to right and left against the high walls tower nine grim figures—five on one side, four on the other—wearing strange crowns with trumpet-shapen ornaments; figures hoary with centuries, and so like to the icon of Enma, which I saw at Kuboyama, that I ask, 'Are all these Enma?' 'Oh, no!' my guide answers; 'these are his attendants only—the Jū-ō, the Ten Kings.' 'But there are only nine?' I query. 'Nine, and Enma completes the number. You have not yet seen Enma.'

Where is he? I see at the farther end of the chamber an altar elevated on a platform approached by wooden steps, but there is no image, only the usual altar furniture of gilded bronze and lacquerware. Behind the altar I see only a curtain about six feet square—a curtain once dark red, now almost without any definite hue—probably veiling some alcove. A temple guardian approaches, and invites us to ascend the platform. I remove my shoes before stepping onto the matted surface, and follow the guardian behind the altar, in front of the curtain. He makes me a sign to look, and lifts the veil with a long rod. And suddenly, out of the blackness of some mysterious profundity masked by that sombre curtain, there glowers over me an apparition at the sight of which I involuntarily start back—a monstrosity exceeding all anticipation—a face.

A face tremendous, menacing, frightful, dull red, as with the redness of heated iron cooling into grey. The first shock of the vision is no doubt partly due to the somewhat theatrical manner in which the work is suddenly revealed out of darkness by the lifting of the curtain. But as the surprise passes I begin to recognise the immense energy of the conception—to look for the secret of the grim artist. The wonder of the creation is not in the tiger frown, nor in the violence of the terrific mouth, nor in the fury and ghastly colour of the head as a whole: it is in the eyes—eyes of nightmare.

Oni

Now this weird old temple has its legend. Seven hundred years ago, it is said, there died the great image maker, the great warrior, Unke Sosei. Unke Sosei signifies 'Unke who returned from the dead.' For when he came before Enma, the Judge of Souls, Enma said to him, 'Living, you made no image of me. Go back to earth and make one, now that you have looked upon me.' And Unke found himself suddenly restored to the world of men; and they who had known him before, astonished to see him alive again, called him Unke Sosei. And Unke Sosei, bearing with him always the memory of the countenance of Enma, wrought this image of him, which still inspires fear in all who behold it. And he made also the images of the grim Jū-ō, the Ten Kings obeying Enma, which sit throned about the temple.

I want to buy a picture of Enma, and make my wish known to the temple guardian. Oh, yes, I may buy a picture of Enma, but I must first see the *oni*. I follow the guardian out of the temple, down the mossy steps, and across the village highway into a little Japanese cottage, where I take my seat on the floor. The guardian disappears behind a screen, and presently returns dragging with him the *oni*— the image of a demon, naked, blood-red, indescribably ugly. The *oni* is about three feet high. He stands in an attitude of menace, brandishing a club. He has a head shaped something like the head of a bulldog, with brazen eyes; and his feet are like the feet of a lion. Very gravely the guardian turns the grotesquery round and round, that I may admire its every aspect; while a naive crowd collects before the open door to look at the stranger and the demon.

Then the guardian finds me a rude woodcut of Enma, with a sacred inscription printed on it; and as soon as I have paid for it, he proceeds to stamp the paper, with the seal of the temple. The seal he keeps in a wonderful lacquered box, covered with many wrappings of soft leather. These having been removed, I inspect the seal—an oblong, vermilion-red polished stone, with the design cut in intaglio on it. He moistens the surface with red ink, presses it on the corner of the paper bearing the grim picture, and the authenticity of my strange purchase is established for ever.

Daibutsu

You do not see the Daibutsu as you enter the grounds of his long-vanished temple, and proceed along a paved path across stretches of lawn; great trees hide him. But very suddenly, at a turn, he comes into full view and you start! No matter how many photographs of the colossus you may have already seen, this first vision of the reality is an astonishment. Then you imagine that you are already too near, though the image is at least a hundred yards away. As for me, I retire at once thirty or forty yards back, to get a better view. And the *jinrikisha* man runs after me, laughing and gesticulating, thinking that I imagine the image alive and am afraid of it.

But, even were that shape alive, none could be afraid of it. The gentleness, the dreamy passionlessness of those features—the immense repose of the whole figure—are full of beauty and charm. And, contrary to all expectation, the nearer you approach the giant Buddha, the greater this charm becomes. You look up into the solemnly beautiful face—into the half-closed eyes that seem to watch you through their eyelids of bronze as gently as those of a child, and you feel that the image typifies all that is tender and calm in the soul of the East. Yet you feel also that only Japanese thought could have created it. Its beauty, its dignity, its perfect repose, reflect the higher life of the race that imagined it; and, though doubtless inspired by some Indian model, as the treatment of the hair and various symbolic marks reveal, the art is Japanese.

So mighty and beautiful the work is, that you will not for some time notice the magnificent lotus plants of bronze, fully fifteen feet high, planted before the figure, on either side of the great tripod in which incense rods are burning.

Through an orifice in the right side of the enormous lotus blossom on which Buddha is seated, you can enter into the statue. The interior contains a little shrine of Kannon, and a statue of the priest Yuten, and a stone tablet bearing in Chinese characters the sacred formula, *Namu Amida Butsu*.

A ladder enables the pilgrim to ascend into the interior of the colossus as high as the shoulders, in which are two little windows commanding a wide prospect of the grounds. A priest, who acts as guide, states the age of the statue to be six hundred and thirty years, and asks for some small contribution to aid in the erection of a new temple to shelter it from the weather.

This Buddha once had a temple. A tidal wave following an earthquake swept walls and roof away, but left the mighty Amida unmoved, still meditating on his lotus.

Hase-dera

And we arrive before the Hasedera, the far-famed Kamakura temple of Kannon, who yielded up her right to eternal peace that she might save the souls of men, and renounced Nirvana to suffer with humanity for other myriad million ages—Kannon, the Goddess of Pity and of Mercy.

I climb three flights of steps leading to the temple, and a young girl, seated at the threshold, rises to greet us. Then she disappears within the temple to summon the guardian priest, a venerable man, white-robed, who makes me a sign to enter.

The temple is large as any that I have yet seen, and, like the others, grey with the wearing of six hundred years. From the roof there hang down votive offerings, inscriptions, and lanterns in multitude, painted with various pleasing colours. Almost opposite to the entrance is a singular statue, a seated figure, of human dimensions and most human aspect, looking upon us with small weird eyes set in a wondrously wrinkled face. This face was originally painted flesh-tint, and the robes of the image pale blue. But now the whole is uniformly grey with age and dust, and its colourlessness harmonises so well with the senility of the figure that one is almost ready to believe one's self gazing at a living mendicant pilgrim. It is Benzuru, the same personage whose famous image at Asakusa has been made featureless by the wearing touch of countless pilgrim fingers. To the left and right of the entrance are the *niō*, enormously muscled, furious of aspect, their crimson bodies speckled with a white scum of paper pellets spat at them by worshippers. Above the altar is a small but very pleasing image of Kannon, her entire figure relieved against an oblong halo of gold, imitating a flickering flame.

But this is not the image for which the temple is famed; there is another to be seen on certain conditions. The old priest presents me with a petition, written in excellent and eloquent English, praying visitors to contribute something to the maintenance of the temple and its pontiff, and appealing to those of another faith to remember that 'any belief that can make men kindly and good is worthy of respect.' I contribute my mite, and I ask to see the great Kannon.

Then the old priest lights a lantern, and leads the way, through a low doorway on the left of the altar, into the interior of the temple, into some very lofty darkness. I follow him cautiously awhile, discerning nothing but the flicker of the lantern. Then we halt before something which gleams. A moment, and my eyes, becoming more accustomed to the darkness, begin to distinguish outlines. The gleaming object defines itself gradually as a foot, an immense golden foot, and I perceive the hem of a golden robe undulating over the instep. Now the other foot appears; the figure is certainly standing. I can perceive that we are in a narrow but also very lofty chamber, and that out of some mysterious blackness overhead ropes are dangling down into the circle of lantern-light illuminating the golden feet. The priest lights two more lanterns, and suspends them on hooks attached to a pair of pendent

ropes about a yard apart; then he pulls up both together slowly. More of
the golden robe is revealed as the lanterns ascend, swinging on their way;
then the outlines of two mighty knees; then the curving of columnar thighs
under chiselled drapery, and, as with the still waving ascent of the lanterns
the golden vision towers ever higher through the gloom, expectation
intensifies. There is no sound but the sound of the invisible pulleys overhead,
which squeak like bats. Now above the golden girdle, the suggestion of a
bosom. Then the glowing of a golden hand uplifted in benediction. Then
another golden hand holding a lotus. And at last a face, golden, smiling with
eternal youth and infinite tenderness, the face of Kannon.

So revealed out of the consecrated darkness, this ideal of divine femin-
ity—creation of a forgotten art and time—is more than impressive. I can
scarcely call the emotion it produces admiration; it is rather reverence. But
the lanterns, which paused awhile at the level of the beautiful face, now
ascend still higher, with a fresh squeaking of pulleys. And lo! the tiara of
the divinity appears with strangest symbolism. It is a pyramid of heads, of
faces-charming faces of maidens, miniature faces of Kannon herself.

For this is the Kannon of the Eleven Faces—Jūichimen Kannon.

Tokudo Shonin

Most sacred this statue is held, and this is its legend:

In the reign of Emperor Gensei, there lived in the province of Yamato a
Buddhist priest, Tokudo Shonin, who had been a *bosatsu* in a previous birth,
but had been reborn among common men to save their souls. Now at that
time, in a valley in Yamato, Tokudo Shonin, walking by night, saw a wonderful
radiance. Going toward he found that it came from the trunk of a great
fallen tree, a *kusunoki*, or camphor tree. A delicious perfume came from the
tree, and the shining of it was like the shining of the moon. And by these
signs Tokudo Shonin knew that the wood was holy, and he decided that he
should have the statue of Kannon carved from it. He recited a *sūtra*, and
repeated the Nenbutsu, praying for inspiration. And even while he prayed
there came and stood before him an aged man and an aged woman, and
these said to him, 'We know that your desire is to have the image of Kannon-
sama carved from this tree with the help of Heaven; continue therefore, to
pray, and we shall carve the statue.'

And Tokudo Shonin did as they bade him. And he saw them easily split the vast trunk into two equal parts, and begin to carve each of the parts into an image. And he saw them labour for three days. And on the third day the work was done—and he saw the two marvellous statues of Kannon made perfect before him. And he said to the strangers, 'Tell me, by what names are you known.' The old man answered, 'I am Kasuga Myōjin.' And the woman answered, 'I am called Tenshōko Daijin; I am the goddess of the sun.' As they spoke both became transfigured and ascended to heaven and vanished from the sight of Tokudo Shonin.

The emperor, hearing of these happenings, sent his representative to Yamato to make offerings, and to have a temple built. Also the great priest, Gyōgi Bosatsu, came and consecrated the images, and dedicated the temple that by order of the emperor was built. And one of the statues he placed in the temple, enshrining it, and commanding it, 'Stay thou here always to save all living creatures!' But the other statue he cast into the sea, saying to it, 'Go whereever it is best, to save all the living.'

Now the statue floated to Kamakura. And there arriving by night it shed a great radiance all about it as if there were sunshine upon the sea; and the fishermen of Kamakura were awakened by the great light. And they went out in boats, and found the statue floating and brought it to shore. And the emperor ordered that a temple should be built for it, the temple called Hase-*dera*, on the mountain called Kaikō-*zan*, at Kamakura.

Roku-Jizō

As we leave the Hase-*dera* behind us, there are no more dwellings visible along the road; the green slopes to left and right become steeper, and the shadows of the great trees deepen over us. But still, at intervals, some flight of venerable mossy steps, a carven Buddhist gateway, or a lofty *torii*, signals the presence of sanctuaries we have no time to visit: countless crumbling shrines are all around us, dumb witnesses to the antique splendour and vastness of the dead capital. And everywhere, mingled with perfume of blossoms, hovers the sweet, resinous smell of Japanese incense. Betimes we pass a scattered multitude of sculptured stones, like segments of four-sided pillars—old *haka*, the forgotten tombs of a long-abandoned cemetery; or the solitary image of some Buddhist deity—a dreaming Amida or faintly smiling Kannon. All are ancient, time-discoloured, mutilated. A few have been weather-worn into unrecognisability. I halt a moment to contemplate something pathetic, a group of six images of the charming divinity who cares for the ghosts of little children—the Roku-Jizō. Oh, how chipped and scurfed and mossed they are! Five stand buried almost up to their shoulders in a heaping of little stones, testifying to the prayers of generations. Votive *yodarekake*, infant bibs of divers colours, have been put about the necks of these for the love of children lost. But one of the gentle god's images lies shattered and overthrown in its own scattered pebble pile broken perhaps by some passing wagon.

Enoshima

The road slopes before us as we go, sinks down between cliffs steep as the walls of a canyon, and curves. Suddenly we emerge from the cliffs, and reach the sea. It is blue like the unclouded sky—a soft dreamy blue.

And our path turns sharply to the right, and winds along cliff summits overlooking a broad beach of dun-coloured sand. The sea wind blows deliciously with a sweet saline scent, urging the lungs to fill themselves to the very utmost. Far away before me, I perceive a beautiful high green mass, an island foliage-covered, rising out of the water about a quarter of a mile from the mainland—Enoshima, the holy island, sacred to the goddess of the sea, the goddess of beauty. I can already distinguish a tiny town, grey-sprinkling its steep slope. Evidently it can be reached today on foot, for the tide is out, and has left bare a long broad reach of sand, extending to it, from the opposite village which we are approaching, like a causeway.

At Katase, the little settlement facing the island, we must leave our *jinrikisha* and walk. The dunes between the village and the beach are too deep to pull the vehicle over. Scores of other *jinrikisha* are waiting here in the little narrow street for pilgrims who have preceded me. But today, I am told, I am the only European who visits the shrine of Benten.

Our two men lead the way over the dunes, and we soon descend on damp firm sand.

As we near the island the architectural details of the little town define delightfully through the faint sea haze—curved bluish sweeps of fantastic roofs, angles of airy balconies, high-peaked curious gables, all above a fluttering of queerly shaped banners covered with mysterious lettering. We pass the sand flats, and the ever-open portal of the sea city, the city of the dragon-goddess, is before us, a beautiful *torii*. All of bronze it is, with *shimenawa* of bronze above it, and a brazen tablet inscribed with characters declaring, 'This is the palace of the goddess of Enoshima.' About the bases of the ponderous pillars are strange designs in relievo, eddyings of waves with tortoises struggling in the flow. This is really the gate of the city, facing the shrine of Benten by the land approach. But it is only the third *torii* of the imposing series through Katase: we did not see the others, having come by way of the coast.

And lo! we are in Enoshima. High before us slopes the single street, a street of broad steps, a street shadowy, full of multi-coloured flags and dank blue drapery dashed with white fantasticalities, which are words, fluttered by the sea wind. It is lined with taverns and miniature shops. At every one I must pause to look; and to dare to look at anything in Japan is to want to buy it. So I buy, and buy, and buy!

For verily 'it is the city of mother-of-pearl, this Enoshima. In every shop, behind the lettered draperies there are miracles of shell-work for sale at absurdly small prices. The glazed cases laid flat on the matted platforms, the shelved cabinets set against the walls, are all opalescent with nacreous things—extraordinary surprises, incredible ingenuities; strings of mother-of-pearl fish, strings of mother-of-pearl birds, all shimmering with rainbow colours. There are little kittens of mother-of-pearl, and little foxes of mother-of-pearl, and little puppies of mother-of-pearl, and girls' hair-combs, and cigarette-holders, and pipes too beautiful to use. There are little tortoises, not larger than a shilling, made of shells, that, when you touch them, however lightly, begin to move head, legs, and tail, all at the same time, alternately withdrawing or protruding their limbs so much like real tortoises as to give one a shock of surprise. There are storks and birds, and beetles and butterflies, and crabs and lobsters, made so cunningly of shells, that only touch convinces you they are not alive. There are bees of shell, poised on flowers of the same material—poised on wire in such a way that they seem to buzz if moved only with the tip of a feather. There is shell-work jewellery indescribable, things that Japanese girls love, enchantments in mother-of-pearl, hairpins carven in a hundred forms, brooches, necklaces. And there are photographs of Enoshima.

Benten

This curious street ends at another *torii*, a wooden *torii*, with a steeper flight of stone steps ascending to it. At the foot of the steps are votive stone lamps and a little well, and a stone tank at which all pilgrims wash their hands and rinse their mouths before approaching the temples of the gods. Hanging beside the tank are bright blue towels, with large white Chinese characters on them.

I ask Akira what these characters signify.

'*Ho-keng* is the sound of the characters in Chinese; but in Japanese the same characters are pronounced *kenji tatetmatsuru*, and signify that those towels are most humbly offered to Benten. They are what you call votive offerings. And there are many kinds of votive offerings made to famous shrines. Some people give towels, some give pictures, some give vases; some offer lanterns of paper, or bronze, or stone. It is common to promise such offerings when making petitions to the gods; and it is usual to promise a *torii*. The *torii* may be small or great according to the wealth of him who gives it; the very rich pilgrim may offer to the gods a *torii* of metal, such as that below, which is the gate of Enoshima.'

'Akira, do the Japanese always keep their vows to the gods?'

Akira smiles a sweet smile, and answers, 'There was a man who promised to build a *torii* of good metal if his prayers were granted. And he obtained all that he desired. And then he built a *torii* with three exceedingly small needles.'

Stones and Serpents

Ascending the steps, we reach a terrace, overlooking all the city roofs. There are Buddhist lions of stone and stone lanterns, mossed and chipped, on either side the *torii*; and the background of the terrace is the sacred hill, covered with foliage. To the left is a balustrade of stone, old and green, surrounding a shallow pool covered with scum of waterweed. And on the farther bank above it, out of the bushes, protrudes a strangely shaped stone slab, poised on edge, and covered with Chinese characters. It is a sacred stone, and is believed to have the form of a great frog, *gama*; wherefore it is called Gamaishi, the frog stone. Here and there along the edge of the terrace are other graven monuments, one of which is the offering of certain pilgrims who visited the shrine of the sea goddess one hundred times. On the right other flights of steps lead to loftier terraces. An old man, who sits at the foot of them, making bird cages of bamboo, offers himself as guide.

We follow him to the next terrace, where there is a school for the children of Enoshima, and another sacred stone, huge and shapeless: Fuku-ishi, the Stone of Good Fortune. In old times pilgrims who rubbed their hands on it believed they would thereby gain riches. The stone is polished and worn by the touch of innumerable palms.

More steps and more green-mossed lions and lanterns, and another terrace with a little shrine in its midst. It is the Hetsu no Miya, the first shrine of Benten. Before it a few stunted palm trees are growing. There is nothing in the shrine of interest, only Shintō emblems. But there is another well beside it with other votive towels, and there is another mysterious monument, a stone shrine brought from China six hundred years ago. Perhaps it contained some far-famed statue before this place of pilgrimage was given over to the priests of Shintō. There is nothing in it nowl the monolith slab forming the back of it has been fractured by the falling of rocks from the cliff above. The inscription has been almost effaced by some kind of scum. Akira reads 'Dainippongoku Enoshima no reiseki ken . . .'; the rest is undecipherable. He says there is a statue in the neighbouring temple, but it is exhibited only once a year, on the fifteenth day of the seventh month.

Leaving the court by a rising path to the left, we proceed along the verge of a cliff overlooking the sea. Perched on this verge are pretty teahouses, all widely open to the sea wind, so that, looking through them, over their matted floors and lacquered balconies one sees the ocean as in a picture-frame, and the pale clear horizon specked with snowy sails, and a faint blue-peaked shape also, like a phantom island, the far vapoury silhouette of Oshima. Then we find another torii, and other steps leading to a terrace almost black with shade of enormous evergreen trees, and surrounded on the sea side by another stone balustrade, velveted with moss. On the right more steps, another torii, another terrace; and more mossed green lions and stone lamps; and a monument inscribed with the record of the change whereby Enoshima passed away from Buddhism to become Shino. Beyond, in the centre of another plateau, is the Nakatsu no Miya, the second shrine of Benten.

But there is no Benten! Benten has been hidden away by Shintō hands. The second shrine is void as the first. Nevertheless, in a building to the left of the temple, strange relics are exhibited. Feudal armour; suits of plate and chain mail; helmets with visors which are demoniac masks of iron; helmets crested with dragons of gold; two-handed swords worthy of giants; and enormous arrows, more than five feet long, with shafts nearly an inch in diameter. One has a crescent head about nine inches from horn to horn, the interior edge of the crescent being sharp as a knife. Such a missile would take off a man's head; and I can scarcely believe Akira's assurance that such ponderous arrows were shot from a bow by hand only. There is a specimen of the writing of Nichiren, the great Buddhist priest—gold characters on a blue ground; and there is, in a lacquered shrine, a gilded dragon said to have been made by that still greater priest and writer and master-wizard, Kōbō Daishi.

A path shaded by overarching trees leads from this plateau to the third shrine. We pass a *torii* and beyond it come to a stone monument covered with figures of monkeys chiselled in relief. What the signification of this monument is, even our guide cannot explain. Then another *torii*. It is of wood; but I am told it replaces one of metal, stolen in the night by thieves. Wonderful thieves! that *torii* must have weighed at least a ton! More stone lanterns. Then an immense count, on the very summit of the mountain. And there, in its midst, the Okutsu no Miya, the third and chief temple of Benten. Before the temple is a large vacant space surrounded by a fence in such manner as to render the shrine totally inaccessible. Vanity and vexation of spirit!

There is a little *haiden*, or place of prayer, with nothing in it but a money box and a bell, before the fence, and facing the temple steps. Here the pilgrims make their offerings and pray. Only a small raised platform covered with a Chinese roof supported on four plain posts, the back of the structure being closed by a lattice about breast high. From this praying station we can look into the temple of Benten, and see that Benten is not there.

But I perceive that the ceiling is arranged in caissons. And in a central caisson I discover a very curious painting—a foreshortened tortoise, gazing down at me. And while I am looking at it I hear Akira and the guide laughing, and the latter exclaims, 'Benten-*sama!*'

A beautiful little damask snake is undulating up the latticework, poking its head through betimes to look at us. It does not seem in the least afraid, nor has it much reason to be, seeing that its kind are deemed the servants and confidants of Benten. Sometimes the great goddess herself assumes the serpent form. Perhaps she has come to see us.

Nearby is a singular stone, set on a pedestal in the court. It has the form of the body of a tortoise, and markings like those of the creature's shell. It is held a sacred thing, and is called the Tortoise Stone. But I fear that in all this place we shall find nothing save stones and serpents!

Ryōjin no Jwaya

Now we are going to visit the Ryōjin no Iwaya, the Dragon Cavern, not so called, Akira says, because the dragon of Benten ever dwelt therein, but because the shape of the cavern is the shape of a dragon. The path descends toward the opposite side of the island, and suddenly breaks into a flight of steps cut out of the pale hard rock—exceedingly steep, and worn, and slippery, and perilous—overlooking the sea. A vision of low pale rocks, and surf bursting among them, and a *tōrō* or votive stone lamp in the centre of them—all seen as in a bird's-eye view, over the verge of an awful precipice. I see also deep, round holes in one of the rocks. There used to be a teahouse below, and the wooden pillars supporting it were fitted into those holes. I descend with caution; the Japanese seldom slip in their straw sandals, but I can only proceed with the aid of the guide. At almost every step I slip. Surely these steps could never have been thus worn away by the straw sandals of pilgrims who came to see only stones and serpents!

At last we reach a plank gallery carried along the face of the cliff above the rocks and pools, and following it round a projection of the cliff enter the sacred cave. The light dims as we advance. The sea waves, running after us into the gloom, make a stupefying roar, multiplied by the extraordinary echo. Looking back, I see the mouth of the cavern like a prodigious sharply angled rent in blackness, showing a fragment of azure sky.

We reach a shrine with no deity in it, pay a fee, and lamps being lighted and given to each of us, we proceed to explore a series of underground passages. So black they are that even with the light of three lamps, I can at first see nothing. In a while I can distinguish stone figures in relief—chiselled on slabs like those I saw in the Buddhist graveyard. These are placed at regular intervals along the rock walls. The guide approaches his light to the face of each one, and utters their names, 'Daikoku-*sama*, Fudo-*sama*, Kannon-*sama*.' Sometimes in lieu of a statue there is an empty shrine only, with a money box before it. These void shrines have names of Shintō gods, Daijingu, Hachiman, Inari-*sama*. All the statues are black, or seem black in the yellow lamplight, and sparkle as if frosted. I feel as if I were in some mortuary pit, some subterranean burial place of dead gods. Interminable the corridor appears, yet there is at last an end—an end with a shrine in it—where the rocky ceiling descends so low that to reach the shrine one must go down on hands and knees. And there is nothing in the shrine. This is the tail of the dragon.

We do not return to the light at once, but enter into other lateral black corridors—the wings of the dragon. More sable effigies of dispossessed gods; more empty shrines; more stone faces covered with saltpetre; and more money-boxes, possible only to reach by stooping, where more offerings should be made. And there is no Benten, either of wood or stone.

I am glad to return to the light. Here our guide strips naked, and suddenly leaps head foremost into a black deep swirling current between rocks. Five minutes later he reappears, and clambering out lays at my feet a living, squirming sea snail and an enormous shrimp. Then he resumes his robe, and we re-ascend the mountain.

Goddes of the Sea

'And this,' the reader may say—'this is all that you went to see: a *torii*, some shells, a small damask snake, some stones?'

It is true. And nevertheless I know that I am bewitched. There is a charm indefinable about the place—the sort of charm that comes with a little ghostly thrill never to be forgotten.

Not of strange sights alone is this charm made, but of numberless subtle sensations and ideas interwoven and interblended: the sweet sharp scents of grove and sea; the blood-brightening, vivifying touch of the free wind; the dumb appeal of ancient mystic mossy things; the vague reverence evoked by the knowledge of treading soil called holy for a thousand years; and a sense of sympathy, as a human duty, compelled by the vision of steps of rock worn down into shapelessness by the pilgrim feet of vanished generations.

And other memories ineffaceable: the first sight of the sea-girt city of pearl through a fairy veil of haze; the windy approach to the lovely island over the velvety soundless brown stretch of sand; the weird majesty of the giant gate of bronze; the queer, high-sloping, fantastic, quaintly gabled street, flinging down sharp shadows of aerial balconies; the flutter of coloured draperies in the sea wind, and of flags with their riddles of lettering; the pearly glimmering of the astonishing shops.

And impressions of the enormous day—the day of the land of the gods— a loftier day than ever our summers know; the glory of the view from those green sacred silent heights between sea and sun; the remembrance of the sky, a sky spiritual as holiness, a sky with clouds ghost-pure and white as the light itself—seeming, indeed, not clouds but dreams, or souls of Bodhisattvas about to melt for ever into some blue Nirvana.

The romance of Benten, too—the Deity of Beauty, the Divinity of Love, the Goddess of Eloquence. Rightly is she likewise named Goddess of the Sea. For is not the sea the most ancient and most excellent of speakers— the eternal poet, chanter of that mystic hymn whose rhythm shakes the world, whose mighty syllables no man may learn?

Tiny Dresses

We return by another route.

For a while the way winds through a long narrow winding valley between wooded hills: the whole extent of bottom land is occupied by rice farms. The air has a humid coolness, and one hears only the chanting of frogs, like a clattering of countless castanets, as the *jinrikisha* jolts over the rugged elevated paths separating the flooded rice fields.

As we skirt the foot of a wooded hill on the right, my Japanese comrade signals to our runners to halt, and himself dismounting, points to the blue peaked roof of a little temple perched high on the green slope. 'Is it really worth while to climb up there in the sun?' I ask. 'Oh, yes!' he answers, 'it is the temple of Kishimojin—Kishimojin, the Mother of Demons!'

We ascend a flight of broad stone steps, meet the Buddhist guardian lions at the summit, and enter the little court in which the temple stands. An elderly woman, with a child clinging to her robe, comes from the adjoining building to open the screens for us. Taking off our footgear we enter the temple. Without, the edifice looked old and dingy. Within all is neat and pretty. The June sun, pouring through the open *shōji*, illuminates an artistic confusion of brasses gracefully shaped and multi-coloured things—images, lanterns, paintings, gilded inscriptions, pendent scrolls. There are three altars.

Above the central altar Amida Buddha sits enthroned on his mystic golden lotus in the attitude of the teacher. On the altar to the right gleams a shrine of five miniature golden steps, where little images stand in rows, tier above tier, some seated, some erect, male and female, attired like goddesses or like *daimyō*: the Sanjūbanjin, or the Thirty Guardians. Below, on the façade of the altar, is the figure of a hero slaying a monster. On the altar to the left is the shrine of the Mother of Demons.

Her story is a legend of horror. For some sin committed in a previous birth, she was born a demon, devouring her own children. But being saved by the teaching of Buddha, she became a divine being, especially loving and protecting infants. Japanese mothers pray to her for their little ones, and wives pray to her for beautiful boys.

The face of Kishimojin is the face of a comely woman. But her eyes are weird. In her right hand she bears a lotus blossom; with her left she supports in a fold of her robe, against her half-veiled breast, a naked baby. At the foot of her shrine stands Jizō-*sama*, leaning on his *shakujō*. But the altar and its images do not form the startling feature of the temple interior. What impresses the visitor in a totally novel way are the votive offerings. High before the shrine, suspended from strings stretched taut between tall poles of bamboo, are scores, no, hundreds, of pretty, tiny dresses—Japanese baby dresses of many colours. Most are made of poor material, for these are the thank-offerings of very poor simple women, poor country mothers, whose prayers to Kishimojin for the blessing of children have been heard.

The sight of all those little dresses, each telling so naively its story of joy and pain—those tiny *kimono* shaped and sewn by docile patient fingers of humble mothers—touches irresistibly, like some unexpected revelation of the universal mother-love. And the tenderness of all the simple hearts that have testified thus to faith and thankfulness seems to thrill all about me softly, like a caress of summer wind.

Outside the world appears to have suddenly grown beautiful; the light is sweeter; it seems to me there is a new charm even in the azure of the eternal day.

Three Apes

Having traversed the valley, we reach a main road so level and so magnificently shaded by huge old trees that I could believe myself in an English lane—a lane in Kent or Surrey, perhaps—but for some exotic detail breaking the illusion at intervals; a *torii*, towering before temple steps descending to the highway, or a signboard lettered with Chinese characters, or the wayside shrine of some unknown god.

All at once I observe by the roadside some unfamiliar sculptures in relief a row of chiselled slabs protected by a little bamboo shed. I dismount to look at them, supposing them to be funereal monuments. They are so old that the lines of their sculpturing are half obliterated; their feet are covered with moss, and their visages are half effaced. But I can discern that these are not *haka*, but six images of one divinity, and my guide knows him—Koshin, the God of Roads. So chipped and covered with scurf he is, that the upper portion of his form has become indefinably vague, his attributes have been worn away. But below his feet, on several slabs, chiselled cunningly, I can still distinguish the figures of the Three Apes, his messengers. And some pious soul has left before one image a humble votive offering— the picture of a black cock and a white hen, painted on a wooden shingle. It must have been left here very long ago; the wood has become almost black, and the painting has been damaged by weather and by the droppings of birds. There are no stones piled at the feet of these images, as before the images of Jizō; they seem like things forgotten, crusted over by the neglect of generations—archaic gods who have lost their worshippers.

But my guide tells me, 'The temple of Koshin is near, in the village of Fujisawa.'

Koshin-dō

The Koshin-dō, the temple of Koshin, is situated in the middle of the village, in a court opening on the main street. A very old wooden temple it is, unpainted, dilapidated, grey with the greyness of all forgotten and weather-beaten things. It is some time before the guardian of the temple can be found, to open the doors. For this temple has doors in lieu of *shōji*— old doors that moan sleepily at being turned on their hinges. It is not necessary to remove one's shoes; the floor is matless, covered with dust, and squeaks under the unaccustomed weight of entering feet. All within is crumbling, mouldering, worn. The shrine has no image, only Shintō emblems, some poor paper lanterns whose once bright colours have vanished under a coating of dust, some vague inscriptions. I see the circular frame of a metal mirror, but the mirror itself is gone. Where?

The guardian says, 'No priest lives now in this temple; and thieves might come in the night to steal the mirror; so we have hidden it away.'

I ask about the image of Koshin.

He answers it is exposed but once in every sixty-one years: so I cannot see it. But there are other statues of the god in the temple court.

I go to look at them: a row of images, much like those on the public highway, but better preserved. One figure of Koshin is different from the others I have seen—apparently made after some Hindoo model, judging by the Indian coiffure, mitre-shaped and lofty. The god has three eyes; one in the centre of his forehead, opening perpendicularly instead of horizontally. He has six arms. With one hand he supports a monkey; with another he grasps a serpent; and the other hands hold out symbolic things—a wheel, a sword, a rosary, a sceptre. Serpents are coiled about his wrists and about his ankles. Under his feet is a monstrous head, the head of a demon, Amanjako, sometimes called Utatesa ('Sadness'). Upon the pedestal below the Three Apes are carven, and the face of an ape appears also on the front of the god's tiara.

I see also tablets of stone, graven only with the god's name—votive offerings. And nearby, in a tiny wooden shrine, is the figure of the Earth God, Kenrō Jijin, grey, primeval, vaguely wrought, holding in one hand a spear, in the other a vessel containing something indistinguishable.

The Three Worlds

To uninitiated eyes these many-headed, many-handed gods at first may seem—as they seem always in the sight of Christian bigotry—only monstrous. But when the knowledge of their meaning comes to one who feels the divine in all religions, then they will be found to make appeal to the higher aestheticism, to the sense of moral beauty, with a force never to be divined by minds knowing nothing of the Orient and its thought. To me the image of Kannon of the Thousand Hands is not less admirable than any other representation of human loveliness idealised bearing her name—the Peerless, the Majestic, the Peace-Giving, or even White Suigetsu, who sails the moonlit waters in her rosy boat made of a single lotus petal; In the triple-headed Shaka I discern and revere the mighty power of that truth, whereby, as by a conjunction of suns, the Three Worlds have been illuminated.

But vain to seek to memorise the names and attributes of all the gods; they seem, self-multiplying, to mock the seeker. Kannon the Merciful is revealed as the Hundred Kannon; the Six Jizō become the Thousand. And as they multiply before research, they vary and change: less multiform, less complex, less elusive the moving of waters than the visions of this Oriental faith. Into it, as into a fathomless sea, mythology after mythology from India and China and the farther East has sunk and been absorbed. The stranger, peering into its deeps, finds himself, as in the tale of Undine, contemplating a flood in whose every surge rises and vanishes a face—weird or beautiful or terrible—a most ancient shoreless sea of forms incomprehensibly inter-changing and intermingling, but symbolising the protean magic of that infinite Unknown that shapes and reshapes for ever all cosmic being.

Ugly Gods

I wonder if I can buy a picture of Koshin. In most Japanese temples little pictures of the tutelar deity are sold to pilgrims, cheap prints on thin paper. But the temple guardian here tells me, with a gesture of despair, that there are no pictures of Koshin for sale. There is only an old *kakemono* on which the god is represented. If I would like to see it he will go home and get it for me. I beg him to do me the favour, and he hurries into the street.

While awaiting his return, I continue to examine the queer old statues, with a feeling of mingled melancholy and pleasure. To have studied and loved an ancient faith only through the labours of palaeographers and archaeologists, and as a something astronomically remote from one's own existence, and then suddenly in afteryears to find the same faith a part of one's human environment—to feel that its mythology, though senescent, is alive all around you—is almost to realise the dream of the Romantics, to have the sensation of returning through twenty centuries into the life of a happier world. For these quaint gods of roads and gods of earth are really living still, though so worn and mossed and feebly worshipped. In this brief moment, at least, I am really in the elder world—perhaps just at that epoch of it when the primal faith is growing a little old-fashioned, crumbling slowly before the corrosive influence of a new philosophy. I know myself a pagan still, loving these simple old gods, these gods of a people's childhood.

They need some human love, these naive, innocent, ugly gods. The beautiful divinities will live for ever by that sweetness of womanhood idealised in the Buddhist art of them: eternal are Kannon and Benten; they need no help of man; they will compel reverence when the great temples shall all have become voiceless and priestless as this shrine of Koshin is. But these kind, queer, artless, mouldering gods, who have given ease to so many troubled minds, who have gladdened so many simple hearts, who have heard so many innocent prayers—how gladly would I prolong their beneficent lives in spite of the so-called 'laws of progress' and the irrefutable philosophy of evolution!

The guardian returns, bringing with him a *kakemono*, very small, very dusty, and so yellow-stained by time that it might be a thousand years old. I am disappointed as I unroll it; there is only a very common print of the god within—all outline. While I am looking at it, I become for the first time conscious that a crowd has gathered about me—tanned kindly-faced labourers from the fields, and mothers with babies on their backs, and school children, and *jinrikisha* men—all wondering that a stranger should be thus interested in their gods. And although the pressure about me is very, very gentle, like a pressure of tepid water for gentleness, I feel a little embarrassed. I give back the old *kakemono* to the guardian, make my offering to the god, and take my leave of Koshin and his good servant.

All the kind oblique eyes follow me as I go. And something like a feeling of remorse seizes me at thus abruptly abandoning the void, dusty, crumbling temple, with its mirrorless altar and its colourless lanterns, and the decaying sculptures of its neglected court, and its kindly guardian whom I see still watching my retreating steps, with the yellow *kakemono* in his hand. The whistle of a locomotive warns me that I shall just have time to catch the train. For Western civilisation has invaded all this primitive peace, with its webs of steel, with its ways of iron. This is not your way, O Koshin!—the old gods are dying along its ash-strewn verge!

Bonichi

Bonichi

It is just past five o'clock in the afternoon. Through the open door of my little study the rising breeze of evening is beginning to disturb the papers on my desk, and the white fire of the Japanese sun is taking that pale amber tone which tells that the heat of the day is over. There is not a cloud in the blue—not even one of those beautiful white filamentary things, like ghosts of silken floss, which usually swim in this most ethereal of earthly skies even in the driest weather.

A sudden shadow at the door. Akira, the young Buddhist student, stands at the threshold slipping his white feet out of his sandal thongs preparatory to entering, and smiling like the god Jizō.

'Ah! *konban, Akira.*'

'Tonight,' says Akira, seating himself on the floor in the posture of Buddha on the Lotus, 'the Bonichi will be held. Perhaps you would like to see it?'

'Oh, Akira, all things in this country I should like to see. But tell me, to what may the Bonichi be likened?'

'The Bonichi,' answers Akira, 'is a market at which will be sold all things required for the Festival of the Dead; and the Festival of the Dead will begin tomorrow, when all the altars of the temples and all the shrines in the homes of good Buddhists will be made beautiful.'

'Then I want to see the Bonichi, Akira, and I should also like to see a Buddhist shrine—a household shrine.'

'Yes, will you come to my room?' asks Akira. 'It is not far—in the Street of the Aged Men, beyond the Street of the Stony River, and near to the

Street Everlasting. There is a *butsuma* there—a household shrine—and on the way I will tell you about the Bon Matsuri.'

So, for the first time, I learn those things I am now about to write.

Offerings

From the 13th to the 15th day of July is held the Festival of the Dead—the Bon Matsuri or Bon Matsuri—by some Europeans called the Feast of Lanterns. But in many places there are two such festivals annually, for those who still follow the ancient reckoning of time by moons hold that the Bon Matsuri should fall on the 13th, 14th, and 15th days of the seventh month of the antique calendar, which corresponds to a later period of the year.

Early on the morning of the 13th, new mats of purest rice straw, woven expressly for the festival, are spread on all Buddhist altars and within each *butsuma* or *butsudan*—the little shrine before which the morning and evening prayers are offered up in every believing home. Shrines and altars are likewise decorated with beautiful embellishments of coloured paper, and with flowers and sprigs of certain hallowed plants—always real lotus flowers when obtainable, otherwise lotus flowers of paper, and fresh branches of *shikimi* (anise) and of *misohagi* (purple loosestrife). Then a tiny lacquered table—a *zen*—such as Japanese meals are usually served on, is placed on the altar, and the food offerings are laid on it. But in the smaller shrines of Japanese homes the offerings are more often simply laid on the rice matting, wrapped in fresh lotus leaves.

These offerings consist of the foods called *sōmen*, resembling our noodles, *gozen*, which is boiled rice, *dango*, a sort of tiny dumpling, eggplant, and fruits according to season—frequently *uri* and *suika*, slices of melon and watermelon, and plums and peaches. Often sweet cakes and dainties are added. Sometimes the offering is only *o-shōjingu* (honourable uncooked food); more usually it is *o-ryōgu* (honourable boiled food). Of course, it never includes fish, meats, or wine. Clear water is given to the shadowy guest, and is sprinkled from time to time on the altar or within the shrine with a branch of *misohagi*. Tea is poured out every hour for the viewless visitors, and everything is daintily served up in little plates and cups and bowls, as for living guests, with *hashi* (chopsticks) laid beside the offering. So for three days the dead are feasted.

At sunset, pine torches, fixed in the ground before each home, are kindled to guide the spirit-visitors. Sometimes, also, on the first evening of the Bon Matsuri, welcome-fires (*mukaebi*) are lighted along the shore of the sea or lake or river by which the village or city is situated—neither more nor less than one hundred and eight fires, this number having some mystic signification in the philosophy of Buddhism. Charming lanterns are suspended each night at the entrances of homes—the lanterns of the Festival of the Dead—lanterns of special forms and colours, beautifully painted with suggestions of landscape and shapes of flowers, and always decorated with a peculiar fringe of paper streamers.

Also, on the same night, those who have dead friends go to the cemeteries and make offerings there, and pray, and burn incense, and pour out water for the ghosts. Flowers are placed there in the bamboo vases set beside each *haka*, and lanterns are lighted and hung up before the tombs, but these lanterns have no designs on them.

At sunset on the evening of the 15th only the offerings called *segaki* are made in the temples. Then are fed the ghosts of the Circle of Penance, called Gakidō, the place of hungry spirits. Then also are fed by the priests those ghosts having no other friends among the living to care for them. Very, very small these offerings are—like the offerings to the gods.

Shōryōbune

Now this, Akira tells me, is the origin of the Segaki, as the same is related in the holy book *Busetsuuran hongyō*:

Mokukenren, the great disciple of Buddha, obtained by merit the six supernatural powers. And by virtue of them it was given him to see the soul of his mother in the Gakidō—the world of spirits doomed to suffer hunger in expiation of faults committed in a previous life. Mokukenren saw that his mother suffered much. He grieved exceedingly because of her pain, and he filled a bowl with choicest food and sent it to her. He saw her try to eat. But each time that she tried to lift the food to her lips it would change into fire and burning embers, so that she could not eat. Then Mokukenren asked the teacher what he could do to relieve his mother from pain. And the teacher made answer, 'On the fifteenth day of the seventh month, feed the ghosts of the great priests of all countries.' And

Mokukenren, having done so, saw that his mother was freed from the state of *gaki*, and that she was dancing for joy. This is the origin also of the dances called Bon Odori, which are danced on the third night of the Festival of the Dead throughout Japan.

On the third and last night there is a weirdly beautiful ceremony, more touching than that of the *segaki*, stranger than the Bon Odori—the ceremony of farewell. All that the living may do to please the dead has been done; the time allotted by the powers of the unseen worlds to the ghostly visitants is well nigh past, and their friends must send them all back again.

Everything has been prepared for them. In each home small boats made of barley straw closely woven have been freighted with supplies of choice food, with tiny lanterns, and written messages of faith and love. Seldom more than two feet in length are these boats; but the dead require little room. And the frail craft are launched on canal, lake, sea, or river—each with a miniature lantern glowing at the prow, and incense burning at the stern. And if the night be fair, they voyage long. Down all the creeks and rivers and canals the phantom fleets go glimmering to the sea. And all the sea sparkles to the horizon with the lights of the dead, and the sea wind is fragrant with incense.

But alas! it is now forbidden in the great seaports to launch the *shōryōbune*, 'the boats of the blessed ghosts.'

Tea

It is so narrow, the Street of the Aged Men, that by stretching out one's arms one can touch the figured sign draperies before its tiny shops on both sides at once. The little ark-shaped houses really seem toy houses. That in which Akira lives is even smaller than the rest, having no shop in it, and no miniature second story. It is all closed up. Akira slides back the wooden *amado* that forms the door, and then the paper-paned screens behind it. The tiny structure, thus opened, with its light unpainted woodwork and painted paper partitions, looks something like a great bird-cage. But the rush matting of the elevated floor is fresh, sweet-smelling, spotless. As we take off our footgear to mount on it I see that all within is neat, curious, and pretty.

'The woman has gone out,' says Akira, setting the *hibachi* in the middle of the floor, and spreading beside it a little mat for me to squat on.

'But what is this, Akira?' I ask, pointing to a thin board suspended by a ribbon on the wall—a board so cut from the middle of a branch as to leave the bark along its edges. There are two columns of mysterious signs exquisitely painted on it.

'Oh, that is a calendar,' answers Akira. 'On the right side are the names of the months having thirty-one days; on the left, the names of those having less. Now here is a household shrine.'

Occupying the alcove, which is an indispensable part of the structure of Japanese guest rooms, is a native cabinet painted with figures of flying birds, and on this cabinet stands the butsuma. It is a small lacquered and gilded shrine, with little doors modelled after those of a temple gate—a shrine very quaint, very much dilapidated (one door has lost its hinges), but still a dainty thing despite its crackled lacquer and faded gilding. Akira opens it with a sort of compassionate smile, and I look inside for the image. There is none, only a wooden tablet with a band of white paper attached to it, bearing Japanese characters—the name of a dead baby girl—and a vase of expiring flowers, a tiny print of Kannon, the Goddess of Mercy, and a cup filled with ashes of incense.

'Tomorrow,' Akira says, 'she will decorate this, and make the offerings of food to the little one.'

Hanging from the ceiling, on the opposite side of the room, and in front of the shrine, is a wonderful, charming, funny, white-and-rosy mask—the face of a laughing, chubby girl with two mysterious spots on her forehead, the face of Otafuku (the deity of good fortune). It twirls round and round in the soft air current coming through the open *shōji*, and every time those funny black eyes, half shut with laughter, look at me, I cannot help smiling. And hanging still higher, I see little Shintō emblems of paper (*shide*), a miniature mitre-shaped cap in likeness of those worn in the sacred dances, a pasteboard emblem of the Magic Gem (Nyō-i Hōjū) the gods bear in their hands, a small Japanese doll, and a little wind-wheel which will spin around with the least puff of air, and other indescribable toys, mostly symbolic, such as are sold on festal days in the courts of the temples—the playthings of the dead child.

'Konban!' exclaims a very gentle voice behind us. The mother is standing there, smiling as if pleased at the stranger's interest in her *butsuma*—a middle-aged woman of the poorest class, not comely, but with a most kindly face. We return her evening greeting, and while I sit down on the little mat laid before the *hibachi*, Akira whispers something to her, with the result that a small kettle is at once set to boil over a very small charcoal furnace. We are probably going to have some tea.

As Akira takes his seat before me, on the other side of the *hibachi*, I ask him, 'What was the name I saw on the tablet?'

'The name which you saw,' he answers, 'was not the real name. The real name is written on the other side. After death another name is given by the priest. A dead boy is called Ryōchi Dōji; a dead girl, Myōyo Dōnyo.'

While we are speaking, the woman approaches the little shrine, opens it, arranges the objects in it, lights the tiny lamp, and with joined hands and bowed head begins to pray. Totally unembarrassed by our presence and our chatter she seems, as one accustomed to do what is right and beautiful heedless of human opinion; praying with that brave, true frankness which belongs to the poor only of this world—those simple souls who never have any secret to hide, either from each other or from heaven, and of whom Ruskin nobly said, 'These are our holiest.' I do not know what words her heart is murmuring: I hear only at moments that soft sibilant sound, made by gently drawing the breath through the lips, which among this kind people is a token of humblest desire to please.

As I watch the tender little rite, I become aware of something dimly astir in the mystery of my own life—vaguely, indefinably familiar, like a memory ancestral, like the revival of a sensation forgotten two thousand years. Blended in some strange way it seems to be with my faint knowledge of an elder world, whose household gods were also the beloved dead. There is a weird sweetness in this place, like a shadowing of Lares.

Then, her brief prayer over, she turns to her miniature furnace again. She talks and laughs with Akira; she prepares the tea, pours it out in tiny cups and serves it to us, kneeling in that graceful attitude—picturesque, traditional—which for six hundred years has been the attitude of the Japanese woman serving tea. Verily, no small part of the life of the woman of Japan is spent thus in serving little cups of tea. Even as a ghost, she appears in popular prints offering to somebody spectral tea cups of spectral tea. Of all Japanese ghost pictures, I know of none more pathetic than that in which the phantom of a woman kneeling humbly offers to her haunted and remorseful murderer a little cup of tea!

'Now let us go to the Bonichi,' says Akira, rising; 'she must go there herself soon, and it is already getting dark. *Sayōnara!*'

It is indeed almost dark as we leave the little house: stars are pointing in the strip of sky above the street. It is a beautiful night for a walk, with a tepid breeze blowing at intervals, and sending long flutterings through the miles of shop draperies. The market is in the narrow street at the verge of the city, just below the hill where the great Buddhist monastery of Zōtoku-*in* stands—in Yokohama's Motomachi, only ten squares away.

Caged Insects

The curious narrow street is one long blaze of lights—of lantern signs, of torches and lamps illuminating unfamiliar rows of little stands and booths set out in the thoroughfare before all the shopfronts on each side, making two far-converging lines of multi-coloured fire. Between these moves a dense throng, filling the night with a clatter of *geta* that drowns even the tide-like murmuring of voices and the cries of the merchant. But how gentle the movement! There is no jostling, no rudeness; everybody, even the weakest and smallest, has a chance to see everything. And there are many things to see.

'*Hasu no hana!*—*hasu no hana!*' Here are the venders of lotus flowers for the tombs and the altars, of lotus leaves in which to wrap the food of the beloved ghosts. The leaves, folded into bundles, are heaped on tiny tables. The lotus flowers, buds and blossoms intermingled, are fixed upright in immense bunches, supported by light frames of bamboo.

'*Ogara!*—*ogara-ya!* White sheaves of long peeled rods. These are hemp sticks. The thinner ends can be broken up into *hashi* for the use of the ghosts; the rest must be consumed in the *mukaebi*. Rightly all these sticks should be made of pine, but pine is too scarce and dear for the poor folk of this district, so the *ogara* are substituted.

'*Kawarake!*—*kawarake-ya!*' The dishes of the ghosts: small red shallow platters of unglazed earthenware; primeval pottery *suku-makemasu!*'

Eh! what is all this? A little booth shaped like a sentry box, all made of laths, covered with a red-and-white chess pattern of paper. Out of this frail structure issues a shrilling keen as the sound of leaking steam.

'Oh, that is only insects,' says Akira, laughing; 'nothing to do with the Bon Matsuri.' Insects, yes!—in cages!

The shrilling is made by scores of huge green crickets, each prisoned in a tiny bamboo cage by itself.

'They are fed with eggplant and melon rind,' continues Akira, 'and sold to children to play with.'

And there are also beautiful little cages full of fireflies—cages covered with brown mosquito-netting, on each of which some simple but very pretty design in bright colours has been dashed by a Japanese brush. One cricket and cage, two cents. Fifteen fireflies and cage, five cents.

Here on a street corner squats a blue-robed boy behind a low wooden table, selling wooden boxes about as big as matchboxes, with red paper hinges. Beside the piles of these little boxes on the table are shallow dishes filled with clear water, in which extraordinary thin flat shapes are floating—shapes of flowers, trees, birds, boats, men, and women. Open a box; it costs only two cents. Inside, wrapped in tissue paper, are bundles of little pale sticks, like round matchsticks, with pink ends. Drop one into the water, it instantly unrolls and expands into the likeness of a lotus flower. Another transforms itself into a fish. A third becomes a boat. A fourth changes to an owl. A fifth becomes a tea plant, covered with leaves and blossoms...

So delicate are these things that, once immersed, you cannot handle them without breaking them. They are made of seaweed.

'*Tsukuribana!—tsukuribana wa irimasen ka?*' The sellers of artificial flowers, marvellous chrysanthemums and lotus plants of paper, imitations of bud and leaf and flower so cunningly wrought that the eye alone cannot detect the beautiful trickery. It is only right that these should cost much more than their living counterparts.

Otafuku

High above the thronging and the clamour and the myriad fires of the merchants, the great Shingon monastery (Zōtoku-*in*) at the end of the radiant street towers on its hill against the starry night, weirdly, like a dream—strangely illuminated by rows of paper lanterns hung all along its curving eaves, and the flowing of the crowd bears me thither. Out of the broad entrance, over a dark gliding mass which I know to be heads and shoulders of crowding worshippers, beams a broad band of yellow light; and before reaching the lion-guarded steps I hear the continuous clanging of the temple gong, each clang the signal of an offering and a prayer. Doubtless a cataract of cash is pouring into the great alms chest, for tonight is the Festival of Yakushi Nyorai, the Physician of Souls. Borne to the steps at last, I find myself able to halt a moment, despite the pressure of the throng, before the stand of a lantern seller selling the most beautiful lanterns that I have ever seen. Each is a gigantic lotus flower of paper, so perfectly made in every detail as to seem a great living blossom freshly plucked; the petals are crimson at their bases, paling to white at their tips; the calyx is a faultless mimicry of nature, and beneath it hangs a beautiful fringe of paper cuttings, coloured with the colours of the flower, green below the calyx, white in the middle, crimson at the ends. In the heart of the blossom is set a microscopic oil lamp of baked clay. This being lighted, all the flower becomes luminous, diaphanous—a lotus of white and crimson fire. There is a slender gilded wooden hoop by which to hang it up, and the price is four cents! How can people afford to make such things for four cents, even in this country of astounding cheapness?

Akira is trying to tell me something about the *hyaku-hachi no mukaebi*, the 'hundred and eight fires,' to be lighted tomorrow evening, which bear some figurative relation to the hundred and eight foolish desires. But I cannot hear him for the clatter of the *geta* and the *komageta*, the wooden clogs and wooden sandals of the worshippers ascending to the shrine of Yakushi Nyorai. The light straw sandals of the poorer men, the *zōri* and the *waraji*, are silent; the great clatter is really made by the delicate feet of women and girls, balancing themselves carefully on their noisy *geta*. Most of these little feet are clad with spotless *tabi*, white as a white lotus. White feet of little blue-robed mothers they mostly are—mothers climbing patiently and smilingly, with pretty placid babies at their backs, up the hill to Buddha.

And while through the tinted lantern light I wander on with the gentle noisy people, up the great steps of stone, between other displays of lotus-blossoms, between other high hedgerows of paper flowers, my thought suddenly goes back to the little broken shrine in the poor woman's room, with the humble playthings hanging before it, and the laughing, twirling mask of Otafuku. I see the happy, funny little eyes, oblique and silky-shadowed like Otafuku's own, which used to look at those toys—toys in which the fresh child senses found a charm that I can but faintly divine, a delight hereditary, ancestral. I see the tender little creature being borne, as it was doubtless borne many times, through just such a peaceful throng as this, in just such a lukewarm, luminous night, peeping over the mother's shoulder, softly clinging at her neck with tiny hands.

Somewhere among this multitude she is—the mother. She will feel again tonight the faint touch of little hands, yet will not turn her head to look and laugh, as in other days.

Bon Odori

tengu

Over the mountains to Izumo, the *kamiyo*, the 'land of the ancient gods.' It is a journey of four days by *kuruma*, with strong runners, from the Pacific to the Sea of Japan, for we have taken the longest and least frequented route. Through valleys most of this long route lies, valleys always open to higher valleys, while the road ascends, valleys between mountains with rice fields ascending their slopes by successions of diked terraces which look like enormous green flights of steps. Above them are shadowing sombre forests of cedar and pine. Above these wooded summits loom indigo shapes of farther hills overtopped by peaked silhouettes of vapoury grey. The air is lukewarm and windless, and distances are gauzed by delicate mists. In this tenderest of blue skies, this Japanese sky which always seems to me loftier than any other sky which I ever saw, there are only, day after day, some few filmy, spectral, diaphanous white wandering things: like ghosts of clouds, riding on the wind.

Sometimes, as the road ascends, the rice fields disappear a while: fields of barley and of indigo, and of rye and of cotton, fringe the route for a little space. Then it plunges into forest shadows. Above all else, the forests of cedar sometimes bordering the way are astonishments; never outside of the tropics did I see any growths comparable for density and perpendicularity with these. Every trunk is straight and bare as a pillar: the whole front presents the spectacle of an immeasurable massing of pallid columns towering up into a cloud of sombre foliage so dense that one can distinguish nothing overhead but branchings lost in shadow. And the profundities beyond the rare gaps in the palisade of blanched trunks are night-black, as in Dore's pictures of fir woods.

No more great towns; only thatched villages nestling in the folds of the hills, each with its Buddhist temple, lifting a tilted roof of blue-grey tiles above the congregation of thatched homesteads, and its *miya*, or Shintō shrine, with a *torii* before it like a great ideograph shaped in stone or wood. But Buddhism still dominates; every hilltop has its tera. As we travel on, statues of Buddhas or Bodhisattvas appear by the roadside with the regularity of milestones. Often a village *tera* is so large that the cottages of the rustic folk about it seem like little outhouses. The traveller wonders how so costly an edifice of prayer can be supported by a community so humble. And everywhere the signs of the gentle faith appear: its ideographs and symbols are chiselled upon the faces of the rocks. Its icons smile on you from every shadowy recess by the way; even the very landscape betimes would seem to have been moulded by the soul of it, where hills rise softly as a prayer. The summits of some are domed like the head of Shaka, and the dark bossy frondage that clothes them might seem the clustering of his curls.

Gradually, with the passing of the days, as we journey into the loftier west, I see fewer and fewer *tera*. Such Buddhist temples as we pass appear small and poor, and the wayside images become rarer and rarer. But the symbols of Shintō are more numerous, and the structure of its *miya* larger and loftier. And the *torii* are visible everywhere, and tower higher, before the approaches to villages, before the entrances of courts guarded by strangely grotesque lions and foxes of stone, before stairways of old mossed rock, upsloping, between dense growths of ancient cedar and pine, to shrines that moulder in the twilight of holy groves.

At one little village I see, just beyond, the *torii* leading to a great Shintō temple, a particularly odd small shrine, and feel impelled by curiosity to examine it. Leaning against its closed doors are many short gnarled sticks in a row, miniature clubs. Irreverently removing these, and opening the little doors, Akira bids me look within. I see only a mask—the mask of a goblin, a *tengu*, grotesque beyond description, with an enormous nose— so grotesque that I feel remorse for having looked at it.

The sticks are votive offerings. By dedicating one to the shrine, it is believed that the *tengu* may be induced to drive one's enemies away.

Goblin-shaped though they appear in all Japanese paintings and carvings of them, the *tengu-sama* are divinities, lesser divinities, lords of the art of fencing and the use of all weapons.

And other changes gradually become manifest. Akira complains that he can no longer understand the language of the people. We are traversing regions of dialects. The houses are also architecturally different from those of the country folk of the northeast; their high thatched roofs are curiously decorated with bundles of straw fastened to a pole of bamboo parallel with the roof-ridge, and elevated about a foot above it. The complexion of the peasantry is darker than in the northeast, and I see no more of those charming rosy faces one observes among the women of the Tokyo districts. The peasants wear different hats, pointed like the straw roofs of those little wayside temples curiously enough called *an* (which means a straw hat).

The weather is more than warm, rendering clothing oppressive. As we pass through the little villages along the road, I see much healthy cleanly nudity: pretty naked children; brown men and boys with only a soft narrow white cloth about their loins, asleep on the matted floors, all the paper screens of the houses having been removed to admit the breeze. The men seem to be lightly and supply built. I see no saliency of muscles; the lines of the figure are always smooth. Before almost every dwelling, indigo, spread out on little mats of rice straw, may be seen drying in the sun.

The country folk gaze wonderingly at the foreigner. At various places where we halt, old men approach to touch my clothes, apologising with humble bows and winning smiles for their very natural curiosity, and asking my interpreter all sorts of odd questions. Gentler and kindlier faces I never beheld. They reflect the souls behind them; never yet have I heard a voice raised in anger, nor observed an unkindly act.

Each day, as we travel, the country becomes more beautiful—beautiful with that fantasticality of landscape only to be found in volcanic lands. But for the dark forests of cedar and pine, and this far faint dreamy sky, and the soft whiteness of the light, there are moments of our journey when I could fancy myself again in the West Indies, ascending some winding way over the mornes of Dominica or of Martinique. And, indeed, I find myself sometimes looking against the horizon glow for shapes of palms and ceibas. But the brighter green of the valleys and of the mountain-slopes beneath the woods is not the green of young cane, but of rice fields—thousands upon thousands of tiny rice fields no larger than cottage gardens, separated from each other by narrow serpentine dikes.

Batō Kannon

In the very heart of a mountain range, while rolling along the verge of a precipice above rice fields, I catch sight of a little shrine in a cavity of the cliff overhanging the way, and halt to examine it. The sides and sloping roof of the shrine are formed by slabs of unhewn rock. Within smiles a rudely chiselled image of Batō Kannon—Kannon with the Horse's Head—and before it bunches of wild flowers have been placed, and an earthen incense-cup, and scattered offerings of dry rice. Contrary to the idea suggested by the strange name, this form of Kannon is not horse-headed. Instead, the head of a horse is sculptured on the tiara worn by the divinity. And the symbolism is fully explained by a large wooden *sotoba* planted beside the shrine, and bearing, among other inscriptions, the words, *Batō Kanzeon Bosatsu, gyūba bodai-han e*, for Batō Kannon protects the horses and the cattle of the peasant. He prays her not only that his dumb servants may be preserved from sickness, but also that their spirits may enter after death, into a happier state of existence. Near the *sotoba* has been erected a wooden framework about four feet square, filled with little tablets of pine set edge to edge so as to form one smooth surface. On these are written, in rows of hundreds, the names of all who subscribed for the statue and its shrine. The number announced is ten thousand. But the whole cost could not have exceeded ten yen. I surmise that each subscriber gave not more than one *rin*—one tenth of one *sen*, or cent. For the peasants are unspeakably poor.

In the midst of these mountain solitudes, the discovery of that little shrine creates a delightful sense of security. Surely nothing save goodness can be expected from a people gentle-hearted enough to pray for the souls of their horses and cows.

As we proceed rapidly down a slope, my *kurumaya* swerves to one side with a suddenness that gives me a violent start, for the road overlooks a sheer depth of several hundred feet. It is merely to avoid hurting a harmless snake making its way across the path. The snake is so little afraid that on reaching the edge of the road it turns its head to look after us.

Roku-Jizō

Strange signs begin to appear in all these rice fields: I see everywhere, sticking up above the ripening grain, objects like white-feathered arrows. Arrows of prayer! I take one up to examine it. The shaft is a thin bamboo, split down for about one-third of its length; into the slit a strip of strong white paper with ideographs on it—an *ofuda*, a Shintō charm—is inserted. The separated ends of the cane are then rejoined and tied together just above it. The whole, at a little distance, has exactly the appearance of a long, light, well-feathered arrow. That which I first examine bears the words, '*Yu asaki jinja gozen sonchū anzen*' (From the god whose shrine is before the village of peace). Another reads, *Miho jinja shogan jōju go-kitto shugo*,' signifying that 'the deity of the Miho shrine fully grants every prayer made to him.' Everywhere, as we proceed, I see the white arrows of prayer glimmering above the green level of the grain; and always they become more numerous. Far as the eye can reach the fields are sprinkled with them, so that they make on the verdant surface a white speckling as of flowers.

Sometimes, also, around a little rice field, I see a sort of magical fence, formed by little bamboo rods supporting a long cord from which long straws hang down, like a fringe, and paper cuttings, which are symbols (*shide*) are suspended at regular intervals. This is the *shimenawa*, sacred emblem of Shintō. Within the consecrated space inclosed by it no blight may enter—no scorching sun wither the young shoots. Where the white arrows glimmer the locust shall not prevail, nor shall hungry birds do evil.

But now I look in vain for the Buddhas. No more great *tera*, no Shaka, no Amida, no Dainichi Nyorai; even the Bosatsu have been left behind. Kannon and her holy kin have disappeared. Koshin, Lord of Roads, is indeed yet with us, but he has changed his name and become a Shintō deity: he is now Saruda Hiko no Mikoto, and his presence is revealed only by the statues of the three mystic apes that are his servants—Mizaru, who sees no evil, covering his eyes with his hands; Kikazaru, who hears no evil, covering his ears with his hands; Iwazaru, who speaks no evil, covering his mouth with his hands.

Yet no! One Bosatsu survives in this atmosphere of magical Shintō: still by the roadside I see at long intervals the image of Jizō-*sama*, the charming playfellow of dead children. But Jizō also is a little changed; even in his sextuple representation, the Roku-Jizō, he appears not standing, but seated on his lotus flower, and I see no stones piled up before him, as in the eastern provinces.

Hōtei

At last, from the verge of an enormous ridge, the roadway suddenly slopes down into a vista of high peaked roofs of thatch and green-mossed eaves— into a village like a coloured print out of old Hiroshige's picture books, a village with all its tints and colours precisely like the tints and colours of the landscape in which it lies. This is Kamiichi, in the land of Hōki.

We halt before a quiet, dingy little inn, whose host, a very aged man, comes forth to salute me. A silent, gentle crowd of villagers, mostly children and women, gather about the *kuruma* to see the stranger, to wonder at him, even to touch his clothes with timid smiling curiosity. One glance at the face of the old innkeeper decides me to accept his invitation. I must remain here until tomorrow: my runners are too wearied to go farther tonight.

Weather-worn as the little inn seemed without, it is delightful within. Its polished stairway and balconies are speckless, reflecting like mirror surfaces the bare feet of the maidservants. Its luminous rooms are fresh and sweet-smelling as when their soft mattings were first laid down. The carven pillars of the alcove (*tokonoma*) in my chamber, leaves and flowers chiselled in some black rich wood, are wonders. The *kakemono* or scroll picture hanging there is an idyll, Hōtei, God of Happiness, drifting in a bark down some shadowy stream into evening mysteries of vapoury purple. Far as this hamlet is from all art centres, there is no object visible in the house which does not reveal the Japanese sense of beauty in form. The old gold-flowered lacquerware, the astonishing box in which sweetmeats (*kashi*) are kept, the diaphanous porcelain wine cups dashed with a single tiny gold figure of a leaping shrimp, the tea cup holders which are curled lotus leaves of bronze, even the iron kettle with its figurings of dragons and clouds, and the brazen *hibachi* whose handles are heads of Buddhist lions, delight the eye and surprise the fancy. Indeed, wherever today in Japan one sees something totally uninteresting in porcelain or metal, something commonplace and ugly, one may be almost sure that detestable something has been shaped under foreign influence. But here I am in ancient Japan; probably no European eyes ever looked on these things before.

A window shaped like a heart peeps out upon the garden, a wonderful little garden with a tiny pond and miniature bridges and dwarf trees, like the landscape of a tea cup. There are also some shapely stones of course, and some graceful stone lanterns, or *tōrō*, such as are placed in the courts of temples. And beyond these, through the warm dusk, I see lights, coloured lights, the lanterns of the Bon Matsuri, suspended before each home to welcome the coming of beloved ghosts; for by the antique calendar, according to which in this antique place the reckoning of time is still made, this is the first night of the Festival of the Dead.

As in all the other little country villages where I have been stopping, I find the people here kind to me with a kindness and a courtesy unimaginable, indescribable, unknown in any other country, and even in Japan itself only in the interior. Their simple politeness is not an art; their goodness is absolutely unconscious goodness; both come straight from the heart. And before I have been two hours among these people, their treatment of me, coupled with the sense of my utter inability to repay such kindness, causes a wicked wish to come into my mind. I wish these charming folk would do me some unexpected wrong, something surprisingly evil, something atrociously unkind, so that I should not be obliged to regret them, which I feel sure I must begin to do as soon as I go away.

While the aged landlord conducts me to the bath, where he insists on washing me himself as if I were a child, the wife prepares for us a charming little repast of rice, eggs, *kometsuki*, and sweetmeats. She is painfully in doubt about her ability to please me, even after I have eaten enough for two men, and apologises too much for not being able to offer me more.

'There is no fish,' she says, 'for today is the first day of the Bon Matsuri, the Festival of the Dead, being the thirteenth day of the month. On the thirteenth, fourteenth, and fifteenth of the month nobody may eat fish. But on the morning of the sixteenth day, the fishermen go out to catch fish. And everybody who has both parents living may eat of it. But if one has lost one's father or mother then one must not eat fish, even on the sixteenth day.'

While the good soul is thus explaining I become aware of a strange remote sound from without, a sound I recognise through memory of tropical dances, a measured clapping of hands. But this clapping is very soft and at long intervals. And at still longer intervals there comes to us a heavy muffled booming, the tap of a great drum, a temple drum.

'Oh! we must go to see it,' cries Akira. 'It is the Bon Odori, the Dance of the Festival of the Dead. And you will see the Bon Odori danced here as it is never danced in cities—the Bon Odori of ancient days. For customs have not changed here, but in the cities all is changed.'

So I hasten out, wearing only, like the people about me, one of those light wide-sleeved summer robes—*yukata*—which are furnished to male guests at all Japanese hotels. The air is so warm that even thus lightly clad, I find myself slightly perspiring. And the night is divine, still, clear, vaster than nights of Europe, with a big white moon flinging down queer shadows of tilted eaves and horned gables and delightful silhouettes of robed Japanese. A little boy, the grandson of our host, leads the way with a crimson paper lantern. The sonorous echoing of *geta*, the *koro-koro* of wooden sandals, fills all the street, for many are going whither we are going, to see the dance.

A little while we proceed along the main street. Then, traversing a narrow passage between two houses, we find ourselves in a great open space flooded by moonlight. This is the dancing place. But the dance has ceased for a time. Looking about me, I perceive that we are in the court of an ancient Buddhist temple. The temple building itself remains intact, a low long peaked silhouette against the starlight; but it is void and dark and unhallowed now. It has been turned, they tell me, into a schoolhouse. The priests are gone; the great bell is gone; the Buddhas and the Bodhisattvas have vanished, all save one—a broken-handed Jizō of stone, smiling with eyelids closed, under the moon.

In the centre of the court is a framework of bamboo supporting a great drum. About it benches have been arranged, benches from the schoolhouse, on which villagers are resting. There is a hum of voices, voices of people speaking very low, as if expecting something solemn. Cries of children betimes, and soft laughter of girls. And far behind the court, beyond a low hedge of sombre evergreen shrubs, I see soft white lights and a host of tall grey shapes throwing long shadows. I know that the lights are the white lanterns of the dead (those hung in cemeteries only), and that the grey shapes are shapes of tombs.

Suddenly a girl rises from her seat, and taps the huge drum once. It is the signal for the Dance of Souls.

Odori

Out of the shadow of the temple a processional line of dancers files into the moonlight and as suddenly halts—all young women or girls, clad in their choicest attire. The tallest leads; her comrades follow in order of stature; little maids of ten or twelve years compose the end of the procession. Figures lightly poised as birds—figures that somehow recall the dreams of shapes circling about certain antique vases; those charming Japanese robes, close-clinging about the knees, might seem, but for the great fantastic drooping sleeves, and the curious broad girdles confining them, designed after the drawing of some Greek or Etruscan artist. At another tap of the drum, there begins a performance impossible to picture in words, something unimaginable, phantasmal—a dance, an astonishment.

All together glide the right foot forward one pace, without lifting the sandal from the ground, and extend both hands to the right, with a strange floating motion and a smiling, mysterious obeisance. Then the right foot is drawn back, with a repetition of the waving of hands and the mysterious bow. Then all advance the left foot and repeat the previous movements, half-turning to the left. Then all take two gliding paces forward, with a single simultaneous soft clap of the hands, and the first performance is reiterated, alternately to right and left. All the sandalled feet are gliding together, all the supple hands waving together, all the pliant bodies bowing and swaying together. And so slowly, weirdly, the processional movement changes into a great round, circling about the moonlit court and around the voiceless crowd of spectators.

And always the white hands sinuously wave together, as if weaving spells, alternately without and within the round, now with palms upward, now with palms downward. All the elfish sleeves hover duskily together, with a shadowing as of wings. And all the feet poise together with such a rhythm of complex motion, that, in watching it, one feels a sensation of hypnotism—as while striving to watch a flowing and shimmering of water.

And this soporous allurement is intensified by a dead hush. No one speaks, not even a spectator. And, in the long intervals between the soft clapping of hands, one hears only the shrilling of the crickets in the trees, and the shu-shu of sandals, lightly stirring the dust. To what, I ask myself, may this be likened? To nothing. Yet it suggests some fancy of somnambulism—dreamers, who dream themselves flying, dreaming on their feet.

There comes to me the thought that I am looking at something immemorially old, something belonging to the unrecorded beginnings of this Oriental life, perhaps to the crepuscular *kamiyo* itself, to the magical age of the gods—a symbolism of motion whereof the meaning has been forgotten for innumerable years. Yet more and more unreal the spectacle appears, with its silent smilings, with its silent bowings, as if obeisance to watchers invisible. I find myself wondering whether, were I to utter but a whisper, all would not vanish for ever save the grey mouldering court and the desolate temple, and the broken statue of Jizō, smiling always the same mysterious smile I see on the faces of the dancers.

Under the wheeling moon, in the midst of the round, I feel as one within the circle of a charm. And verily this is enchantment. I am bewitched, bewitched by the ghostly weaving of hands, by the rhythmic gliding of feet, above all by the flitting of the marvellous sleeves—apparitional, soundless, velvety as a flitting of great tropical bats. No, nothing I ever dreamed of could be likened to this. And with the consciousness of the ancient *hakaba* behind me, and the weird invitation of its lanterns, and the ghostly beliefs of the hour and the place there creeps upon me a nameless, tingling sense of being haunted. But no! these gracious, silent, waving, weaving shapes are not of the Shadowy Folk, for whose coming the white fires were kindled: a strain of song, full of sweet, clear quavering, like the call of a bird, gushes from some girlish mouth, and fifty soft voices join the chant:

Sorotta soroimashita odoriko ga sorotta, Soroi kite, kita hare yukata.

'Uniform to view, as ears of young rice ripening in the field, all clad alike in summer festal robes, the company of dancers have assembled.'

Again only the shrilling of the crickets, the shu-shu of feet, the gentle clapping. The wavering hovering measure proceeds in silence, with mesmeric lentor—with a strange grace, which, by its very naivete, seems old as the encircling hills.

Those who sleep the sleep of centuries out there, under the grey stones where the white lanterns are, and their fathers, and the fathers of their fathers' fathers, and the unknown generations behind them, buried in cemeteries of which the place has been forgotten for a thousand years, doubtless looked upon a scene like this. Nay! The dust stirred by those young feet was human life, and so smiled and so sang under this self-same moon, 'with woven paces, and with waving hands.'

Suddenly a deep male chant breaks the hush. Two giants have joined the round, and now lead it, two superb young mountain peasants nearly nude, towering head and shoulders above the whole of the assembly. Their *kimono* are rolled about their waistlike girdles, leaving their bronzed limbs and torsos naked to the warm air. They wear nothing else save their immense straw hats, and white *tabi*, donned expressly for the festival. Never before among these people saw I such men, such thews. But their smiling beardless faces are comely and kindly as those of Japanese boys. They seem brothers, so like in frame, in movement, in the timbre of their voices, as they intone the same song:

No demo yama demo ko wa umiokeyo, senryō no kura yori ko ga takara.

'Whether brought forth upon the mountain or in the field, it matters nothing: more than a treasure of one thousand *ryō*, a baby precious is.'

And Jizō the lover of children's ghosts, smiles across the silence.

Souls close to nature's Soul are these, artless and touching their thought, like the worship of that Kishimojin to whom wives pray. And after the silence, the sweet thin voices of the women answer:

Oomu otoko ni sowasanu oya wa, Kaide gozaranu ko no kataki.

'The parents who will not allow their girl to be united with her lover; they are not the parents, but the enemies of their child.'

And song follows song; and the round ever becomes larger; and the hours pass unfelt, unheard, while the moon wheels slowly down the blue steeps of the night.

A deep low boom rolls suddenly across the court, the rich tone of some temple bell telling the twelfth hour. Instantly the witchcraft ends, like the wonder of some dream broken by a sound; the chanting ceases; the round dissolves in an outburst of happy laughter, and chatting, and softly-vowelled callings of flower names that are names of girls, and farewell cries of 'sayonara!' as dancers and spectators alike go homeward, with a great koro-koro of *geta*.

And I, moving with the throng, in the bewildered manner of one suddenly roused from sleep, feel ungrateful. These silvery-laughing folk who now toddle along beside me on their noisy little clogs, stepping very fast to get a peep at my foreign face, these but a moment ago were visions of archaic grace, illusions of necromancy, delightful phantoms. I feel a vague resentment against them for thus materialising into simple country girls.

Cry of the Land

Lying down to rest, I ask myself the reason of the singular emotion inspired by that simple peasant chorus. Utterly impossible to recall the air, with its fantastic intervals and fractional tones—as well attempt to fix in memory the purlings of a bird. But the indefinable charm of it lingers with me still.

Melodies of Europe awaken within us feelings we can utter, sensations familiar as mother-speech, inherited from all the generations behind us. But how explain the emotion evoked by a primitive chant totally unlike anything in Western melody—impossible even to write in those tones which are the ideographs of our music-tongue?

And the emotion itself—what is it? I know not. I feel it to be something infinitely more old than I—something not of only one place or time, but vibrant to all common joy or pain of being, under the universal sun. Then I wonder if the secret does not lie in some untaught spontaneous harmony of that chant with nature's most ancient song, in some unconscious kinship to the music of solitudes—all trillings of summer life that blend to make the great sweet cry of the land.

Matsue

Kometsuki

The first of the noises of a Matsue day comes to the sleeper like the throbbing of a slow, enormous pulse exactly under his ear. It is a great, soft, dull buffet of sound—like a heartbeat in its regularity, in its muffled depth, in the way it quakes up through one's pillow so as to be felt rather than heard. It is simply the pounding of the ponderous pestle of the *kometsuki*, the cleaner of rice—a sort of colossal wooden mallet with a handle about fifteen feet long horizontally balanced on a pivot. By treading with all his force on the end of the handle, the naked *kometsuki* elevates the pestle, which is then allowed to fall back by its own weight into the rice tub. The measured muffled echoing of its fall seems to me the most pathetic of all sounds of Japanese life; it is the beating, indeed, of the pulse of the land.

Then the boom of the great bell of Tōkō-*ji* the Zen sect temple, shakes over the town; then come melancholy echoes of drumming from the tiny little temple of Jizō in the street Zaimokuchō, near my house, signalling the Buddhist hour of morning prayer. And finally the cries of the earliest itinerant venders begin—'*Daikoyai! kabuya-kabu!*'—the sellers of *daikon* and other strange *kometsuki*. '*Moyaya-moya!*'—the plaintive call of the women who sell little thin slips of kindling-wood for the lighting of charcoal fires.

The Ghost of a Junk

Roused thus by these earliest sounds of the city's wakening life, I slide open my little Japanese paper window to look out upon the morning over a soft green cloud of spring foliage rising from the river-bounded garden below.

Before me, tremulously mirroring everything on its farther side, glimmers the broad glassy mouth of the Ohashi River, opening into the grand Shinji Lake, which spreads out broadly to the right in a dim grey frame of peaks. Just opposite to me, across the stream, the blue-pointed Japanese dwellings have their *to* (a thick solid sliding shutters of unpainted wood) all closed. They are still shut up like boxes, for it is not yet sunrise, although it is day.

But oh, the charm of the vision—those first ghostly love colours of a morning steeped in mist soft as sleep itself resolved into a visible exhalation! Long reaches of faintly tinted vapour cloud the far lake verge—long nebulous bands, as you may have seen in old Japanese picture books and deemed artistic whimsicalities unless you had seen the real phenomena. All the bases of the mountains are veiled by them, and they stretch across the loftier peaks at different heights like immeasurable lengths of gauze (this singular appearance the Japanese term 'shelving' (*tanabiku*), so that the lake appears incomparably larger than it really is, and not an actual lake, but a beautiful spectral sea of the same tint as the dawn-sky and mixing with it, while peak tips rise like islands from the brume, and visionary strips of hill-ranges figure as league-long causeways stretching out of sight—an exquisite chaos, ever-changing aspect as the delicate fogs rise, slowly, very slowly. As the sun's yellow rim comes into sight, fine thin lines of warmer tone—spectral violets and opalines—shoot across the flood, treetops take tender fire, and the unpainted façades of high edifices across the water change their wood colour to vapoury gold through the delicious haze.

Looking sunward, up the long Ohashi-*gawa*, beyond the many-pillared wooden bridge, one high-pooped junk, just hoisting sail, seems to me the most fantastically beautiful craft I ever saw—a dream of Orient seas, so idealised by the vapour is it; the ghost of a junk, but a ghost that catches the light as clouds do; a shape of gold mist, seemingly semi-diaphanous, suspended in pale blue light.

Prayer

And now from the river-front touching my garden there rises to me a sound of clapping of hand—one, two, three, four claps—but the owner of the hands is screened from view by the shrubbery. At the same time, I see men and women descending the stone steps of the wharves on the opposite side of the Ohashigawa, all with little blue towels tucked into their girdles. They wash their faces and hands and rinse their mouths—the customary ablution preliminary to Shintō prayer. Then they turn their faces to the sunrise and clap their hands four times and pray. From the long high white bridge come other clappings, like echoes, and others again from far light graceful craft, curved like new moons—extraordinary boats, in which I see bare-limbed fishermen standing with foreheads bowed to the golden east. Now the clappings multiply—multiply at last into an almost continuous volleying of sharp sounds. For all the population are saluting the rising sun, *o-Hi-san*, the Lady of Fire—Amaterasu Ōmikami, the the Heaven-Shining Great August Divinity. '*Konnichi-sama!* Hail this day to you, divinest day-maker! Thanks unutterable to you, for this your sweet light, making beautiful the world!' So, doubtless, the thought, if not the utterance, of countless hearts.

Some turn to the sun only, clapping their hands. Yet many turn also to the west, to the holy Izumo Ōyashiro, the immemorial shrine and not a few turn their faces successively to all the points of heaven, murmuring the names of a hundred gods. Others, again, after having saluted the Lady of Fire, look toward high Ichibata, toward the place of the great temple of Yakushi Nyorai, who gives sight to the blind—not clapping their hands as in Shintō worship, but only rubbing the palms softly together after the Buddhist manner. But all—for in this most antique province of Japan all Buddhists are Shintōists likewise—utter the archaic words of Shintō prayer, '*Harai tamai kiyome tamai to kami imi tami.*'

Prayer to the most ancient gods who reigned before the coming of the Buddha, and who still reign here in their own Izumo land—in the land of reed plains, the place of the Issuing of Clouds (Izumo). Prayer to the deities of primal chaos and primeval sea and of the beginnings of the world—strange gods with long weird names, kindred of Uhijini no Kami, the First Mud Lord, kindred of Suhijini no Kanii, the First Sand Lady. Prayer to those who came after them—the gods of strength and beauty, the world-fashioners, makers of the mountains and the isles, ancestors of those sovereigns whose lineage still is named 'The sun's succession.' Prayer to the three thousand gods 'residing within the provinces,' and to the eight hundred myriads who dwell in the azure *takama no hara*—in the blue plain of high heaven. '*Nippon-kokuchū yaoyorozu no Kamigami-sama!*'

Uguisu

'*Ho——ke-kyō!*'

My *uguisu* is awake at last, and utters his morning prayer. You do not know what an uguisu is? An *uguisu* is a holy little bird that professes Buddhism. All *uguisu* have professed Buddhism from time immemorial; all *uguisu* preach alike to men the excellence of the divine *sūtra*.

' *Ho——ke-kyō!*'

In the Japanese tongue, *Hoke-kyō*; in Sanscrit, Saddharma Pundarika: the *sūtra* of the Lotus of the Good Law,' the divine book of the Nichiren sect. Very brief, indeed, is my little feathered Buddhist's confession of faith—only the sacred name reiterated over and over again like a litany, with liquid bursts of twittering between.

' *Ho——ke-kyō!*'

Only this one phrase, but how deliciously he utters it! With what slow amorous ecstasy he dwells on its golden syllables! It has been written, 'He who shall keep, read, teach, or write this *sūtra* shall obtain eight hundred good qualities of the eye. He shall see the whole triple universe down to the great hell Aviki, and up to the extremity of existence. He shall obtain twelve hundred good qualities of the ear. He shall hear all sounds in the triple universe—sounds of gods, goblins, demons, and beings not human.'

' *Ho——ke-kyō!*'

A single word only. But it is also written, 'He who shall joyfully accept but a single word from this *sūtra*, incalculably greater shall be his merit than the merit of one who should supply all beings in the four hundred thousand Asankhyeyas of worlds with all the necessaries for happiness.'

' *Ho——ke-kyō!*'

Always he makes a reverent little pause after uttering it and before shrilling out his ecstatic warble—his bird-hymn of praise. First the warble; then a pause of about five seconds; then a slow, sweet, solemn utterance of the holy name in a tone as of meditative wonder; then another pause; then another wild, rich, passionate warble. Could you see him, you would marvel how so powerful and penetrating a soprano could ripple from so minute a throat. For he is one of the very tiniest of all feathered singers, yet his chant can be heard far across the broad river, and children going to school pause daily on the bridge, a whole *chō* away, to listen to his song.

And uncomely withal: a neutral-tinted mite, almost lost in his immense box cage of *hinoki* wood, darkened with paper screens over its little wire-grated windows, for he loves the gloom.

Delicate he is and exacting even to tyranny. All his diet must be laboriously triturated and weighed in scales, and measured out to him at precisely the same hour each day. It demands all possible care and attention merely to keep him alive. He is precious, nevertheless. 'Far and from the uttermost coasts is the price of him,' so rare he is. Indeed, I could not have afforded to buy him. He was sent to me by one of the sweetest ladies in Japan, daughter of the governor of Izumo, who, thinking the foreign teacher might feel lonesome during a brief illness, made him the exquisite gift of this dainty creature.

Geta

The clapping of hands has ceased; the toil of the day begins; continually louder and louder the pattering of *geta* over the bridge. It is a sound never to be forgotten, this pattering of *geta* over the Ohashi River—rapid, merry, musical, like the sound of an enormous dance; and a dance it veritably is. The whole population is moving on tiptoe, and the multitudinous twinkling of feet over the verge of the sunlit roadway is an astonishment. All those feet are small, symmetrical—light as the feet of figures painted on Greek vases— and the step is always taken toes first; indeed, with *geta* it could be taken no other way, for the heel touches neither the *geta* nor the ground, and the foot is tilted forward by the wedge-shaped wooden sole. Merely to stand on a pair of *geta* is difficult for one unaccustomed to their use, yet you see Japanese children running at full speed in *geta* with soles at least three inches high, held to the foot only by a forestrap fastened between the great toe and the other toes, and they never trip and the *geta* never falls off. Still more curious is the spectacle of men walking in *bokkuri* or *takageta*, a wooden sole with wooden supports at least five inches high fitted underneath it so as to make the whole structure seem the lacquered model of a wooden bench. But the wearers stride as freely as if they had nothing on their feet.

Now children begin to appear, hurrying to school. The undulation of the wide sleeves of their pretty speckled robes, as they run, looks precisely like a fluttering of extraordinary butterflies. The junks spread their great white or yellow wings, and the funnels of the little steamers which have been slumbering all night by the wharves begin to smoke.

One of the tiny lake steamers lying at the opposite wharf has just opened its steam throat to utter the most unimaginable, piercing, desperate, furious howl. When that cry is heard everybody laughs. The other little steamboats utter only plaintive mooings, but to this particular vessel—newly built and launched by a rival company—there has been given a voice expressive to the most amazing degree of reckless hostility and savage defiance. The good people of Matsue, on hearing its voice for the first time, gave it forthwith a new and just name—Okami-maru. '*Maru*' signifies a steamship. 'Okami' signifies a wolf.

Kawarake

A very curious little object now comes slowly floating down the river, and I do not think that you could possibly guess what it is.

The Hotoke, or Buddhas, and the beneficent *kami* are not the only divinities worshipped by the Japanese of the poorer classes. The deities of evil, or at least some of them, are duly propitiated on certain occasions, and requited by offerings whenever they graciously vouchsafe to inflict a temporary ill instead of an irremediable misfortune. (After all, this is no more irrational than the thanksgiving prayer at the close of the hurricane season in the West Indies, after the destruction by storm of twenty-two thousand lives.) So men sometimes pray to Ekibyōgami, the God of Pestilence, and to Kaze no Kami, the God of Wind and of Bad Colds, and to Hoso no Kami, the God of Smallpox, and to divers evil genii.

Now when a person is certainly going to get well of smallpox a feast is given to the Hoso no Kami, much as a feast is given to the Fox God when a possessing fox has promised to allow himself to be cast out. On a *sando-wara*, or small straw mat, such as is used to close the end of a rice bale, one or more *kawarake*, or small earthenware vessels, are placed. These are filled with a preparation of rice and red beans, called *azukimeshi*, whereof both Inari-*sama* and Hoso no Kami are supposed to be very fond. Little bamboo wands (*gohei*) with *shide* (paper streamers) fastened to them are then planted either in the mat or in the *azukimeshi*, and the colour of these *gohei* must be red. (Be it observed that the *gohei* of other *kami* are always white.) This offering is then either suspended to a tree, or set afloat in some running stream at a considerable distance from the home of the convalescent. This is called 'seeing the god off.'

Gensuke-bashi

The long white bridge with its pillars of iron is recognisably modern. It was, in fact, opened to the public only last spring with great ceremony. According to some most ancient custom, when a new bridge has been built the first persons to pass over it must be the happiest of the community. So the authorities of Matsue sought for the happiest folk, and selected two aged men who had both been married for more than half a century, and who had had not less than twelve children, and had never lost any of them. These good patriarchs first crossed the bridge, accompanied by their venerable wives, and followed by their grown-up children, grandchildren, and great-grandchildren, amidst a great clamour of rejoicing, the showering of fireworks, and the firing of cannon.

But the ancient bridge so recently replaced by this structure was much more picturesque, curving across the flood and supported on multitudinous feet, like a long-legged centipede of the innocuous kind. For three hundred years it had stood over the stream firmly and well, and it had its particular tradition.

When Horio Yoshiharu, the great general who became *daimyō* of Izumo in the Keichō era (1596–1615), first undertook to put a bridge over the mouth of this river, the builders laboured in vain, for there appeared to be no solid bottom for the pillars of the bridge to rest upon. Millions of great stones were cast into the river to no purpose, for the work constructed by day was swept away or swallowed up by night. Nevertheless, at last the bridge was built, but the pillars began to sink soon after it was finished; then a flood carried half of it away and as often as it was repaired so often it was wrecked. Then a human sacrifice was made to appease the vexed spirits of the flood. A man was buried alive in the riverbed below the place of the middle pillar, where the current is most treacherous, and thereafter the bridge remained immovable for three hundred years.

This victim was one Gensuke, who had lived in the street Saikamachi, for it had been determined that the victim would be the first man who should cross the bridge wearing *hakama* without a *machi*, a stiff pasteboard sewn into the waist of the *hakama* at the back, so as to keep the folds of the garment perpendicular and neat-looking. Gensuke sought to pass over not having a *machi* in his *hakama*, so they sacrificed him For this reason the midmost pillar of the bridge was for three hundred years called by his name—Gensuke-*bashi*. It is said that on moonless nights a ghostly fire flitted about that pillar—always in the dead watch hour between two and three. The colour of the light was red, though I am assured that in Japan, as in other lands, the fires of the dead are most often blue.

Benten no Shima

Now some say that Gensuke was not the name of a man, but the name of an era, corrupted by local dialect into the semblance of a personal appellation. Yet so profoundly is the legend believed, that when the new bridge was being built thousands of country folk were afraid to come to town, for a rumour arose that a new victim was needed, who was to be chosen from among them, and that it had been determined to make the choice from those who still wore their hair in queues after the ancient manner. Wherefore hundreds of aged men cut off their queues. Then another rumour was circulated to the effect that the police had been secretly instructed to seize the one-thousandth person of those who crossed the new bridge the first day, and to treat him after the manner of Gensuke. And at the time of the great festival of the rice god, when the city is usually thronged by farmers coming to worship at the many shrines of Inari this year there came but few, and the loss to local commerce was estimated at several thousand yen.

The vapours have vanished, sharply revealing a beautiful little islet in the lake, lying scarcely half a mile away—a low, narrow strip of land with a Shintō shrine on it, shadowed by giant pines; not pines like ours, but huge, gnarled, shaggy, tortuous shapes, vast-reaching like ancient oaks. Through a glass one can easily discern a *torii*, and before it two symbolic lions of stone (*karashishi*), one with its head broken off, doubtless by its having been overturned and dashed about by heavy waves during some great storm. This islet is sacred to Benten, the Goddess of Eloquence and Beauty, wherefore it is called Benten no Shima. But it is more commonly called

Yomega-shima, or 'The Island of the Young Wife,' by reason of a legend. It is said that it arose in one night, noiselessly as a dream, bearing up from the depths of the lake the body of a drowned woman who had been very lovely, very pious, and very unhappy. The people, deeming this a sign from heaven, consecrated the islet to Benten. On it they built a shrine to her, planted trees about it, set a *torii* before it, and made a rampart about it with great curiously-shaped stones, and there they buried the drowned woman.

Now the sky is blue down to the horizon, the air is a caress of spring. I go forth to wander through the queer old city.

Ofuda

I perceive that on the sliding doors, or immediately above the principal entrance of nearly every house, are pasted oblong white papers bearing ideographic inscriptions. Overhanging every threshold I see the sacred emblem of Shintō, the little rice straw rope with its long fringe of pendent stalks. The white papers at once interest me, for they are *ofuda*, or holy texts and charms, of which I am a devout collector. Nearly all are from temples in Matsue or its vicinity. The Buddhist ones indicate by the sacred words on them to what particular sect the family belong, for nearly every soul in this community professes some form of Buddhism as well as the all-dominant and more ancient faith of Shintō. And even one quite ignorant of Japanese ideographs can nearly always distinguish at a glance the formula of the great Nichiren sect from the peculiar appearance of the column of characters composing it, all bristling with long sharp points and banneret zigzags, like an army—the famous text *Namu myōhō rengekyō* inscribed of old on the flag of the great captain Katō Kiyomasa, the extirpator of Spanish Christianity, the glorious *vir ter execrandus* of the Jesuits. Any pilgrim belonging to this sect has the right to call at whatever door bears the above formula and ask for alms or food.

But by far the greater number of the *ofuda* are Shintō. On almost every door there is one *ofuda* especially likely to attract the attention of a stranger, because at the foot of the column of ideographs composing its text there are two small figures of foxes, a black and a white fox, facing each other in a sitting posture, each with a little bunch of rice straw in its mouth, instead of the more usual emblematic key. These *ofuda* are from the great

Inari temple of Oshiroyama, within the castle grounds, and are charms against fire. They represent, indeed, the only form of assurance against fire yet known in Matsue, so far, at least, as wooden dwellings are concerned. And although a single spark and a high wind are sufficient in combination to obliterate a larger city in one day, great fires are unknown in Matsue, and small ones are of rare occurrence.

The charm is peculiar to the city; and of the Inari in question this tradition exists:

When Matsudaira Naomasa, the grandson of Tokugawa Iyeyasu, first came to Matsue to rule the province, there entered into his presence a beautiful boy, who said, 'I came hither from the home of your august father in Echizen, to protect you from all harm. But I have no dwelling place, and am staying therefore at the Buddhist monastery of Fumon-*in*. Now if you will make for me a dwelling within the castle grounds, I will protect from fire the buildings there and the houses of the city, and your other residence likewise which is in the capital. For I am Inari Shinemon.' With these words he vanished from sight. Therefore Naomasa dedicated to him the great temple which still stands in the castle grounds, surrounded by one thousand foxes of stone.

Nets

I now turn into a narrow little street, which, although so ancient that its dwarfed two-story houses have the look of things grown up from the ground, is called the Street of the New Timber. New the timber may have been one hundred and fifty years ago, but the tints of the structures would ravish an artist—the sombre ashen tones of the woodwork, the furry browns of old thatch, ribbed and patched and edged with the warm soft green of those velvety herbs and mosses that flourish on Japanesese roofs.

The perspective of the street frames in a vision more surprising than any details of its mouldering homes. Between very lofty bamboo poles, higher than any of the dwellings, and planted on both sides of the street in lines, extraordinary black nets are stretched, like prodigious cobwebs against the sky, evoking sudden memories of those monster spiders that figure in Japanese mythology and in the picture books of the old artists. But these are only fishing nets of silken thread. This is the street of the fishermen. I take my way to the great bridge.

Izumo Fuji

A stupendous ghost!

Looking eastward from the great bridge over those sharply beautiful mountains, green and blue, which tooth the horizon, I see a glorious spectre towering to the sky. Its base is effaced by far mists: out of the air the thing would seem to have shaped itself—a phantom cone, diaphanously grey below, vaporously white above, with a dream of perpetual snow—the mighty mountain of Daisen.

At the first approach of winter it will in one night become all blanched from foot to crest. Its snowy pyramid so much resembles that Sacred Mountain, often compared by poets to a white inverted fan, half opened, hanging in the sky, that it is called Izumo Fuji, 'the Fuji of Izumo.' But it is really in Hoki, not in Izumo, though it cannot be seen from any part of Hoki to such advantage as from here. It is the one sublime spectacle of this charming land, visible only when the air is very pure. Many are the marvellous legends related concerning it, and somewhere on its mysterious summit the *tengu* are believed to dwell.

Lotus

At the farther end of the bridge, close to the wharf where the little steamboats are, is a very small Jizō temple. Here are kept many bronze drags, and whenever anyone has been drowned and the body not recovered, these are borrowed from the little temple and the river is dragged. If the body is found, a new drag must be presented to the temple.

From here, half a mile southward to the great Shintō temple of Tenjin, deity of scholarship and calligraphy, broadly stretches Tenjinmachi, the Street of the Rich Merchants, all draped on either side with dark blue hangings, over which undulate with every windy palpitation from the lake white wondrous ideographs, which are names and signs, while down the wide way, in white perspective, diminishes a long line of telegraph poles.

Beyond the temple of Tenjin the city is again divided by a river, the Shindotegawa, over which arches the bridge Tenjin-*bashi*. Again beyond this other large quarters extend to the hills and curve along the lake shore. But in the space between the two rivers is the richest and busiest life of the city, and also the vast and curious quarter of the temples. In this islanded district are likewise the theatres, and the place where wrestling matches are held, and most of the resorts of pleasure.

Parallel with Tenjinmachi runs the great street of the Buddhist temples, or Teramachi, of which the eastern side is one unbroken succession of temples—a solid front of court walls tile-capped, with imposing gateways at regular intervals. Above this long stretch of tile-capped wall rise the beautiful tilted massive lines of grey-blue temple roofs against the sky. Here all the sects (*shū*) dwell side by side in harmony—Nichiren-*shū*, Shingon-*shū*, Zen-*shū*, Tendai-*shū*, even that Shin-*shū*, unpopular in Izumo because those who follow its teaching strictly must not worship the *kami*. Behind each temple court there is a cemetery, or *hakaba*. Eastward beyond these are other temples, and beyond them yet others—masses of Buddhist architecture mixed with shreds of gardens and miniature homesteads, a huge labyrinth of mouldering courts and fragments of streets.

Today, as usual, I find I can pass a few hours very profitably in visiting the temples. Looking at the ancient images seated within the cups of golden lotus flowers under their aureoles of gold; in buying curious *mamori*; in examining the sculptures of the cemeteries, where I can nearly always find some dreaming Kannon or smiling Jizō well worth the visit.

The great courts of Buddhist temples are places of rare interest for one who loves to watch the life of the people. For unremembered centuries they have been the playing places of children. Generations of happy infants have been amused in them. All the nurses, and little girls who carry tiny brothers or sisters on their backs, go thither every morning that the sun shines. Hundreds of children join them, and they play at strange, funny games— *onigokko,* or the game of devil, *kageoni*, which signifies the shadow and the demon, and *mekusangokko*, which is a sort of blindman's buff.

During the long summer evenings, these temples are wrestling grounds, free to all who love wrestling. In many of them there is a *dohyōba*, a wrestling ring. Robust young labourers and sinewy artisans come to these courts to test their strength after the day's tasks are done, and here the fame of more than one now noted wrestler was first made. When a youth has shown himself able to overmatch at wrestling all others in his own district, he is challenged by champions of other district. If he can overcome these also, he may hope eventually to become a professional wrestler.

It is also in the temple courts that the sacred dances are performed and that public speeches are made. It is in the temple courts, too, that the most curious toys are sold, on the occasion of the great holidays—toys most of which have a religious signification. There are grand old trees, and ponds full of tame fish, which put up their heads to beg for food when your shadow falls on the water. The holy lotus is cultivated therein.

> Though growing in the foulest slime,
> the flower remains pure and undefiled.
> And the soul of him who remains ever pure
> in the midst of temptation is likened to the lotus.
> Therefore is the lotus carven or painted
> on the furniture of temples;
> therefore also does it appear
> in all the representations of our Lord Buddha.
> 'In Paradise the blessed shall sit
> at ease enthroned on the cups of golden lotus flowers.

The above is from an English composition by one of my Japanese pupils.

A bugle call rings through the quaint street, and round the corner of the last temple come marching a troop of handsome young riflemen, uniformed somewhat like French light infantry, marching by fours so perfectly that all the gaitered legs move as if belonging to a single body, and every sword-bayonet catches the sun at exactly the same angle, as the column wheels into view. These are the students of the *shihan gakkō*, the college of teachers, performing their daily military exercises. Their professors give them lectures on the microscopic study of cellular tissues, on the segregation of developing nerve structure, on spectrum analysis, on the evolution of the colour sense, and on the cultivation of bacteria in glycerine infusions. And they are none the less modest and knightly in manner for all their modern knowledge, nor the less reverentially devoted to their dear old fathers and mothers whose ideas were shaped in the era of feudalism.

Pilgrimage

Here come a band of pilgrims, with yellow straw overcoats, rain coats (*mino*), and enormous yellow straw hats, mushroom-shaped, of which the down-curving rim partly hides the face. All carry staffs, and wear their robes well girded up so as to leave free the lower limbs, which are inclosed in white cotton leggings of a peculiar and indescribable kind. Precisely the same sort of costume was worn by the same class of travellers many centuries ago. Just as you now see them trooping by—whole families wandering together, the pilgrim child clinging to the father's hands—so may you see them pass in quaint procession across the faded pages of Japanese picture-books a hundred years old.

At intervals they halt before some shopfront to look at the many curious things which they greatly enjoy seeing, but which they have no money to buy.

I myself have become so accustomed to surprises, to interesting or extraordinary sights, that when a day happens to pass during which nothing remarkable has been heard or seen I feel vaguely discontented. But such blank days are rare: they occur in my own case only when the weather is too detestable to go out-of-doors. For with ever so little money one can always obtain the pleasure of looking at curious things. And this has been one of the chief pleasures of the people in Japan for centuries and centuries, for the nation has passed its generations of lives in making or seeking such things. To divert one's self seems, indeed, the main purpose of Japanese existence, beginning with the opening of the baby's wondering eyes. The faces of the people have an indescribable look of patient expectancy—the air of waiting for something interesting to make its appearance. If it fail to appear, they will travel to find it: they are astonishing pedestrians and tireless pilgrims, and I think they make pilgrimages not more for the sake of pleasing the gods than of pleasing themselves by the sight of rare and pretty things. For every temple is a museum, and every hill and valley throughout the land has its temple and its wonders.

Even the poorest farmer, one so poor that he cannot afford to eat a grain of his own rice, can afford to make a pilgrimage of a month's duration; and during that season when the growing rice needs least attention hundreds of thousands of the poorest go on pilgrimages. This is possible, because from ancient times it has been the custom for everybody to help pilgrims a little. They can always find rest and shelter at particular inns (*kichinyado*) which receive pilgrims only, and where they are charged merely the cost of the wood used to cook their food.

But multitudes of the poor undertake pilgrimages requiring much more than a month to perform, such as the pilgrimage to the thirty-three great temples of Kannon, or that to the eighty-eight temples of Kōbō Daishi; and these, though years be needed to accomplish them, are as nothing compared to the enormous Sengaji, the pilgrimage to the thousand temples of the Nichiren sect. The time of a generation may pass ere this can be made. One may begin it in early youth, and complete it only when youth is long past. Yet there are several in Matsue, men and women, who have made this tremendous pilgrimage, seeing all Japan, and supporting themselves not merely by begging, but by some kinds of itinerant peddling.

The pilgrim who desires to perform this pilgrimage carries on his shoulders a small box, shaped like a Buddhist shrine, in which he keeps his spare clothes and food. He also carries a little brazen gong, which he constantly sounds while passing through a city or village, at the same time chanting the *Namu myōhō rengekyō*; and he always bears with him a little blank book, in which the priest of every temple visited stamps the temple seal in red ink. The pilgrimage over, this book with its one thousand seal impressions becomes an heirloom in the family of the pilgrim.

Straw Sandals

I too must make divers pilgrimages, for all about the city, beyond the waters or beyond the hills, lie holy places immemorially old.

Izumo Ōyashiro, founded by the ancient gods, who 'made stout the pillars on the nethermost rock bottom, and made high the cross-beams to the plain of high heaven'—Izumo Ōyashiro, the holy of holies, whose high priest claims descent from the goddess of the sun.

And Ichibata, famed shrine of Yakushi Nyorai, who gives sight to the blind—Ichibata no Yakushi, whose lofty temple is approached by six hundred and forty steps of stone. And Kiyomizu, shrine of Kannon of the Eleven Faces, before whose altar the sacred fire has burned without ceasing for a thousand years. And Sada, where the sacred snake lies coiled for ever on the *sanbō* of the gods. And Oba, with its temples of Izanami and Izanagi, parents of gods and men, the makers of the world. And Yaegaki, where lovers go to pray for unions with the beloved. And Kaka and its cave—all these I hope to see.

But of all places, Kaka! Assuredly I must go to Kaka. Few pilgrims go thither by sea, and boatmen are forbidden to go there if there be even wind enough 'to move three hairs.' So that whosoever wishes to visit Kaka must either wait for a period of dead calm—very rare on the coast of the Japanese Sea—or journey by land, and by land the way is difficult and wearisome. But I must see Kaka. For at Kaka, in a great cavern by the sea, there is a famous Jizō of stone. Each night, it is said, the ghosts of little children climb to the high cavern and pile up before the statue small heaps of pebbles. And every morning, in the soft sand, there may be seen the fresh prints of tiny naked feet, the feet of the infant ghosts. It is also said that in the cavern there is a rock out of which comes a stream of milk, as from a woman's breast. The white stream flows for ever, and the phantom children drink of it. Pilgrims bring with them gifts of small straw sandals—the *zōri* that children wear—and leave them before the cavern, that the feet of the little ghosts may not be wounded by the sharp rocks. And the pilgrim treads with caution, lest he should overturn any of the many heaps of stones, for if this be done the children cry.

Oshiroyama

The city proper is as level as a table, bounded on two sides by low demilunes of charming hills shadowed with evergreen foliage and crowned with temples or shrines. Thirty-five thousand souls dwel in ten thousand houses forming thirty-three principal and many smaller streets. From each end of almost every street, beyond the hills, the lake, or the eastern rice fields, a mountain summit is always visible—green, blue, or grey according to distance. One may ride, walk, or go by boat to any quarter of the town, for it is not only divided by two rivers, but also intersected by numbers of canals crossed by queer little bridges curved like a well-bent bow.

Architecturally (despite such constructions in European style as the College of Teachers, the great public school, the prefectural office, the new post-office), it is much like other quaint Japanese towns; the structure of its temples, taverns, shops, and private dwellings is the same as in other cities of the western coast. But doubtless owing to the fact that Matsue remained a feudal stronghold until a time within the memory of thousands still living, those feudal distinctions of caste so sharply drawn in ancient times are yet indicated with singular exactness by the varying architecture of different districts.

The city can be definitely divided into three architectural quarters: the district of the merchants and shop-keepers, forming the heart of the settlement, where all the houses are two stories high; the district of the temples, including nearly the whole southeastern part of the town; and the district or districts of the *shizoku*, or nobility (formerly called samurai), comprising a vast number of large, roomy, garden-girt, one-story dwellings. From these elegant homes, in feudal days, could be summoned at a moment's notice five thousand 'two-sworded men' with their armed retainers, making a fighting total for the city alone of probably not less than thirteen thousand warriors.

More than one-third of all the city buildings were then samurai homes, for Matsue was the military centre of the most ancient province of Japan. At both ends of the town, which curves in a crescent along the lake shore, were the two main settlements of samurai. But just as some of the most important temples are situated outside of the temple district, so were many of the finest homesteads of this knightly caste situated in other quarters. They mustered most thickly about the castle, which stands today on the summit of its citadel hill—the Oshiroyama—solid as when first built long centuries ago, a vast and sinister shape, all iron-grey, rising against the sky from a cyclopean foundation of stone. Fantastically grim the thing is, and grotesquely complex in detail, looking somewhat like a huge pagoda, of which the second, third, and fourth stories have been squeezed down and telescoped into one another by their own weight.

Crested at its summit, like a feudal helmet, with two colossal fishes of bronze lifting their curved bodies skyward from either angle of the roof, and bristling with horned gables and gargoyled eaves and tilted puzzles of tiled roofing at every story, the creation is a veritable architectural dragon, made up of magnificent monstrosities—a dragon, moreover, full of eyes set at all conceivable angles, above below, and on every side. From under the black scowl of the loftiest eaves, looking east and south, the whole city can be seen at a single glance, as in the vision of a soaring hawk; and from the northern angle the view plunges down three hundred feet to the castle road, where walking figures of men appear no larger than flies.

Matsue Castle

The grim castle of Matsue has its legend.

It is related that, in accordance with some primitive and barbarous custom, precisely like that of which so terrible a souvenir has been preserved for us in the most pathetic of Servian ballads, 'The Foundation of Skadra,' a maiden of Matsue was interred alive under the walls of the castle at the time of its erection, as a sacrifice to some forgotten gods. Her name has never been recorded; nothing concerning her is remembered except that she was beautiful and very fond of dancing.

Now after the castle had been built, it is said that a law had to be passed forbidding that any girl should dance in the streets of Matsue. For whenever any maiden danced the hill Oshiroyama would shudder, and the great castle quiver from basement to summit.

Kakitsuba

One may still sometimes hear in the streets a very humorous song, which every one in town formerly knew by heart, celebrating the seven Wonders of Matsue. For Matsue was formerly divided into seven quarters, in each of which some extraordinary object or person was to be seen. It is now divided into five religious districts, each containing a temple of the state religion. People living within those districts are called *ujiko*, and the temple the *ujigami*, or dwelling place of the tutelary god. The *ujiko* must support the *ujigami* (every village and town has at least one *ujigami*).

There is probably not one of the multitudinous temples of Matsue which has not some marvellous tradition attached to it. Each of the districts has many legends, and I think that each of the thirty-three streets has its own special ghost story. Of these ghost stories I cite two specimens: they are quite representative of one variety of Japanese folklore.

Near to the Fumon-in monastery, which is in the northeastern quarter, there is a bridge called Azukitogi-*bashi*, or The Bridge of the Washing of Peas. For it was said in other years that nightly a phantom woman sat beneath that bridge washing phantom peas. There is an exquisite Japanese iris-flower, of rainbow-violet colour, which flower is named *kakitsubata*. There is a song about that flower called Kakitsubata no Uta. Now this song must never be sung near the Adzukitogi-*bashi*, because, for some strange reason which seems to have been forgotten, the ghosts haunting that place become so angry on hearing it that to sing it there is to expose one's self to the most frightful calamities. There was once a samurai who feared nothing, who one night went to that bridge and loudly sang the song. No ghost appearing, he laughed and went home. At the gate of his house he met a beautiful tall woman whom he had never seen before, and who, bowing, presented him with a lacquered box *fumibako*—such as women keep their letters in.

He bowed to her in his knightly way.

But she said, 'I am only the servant—this is my mistress's gift,' and vanished out of his sight.

Opening the box, he saw the bleeding head of a young child. Entering his house, he found on the floor of the guest room the dead body of his own infant son with the head torn off.

Mizuame

Of the cemetery Dai Oji, which is in the street called Nakabaramachi, this story is told:

In Nakabaramachi there is an *ameya*, or little shop in which *mizuame* is sold—the amber-tinted syrup, made of malt, which is given to children when milk cannot be obtained for them. Every night at a late hour there came to that shop a very pale woman, all in white, to buy one *rin* worth of *mizuame*. The *ame*-seller wondered that she was so thin and pale, and often questioned her kindly, but she answered nothing. At last one night he followed her, out of curiosity. She went to the cemetery, and he became afraid and returned.

The next night the woman came again, but bought no *mizuame*, and only beckoned to the man to go with her. He followed her, with friends, into the cemetery. She walked to a certain tomb, and there disappeared, and they heard, under the ground, the crying of a child. Opening the tomb, they saw within it the corpse of the woman who nightly visited the *ameya*, with a living infant, laughing to see the lantern light, and beside the infant a little cup of *mizuame*. For the mother had been prematurely buried; the child was born in the tomb, and the ghost of the mother had thus provided for it—love being stronger than death.

Sobaya

Over the Tenjin-*bashi*, or Bridge of Tenjin, and through small streets and narrow of densely populated districts, and past many a tenantless and mouldering feudal homestead, I make my way to the extreme southwestern end of the city, to watch the sunset from a little *sobaya* (noodle inn) facing the lake. For to see the sun sink from this *sobaya* is one of the delights of Matsue.

There are no such sunsets in Japan as in the tropics: the light is gentle as a light of dreams; there are no furies of colour; there are no chromatic violences in nature in this Orient. All in sea or sky is tint rather than colour, and tint vapour-toned. I think that the exquisite taste of the race in the matter of colours and of tints, as exemplified in the dyes of their wonderful textures, is largely attributable to the sober and delicate beauty of nature's tones in this all-temperate world where nothing is garish.

Before me the fair vast lake sleeps, softly luminous, far-ringed with chains of blue volcanic hills shaped like a sierra. On my right, at its eastern end, the most ancient quarter of the city spreads its roofs of blue-grey tile; the houses crowd thickly down to the shore, to dip their wooden feet into the flood. With a glass I can see my own windows and the far-spreading of the roofs beyond, and above all else the green citadel with its grim castle, grotesquely peaked. The sun begins to set, and exquisite astonishments of tinting appear in water and sky.

Dead rich purples cloud broadly behind and above the indigo blackness of the serrated hills—mist purples, fading upward smokily into faint vermilions and dim gold, which again melt up through ghostliest greens into the blue. The deeper waters of the lake, far away, take a tender violet indescribable, and the silhouette of the pine-shadowed island seems to float in that sea of soft sweet colour. But the shallower and nearer is cut from the deeper water by the current as sharply as by a line drawn, and all the surface on this side of that line is a shimmering bronze—old rich ruddy gold-bronze.

All the fainter colours change every five minutes—wondrously change and shift like tones and shades of fine shot-silks.

Flower Displays

Often in the streets at night, especially on the nights of sacred festivals (*matsuri*), one's attention will be attracted to some small booth by the spectacle of an admiring and perfectly silent crowd pressing before it. As soon as one can get a chance to look one finds there is nothing to look at but a few vases containing sprays of flowers, or perhaps some light gracious branches freshly cut from a blossoming tree. It is simply a little flower-show, or, more correctly, a free exhibition of master skill in the arrangement of flowers. For the Japanese do not brutally chop off flower heads to work them up into meaningless masses of colour, as we barbarians do: they love nature too well for that. They know how much the natural charm of the flower depends on its setting and mounting, its relation to leaf and stem, and they select a single graceful branch or spray just as nature made it.

At first you will not, as a Western stranger, comprehend such an exhibition at all: you are yet a savage in such matters compared with the commonest coolies about you. But even while you are still wondering at popular interest in this simple little show, the charm of it will begin to grow on you, will become a revelation to you; and, despite your Occidental idea of self-superiority, you will feel humbled by the discovery that all flower displays you have ever seen abroad were only monstrosities in comparison with the natural beauty of those few simple sprays. You will also observe how much the white or pale blue screen behind the flowers enhances the effect by lamp or lantern light. For the screen has been arranged with the special purpose of showing the exquisiteness of plant shadows. The sharp silhouettes of sprays and blossoms cast thereon are beautiful beyond the imagining of any Western decorative artist.

The Praying Woman

It is still the season of mists in this land whose most ancient name signifies the 'place of the issuing of clouds.' With the passing of twilight a faint ghostly brume rises over lake and landscape, spectrally veiling surfaces, slowly obliterating distances. As I lean over the parapet of the Tenjin-*bashi*, on my homeward way, to take one last look eastward, I find that the mountains have already been effaced. Before me there is only a shadowy flood far vanishing into vagueness without a horizon—the phantom of a sea. And I become suddenly aware that little white things are fluttering slowly down into it from the fingers of a woman standing on the bridge beside me, and murmuring something in a low sweet voice. She is praying for her dead child. Each of those little papers she is dropping into the current bears a tiny picture of Jizō and perhaps a little inscription. For when a child dies the mother buys a small woodcut (hankō) of Jizō, and with it prints the image of the divinity on one hundred little papers. And she sometimes also writes on the papers words signifying 'For the sake of...'—inscribing never the living, but the kaimyō or 'soul name' only, which the Buddhist priest has given to the dead, and which is written also on the little commemorative tablet kept within the Buddhist household shrine, or butsuma. Then, on a fixed day (most commonly the forty-ninth day after the burial), she goes to some place of running water and drops the little papers therein one by one; repeating, as each slips through her fingers, the holy invocation, 'Namu Jizō, Dai Bosatsu!'

Doubtless this pious little woman, praying beside me in the dusk, is very poor. Were she not, she would hire a boat and scatter her tiny papers far away on the bosom of the lake. (It is now only after dark that this may be done; for the police—I know not why—have been instructed to prevent the pretty rite, just as in the open ports they have been instructed to prohibit the launching of the little straw boats of the dead, the shōryōbune.)

But why should the papers be cast into running water? A good old Tendai priest tells me that originally the rite was only for the souls of the drowned. But now these gentle hearts believe that all waters flow downward to the Shadow-world and through the Sai no Kawara, where Jizō is.

Dusk

At home again, I slide open once more my little paper window, and look out upon the night. I see the paper lanterns flitting over the bridge, like a long shimmering of fireflies. I see the spectres of a hundred lights trembling on the black flood. I see the broad shōji of dwellings beyond the river suffused with the soft yellow radiance of invisible lamps. On those lighted spaces I can discern slender moving shadows, silhouettes of graceful women. Devoutly do I pray that glass may never become universally adopted in Japan—there would be no more delicious shadows.

I listen to the voices of the city awhile. I hear the great bell of Tōkō-*ji* rolling its soft Buddhist thunder across the dark, and the songs of the night-walkers whose hearts have been made merry with wine, and the long sonorous chanting of the night peddlers.

'*Umudon-yai, soba-yai!*' It is the seller of hot soba, Japanese buckwheat, making his last round.

'*Umai handan, machibito endan, usemono ninsō kaso kichikyō no urainai!*' The cry of the itinerant fortune teller.

'*Ame-yu!*' The musical cry of the seller of *mizuame*, the sweet amber syrup which children love.

'*Amai!*' The shrilling call of the seller of *amazake*, sweet rice wine.

'*Kawachi no kuni hyōtan-yama koi-no tsujiura!*' The peddler of love papers, of divining papers, pretty tinted things with little shadowy pictures on them. When held near a fire or a lamp, words written on them with invisible ink begin to appear. These are always about sweethearts, and sometimes tell you what you do not wish to know. The fortunate ones who read them believe themselves still more fortunate; the unlucky abandon all hope; the jealous become even more jealous than they were before.

From all over the city there rises into the night a sound like the bubbling and booming of great frogs in a march—the echoing of the tiny drums of the dancing girls, of the charming *geisha*. Like the rolling of a waterfall continually reverberates the multitudinous pattering of *geta* on the bridge. A new light rises in the east; the moon is wheeling up from behind the peaks, very large and weird and wan through the white vapours. Again I hear the sounds of the clapping of many hands. For the wayfarers are paying obeisance to o-Tsuki-*san*: from the long bridge they are saluting the coming of the White Moon Lady.

I sleep, to dream of little children, in some mouldering mossy temple court, playing at the game of shadows and of demons.

Izumo

Izumo

Shinkoku is the sacred name of Japan—Shinkoku, 'The Country of the Gods.' Of all Shinkoku the most holy ground is the land of Izumo. Hither from the blue plain of high heaven first came to dwell a while the earth-makers, Izanagi and Izanami, the parents of gods and of men. Somewhere on the border of this land Izanami was buried. Out of this land into the black realm of the dead Izanagi followed her, and sought in vain to bring her back again. Is not the tale of his descent into that strange nether world, and of what befell him there, written in the *Kojiki*? And of all legends primeval concerning the underworld this story is one of the weirdest—more weird than even the Assyrian legend of the descent of Ishtar.

Even as Izumo is especially the province of the gods, and the place of the childhood of the race by whom Izanagi and Izanami are yet worshiped, so is the Izumo Ōyashiro especially the city of the gods, and its immemorial temple the earliest home of the ancient faith, the great religion of Shintō.

To visit the Izumo Ōyashiro has been my most earnest ambition since I learned the legends of the *Kojiki* concerning it. And this ambition has been stimulated by the discovery that very few Europeans have visited the Izumo Ōyashiro, and that none have been admitted into the great temple itself. Some, indeed, were not allowed even to approach the temple court. But I trust that I shall be somewhat more fortunate, for I have a letter of introduction from my dear friend Nishida Sentaro, who is also a personal friend of the high pontiff of the Izumo Ōyashiro. I am thus assured that even should I not be permitted to enter the temple—a privilege accorded to but few among the Japanese themselves—I shall at least have the honour of an interview with the *guji*, or head priest of the Izumo Ōyashiro, Senke Takanori, whose princely family trace back their descent to the goddess of the sun.

Kami

I leave Matsue for Izumo early in the afternoon of a beautiful September day. Taking passage on a tiny steamer in which everything, from engines to awnings, is Lilliputian. In the cabin one must kneel. Under the awnings one cannot possibly stand upright. But the miniature craft is neat and pretty as a toy model, and moves with surprising swiftness and steadiness. A handsome naked boy is busy serving the passengers with cups of tea and with cakes, and setting little charcoal furnaces before those who desire to smoke: for all of which a payment of about three-quarters of a cent is expected.

I escape from the awnings to climb on the cabin roof for a view, and the view is indescribably lovely. Over the lucent level of the lake we are steaming toward a far-away heaping of beautiful shapes, coloured with that strangely delicate blue which tints all distances in the Japanese atmosphere—shapes of peaks and headlands looming up from the lake verge against a porcelain-white horizon. They show no details, whatever. Silhouettes only they are— masses of absolutely pure colour. To left and right, framing in the Shinji Lake, are superb green surgings of wooded hills. Great Yakuno-*san* is the loftiest mountain before us, northwest. Southeast, behind us, the city has vanished. But proudly towering beyond looms Daisen—enormous, ghostly blue and ghostly white, lifting the cusps of its dead crater into the region of eternal snow. Over all arches a sky of colour faint as a dream.

There seems to be a sense of divine magic in the very atmosphere, through all the luminous day, brooding over the vapoury land, over the ghostly blue of the flood—a sense of Shintō. With my fancy full of the legends of the *Kojiki*, the rhythmic chant of the engines comes to my ears as the rhythm of a Shintō ritual mingled with the names of gods: Kotoshironushi no Kami, Ōkuninushi no Kami.

Binbōgami

The great range on the right grows loftier as we steam on. Its hills, always slowly advancing toward us, begin to reveal all the rich details of their foliage. And lo! on the tip of one grand wood-clad peak is visible against the pure sky the many-angled roof of a great Buddhist temple. That is the temple of Ichibata, on Mount Ichibata, the temple of Yakushi Nyorai, the Physician of Souls. But at Ichibata he reveals himself more specially as the healer of bodies, the Buddha who gives sight to the blind. It is believed that whosoever has an affection of the eyes will be made well by praying earnestly at that great shrine. From many distant provinces afflicted thousands make the pilgrimage, ascending the long weary mountain path and the six hundred and forty steps of stone leading to the windy temple court on the summit, whence may be seen one of the loveliest landscapes in Japan. There the pilgrims wash their eyes with the water of the sacred spring, and kneel before the shrine and murmur the holy formula of Ichibata, '*On koro-koro sendai matoki sowaka*'—words of which the meaning has long been forgotten, like that of many a Buddhist invocation. They are Sanscrit words transliterated into Chinese, and into Japanese, which are understood by learned priests alone, yet are known by heart throughout the land, and uttered with the utmost fervour of devotion.

I descend from the cabin roof, and squat on the deck, under the awnings, to have a smoke with Akira. And I ask:

'How many Buddhas are there, Akira? Is their number known?'

'Countless the Buddhas are,' makes answer Akira. 'Yet there is truly but one Buddha; the many are forms only. Each of us contains a future Buddha. Alike we all are except in that we are more or less unconscious of the truth. But the vulgar may not understand these things, and so seek refuge in symbols and in forms.'

'And the *kami*—the deities of Shintō?'

'Of Shintō I know little. But there are eight hundred myriads of *kami* in the plain of high heaven—so says the Ancient Book. Of these, three thousand one hundred and thirty and two dwell in the various provinces of the land. Being enshrined in two thousand eight hundred and sixty-one temples. And the tenth month of our year is called the "no-god-month," because in that month all the deities leave their temples to assemble in the province of Izumo, at the great temple of Izumo Ōyashiro. For the same reason that month is called in Izumo, and only in Izumo, the "god-is-month." But educated persons sometimes call it the "god-present-festival," using Chinese words. Then it is believed the serpents come from the sea to the land, and coil on the *sanbō*, which is the table of the gods, for the serpents announce the coming. And the dragon king sends messengers to the temples of Izanagi and Izanami, the parents of gods and men.'

'O Akira, many millions of *kami* there must be of whom I shall always remain ignorant, for there is a limit to the power of memory. But tell me something of the gods whose names are most seldom uttered, the deities of strange places and of strange things, the most extraordinary gods.'

'You cannot learn much about them from me,' replies Akira. 'You will have to ask others more learned than I. But there are gods with whom it is not desirable to become acquainted. Such are the God of Poverty, and the God of Hunger, and the God of Penuriousness, and the God of Hindrances and Obstacles. These are of dark colour, like the clouds of gloomy days, and their faces are like the faces of *gaki*.'

'With the God of Hindrances and Obstacles I have had more than a passing acquaintance. Tell me of the others.'

'I know little about any of them,' answers Akira, 'excepting Binbōgami. It is said there are two gods who always go together—Fuku no Kami, who is the God of Luck, and Binbōgami, who is the God of Poverty. The first is white, and the second is black.'

'Because the last,' I venture to interrupt, 'is only the shadow of the first. Fuku no Kami is the Shadow-caster, and Binbōgami the Shadow. I have observed, in wandering about this world, that wherever the one goeth, eternally followeth after him the other.'

Akira refuses his assent to this interpretation, and resumes:

'When Binbōgami once begins to follow anyone it is extremely difficult to be free from him again. In the village of Umitsu, which is in the province of Omi, and not far from Kyoto, there once lived a Buddhist priest who during many years was grievously tormented by Binbōgami. He tried oftentimes without avail to drive him away. Then he strove to deceive him by proclaiming aloud to all the people that he was going to Kyoto. But instead of going to Kyoto he went to Tsuruga, in the province of Echizen. When he reached the inn at Tsuruga there came forth to meet him a boy lean and wan like a *gaki*. The boy said to him, "I have been waiting for you"— and the boy was Binbōgami.

'There was another priest who for sixty years had tried in vain to get rid of Binbōgami, and who resolved at last to go to a distant province. On the night after he had formed this resolve he had a strange dream, in which he saw a very much emaciated boy, naked and dirty, weaving sandals of straw (*waraji*), such as pilgrims and runners wear. And he made so many that the priest wondered, and asked him, "For what purpose are you making so many sandals?" And the boy answered, "I am going to travel with you. I am Binbōgami."'

'Then is there no way, Akira, by which Binbōgami may be driven away?'

'It is written,' replies Akira, 'in the book called *Jizō-kyō kōsui* that the aged Enjōbō Sōen, a priest dwelling in the province of Owari, was able to get rid of Binbōgami by means of a charm. On the last day of the last month of the year he and his disciples and other priests of the Shingon sect took branches of peach trees and recited a formula. Then, with the branches, he imitated the action of driving a person out of the temple, after which they shut all the gates and recited other formulas. The same night Enjōbō dreamed of a skeleton priest in a broken temple weeping alone. And the skeleton priest said to him, "After I had been with you for so many years, how could you drive me away?" But always thereafter until the day of his death, Enjōbō lived in prosperity.'

The holy City

For an hour and a half the ranges to left and right alternately recede and approach. Beautiful blue shapes glide toward us, change to green, and then, slowly drifting behind us, are all blue again. But the far mountains immediately before us—immovable, unchanging—always remain ghosts. Suddenly the little steamer turns straight into the land—a land so low that it came into sight quite unexpectedly—and we puff up a narrow stream between rice fields to a queer, quaint, pretty village on the canal bank—Shobara. Here I must hire *jinrikisha* to take us to Izumo.

There is not time to see much of Shobara if I hope to reach Izumo before bedtime, and I have only a flying vision of one long wide street (so picturesque that I wish I could pass a day in it), as our *kuruma* rush through the little town into the open country, into a vast plain covered with rice fields. The road itself is only a broad dike, barely wide enough for two *jinrikisha* to pass each other on it. On each side the superb plain is bounded by a mountain range shutting off the white horizon. There is a vast silence, an immense sense of dreamy peace, and a glorious soft vapoury light over everything, as we roll into the country of Hyasugi to Kaminawoe. The jagged range on the left is Shusai-*yama*, all sharply green, with the giant Daikoku-*yama* overtopping all. Its peaks bear the names of gods. Much more remote, on our right, enormous, pansy-purple, tower the shapes of the Kita-*yama*, or northern range. Filing away in tremendous procession toward the sunset, fading more and more as they stretch west, to vanish suddenly at last, after the ghostliest conceivable manner, into the uttermost day.

All this is beautiful. Yet there is no change while hours pass. Always the way winds on through miles of rice fields, white-speckled with paper-winged shafts which are arrows of prayer. Always the voice of frogs—a sound as of infinite bubbling. Always the green range on the left, the purple on the right, fading westward into a tall file of tinted spectres which always melt into nothing at last, as if they were made of air. The monotony of the scene is broken only by our occasional passing through some pretty Japanese village, or by the appearance of a curious statue or monument at an angle of the path, a roadside Jizō, or the grave of a wrestler, such as may be seen on the bank of the Hiagawa, a huge slab of granite sculptured with the words, '*Ikumo matsu kikusuki.*'

But after reaching Kandogori, and passing over a broad but shallow river, a fresh detail appears in the landscape. Above the mountain chain on our left looms a colossal blue silhouette, almost saddle-shaped, recognisable by its outline as a once mighty volcano. It is now known by various names, but it was called in ancient times Sahime-*yama*, and it has its Shintō legend.

It is said that in the beginning the God of Izumo, gazing over the land, said, 'This new land of Izumo is a land of but small extent, so I will make it a larger land by adding to it.' Having said so, he looked about him over to Korea, and there he saw land which was good for the purpose. With a great rope he dragged away four islands, and added them to Izumo. The first island was called Yaoyone, and it formed the land where Izumo now is. The second island was called Sada no Kuni, and is at this day the site of the holy temple where all the gods do yearly hold their second assembly, after having first gathered together at Izumo. The third island was called in its new place

Kurami no Kuni, which now forms Shimanegori. The fourth island became that place where stands the temple of the great god at whose shrine are delivered to the faithful the charms which protect the rice fields.

Now in drawing these islands across the sea into their several places the god looped his rope over the mighty mountain of Daisen and over the mountain Sahime-*yama*. They both bear the marks of that wondrous rope even to this day. As for the rope itself, part of it was changed into the long island of ancient times called Yomigahama, and a part into the long beach of Sono.

After we pass the Hori River the road narrows and becomes rougher and rougher, but always draws nearer to the Kitayama range. Toward sundown we have come close enough to the great hills to discern the details of their foliage. The path begins to rise; we ascend slowly through the gathering dusk. At last there appears before us a great multitude of twinkling lights. We have reached Izumo, the holy city.

Torii

Over a long bridge and under a tall *torii* we roll into upward-sloping streets. Like Enoshima, Izumo has a *torii* for its city gate, but the *torii* is not of bronze. Then a flying vision of open lamp-lighted shopfronts, and lines of luminous *shōji* under high-tilted eaves, and Buddhist gateways guarded by lions of stone, and long, low, tile-coped walls of temple courts overtopped by garden shrubbery, and Shintō shrines prefaced by other tall *torii*. But no sign of the great temple itself. It lies toward the rear of the city proper, at the foot of the wooded mountains; and we are too tired and hungry to visit it now. So we halt before a spacious and comfortable-seeming inn—the best, indeed, in Izumo—and rest ourselves and eat, and drink sake out of exquisite little porcelain cups, the gift of some pretty singing-girl to the hotel. Thereafter, as it has become much too late to visit the *guji*, I send to his residence by a messenger my letter of introduction, with an humble request in Akira's handwriting, that I may be allowed to present myself at the house before noon the next day.

Then the landlord of the hotel, who seems to be a very kindly person, comes to us with lighted paper lanterns, and invites us to accompany him to the Izumo Ōyashiro, the great shrine of Izumo.

Most of the houses have already closed their wooden sliding doors for the night, so that the streets are dark, and the lanterns of our landlord indispensable, for there is no moon, and the night is starless. We walk along the main street for a distance of about six squares. Then, making a turn, we find ourselves before a superb bronze *torii*, the gateway to the great temple avenue.

Ōnushi no Kami

Effacing colours and obliterating distances, night always magnifies by suggestion the aspect of large spaces and the effect of large objects. Viewed by the vague light of paper lanterns, the approach to the great shrine is an imposing surprise—such a surprise that I feel regret at the mere thought of having to see it tomorrow by disenchanting day: a superb avenue lined with colossal trees, and ranging away out of sight under a succession of giant *torii*, from which are suspended enormous *shimenawa*, well worthy the grasp of that heavenly hand-strength deity whose symbols they are. But, more than by the *torii* and their festooned symbols, the dim majesty of the huge avenue is enhanced by the prodigious trees—many perhaps thousands of years old—gnarled pines whose shaggy summits are lost in darkness. Some of the mighty trunks are surrounded with a rope of straw: these trees are sacred. The vast roots, far-reaching in every direction, look in the lantern light like a writing and crawling of dragons.

The avenue is certainly not less than a quarter of a mile in length; it crosses two bridges and passes between two sacred groves. All the broad lands on either side of it belong to the temple. Formerly no foreigner was permitted to pass beyond the middle *torii*. The avenue terminates at a lofty wall pierced by a gateway resembling the gateways of Buddhist temple courts, but very massive. This is the entrance to the outer court; the ponderous doors are still open, and many shadowy figures are passing in or out.

Within the court all is darkness, against which pale yellow lights are gliding to and fro like a multitude of enormous fireflies—the lanterns of pilgrims. I can distinguish only the looming of immense buildings to left and right, constructed with colossal timbers. Our guide traverses a very large court, passes into a second, and halts before an imposing structure whose doors are still open. Above them, by the lantern glow, I can see a marvellous frieze of dragons and water, carved in some rich wood by the hand of a master. Within I can see the symbols of Shintō, in a side shrine on the left; and directly before us the lanterns reveal a surface of matted floor vaster than anything I had expected to find. Therefrom I can divine the scale of the edifice which I suppose to be the temple. But the landlord tells us this is not the temple, but only the *haiden* or hall of prayer, before which the people make their orisons, By day, through the open doors, the temple can be seen. But we cannot see it tonight, and but few visitors are permitted to go in. 'The people do not enter even the court of the great shrine, for the most part,' interprets Akira. 'They pray before it at a distance. Listen!'

All about me in the shadow I hear a sound like the plashing and dashing of water—the clapping of many hands in Shintō prayer.

'But this is nothing,' says the landlord; 'there are but few here now. Wait until tomorrow, which is a festival day.'

As we wend our way back along the great avenue, under the *torii* and the giant trees, Akira interprets for me what our landlord tells him about the sacred serpent.

'The little serpent,' he says, 'is called by the people the august dragon serpent, for it is sent by the dragon king to announce the coming of the gods. The sea darkens and rises and roars before the coming of Ryūja-*sama*. Rūja-*sama* we call it because it is the messenger of Ryōgujō, the palace of the dragons. It is also called Hakuja, or the 'White Serpent.'

'Does the little serpent come to the temple of its own accord?'

'Oh, no. It is caught by the fishermen. And only one can be caught in a year, because only one is sent. Whoever catches it and brings it either to the Izumo Ōyashiro, or to the Sada temple, where the gods hold their second assembly during *kamiarizuki*, the month of the gods, receives one *hyo* (2 1/2 *hyo* make one *koku*) of rice in recompense. It costs much labour and time to catch a serpent, but whoever captures one is sure to become rich in after time.'

'There are many deities enshrined at the Izumo Ōyashiro, are there not?' I ask.

'Yes; but the great deity of Izumo Ōyashiro is Ōkuninushi no Kami, whom the people more commonly call Daikoku. Here also is worshipped his son, whom many call Ebisu. These deities are usually pictured together:

Daikoku seated on bales of rice, holding the red sun against his breast with one hand, and in the other grasping the magical mallet of which a single stroke gives wealth. And Ebisu bearing a fishing rod, holding under his arm a great sea bream. These gods are always represented with smiling faces. Both have great ears, which are the sign of wealth and fortune.'

The Messenger

A little wearied by the day's journeying, I get to bed early, and sleep as dreamlessly as a plant until I am awakened about daylight by a heavy, regular, bumping sound, shaking the wooden pillow on which my ear rests—the sound of the *kometsuki* (rice polisher) beginning his eternal labour of rice cleaning. Then the pretty musume of the inn opens the chamber to the fresh mountain air and the early sun, rolls back all the wooden shutters into their casings behind the gallery, takes down the brown mosquito net, brings a *hibachi* with freshly kindled charcoal for my morning smoke, and trips away to get our breakfast.

Early as it is when she returns, she brings word that a messenger has already arrived from the *guji*, Senke Takanori, high descendant of the goddess of the sun. The messenger is a dignified young Shintō priest, clad in the ordinary Japanese full costume, but wearing also a superb pair of blue silken *hakama*, or Japanese ceremonial trousers, widening picturesquely towards the feet. He accepts my invitation to a cup of tea, and informs me that his august master is waiting for us at the temple.

This is delightful news, but we cannot go at once. Akira's attire is pronounced by the messenger to be defective. Akira must don fresh white *tabi* and put on hakama before going into the august presence: no one may enter thereinto without *hakama*. Happily Akira is able to borrow a pair of *hakama* from the landlord. After having arranged ourselves as neatly as we can, we take our way to the temple, guided by the messenger.

Ikigami

I am agreeably surprised to find, as we pass again under a magnificent bronze *torii* I admired the night before, that the approaches to the temple lose very little of their imposing character when seen for the first time by sunlight. The majesty of the trees remains astonishing. The vista of the avenue is grand, and the vast spaces of groves and grounds to right and left are even more impressive than I had imagined. Multitudes of pilgrims are going and coming, but the whole population of a province might move along such an avenue without jostling. Before the gate of the first court a Shintō priest in full sacerdotal costume waits to receive us: an elderly man, with a pleasant kindly face. The messenger commits us to his charge and vanishes through the gateway, while the elderly priest, whose name is Sasa, leads the way.

Already I can hear a heavy sound, as of surf, within the temple court. As we advance the sound becomes sharper and recognisable—a volleying of handclaps. And passing the great gate, I see thousands of pilgrims before the *haiden*, the same huge structure which I visited last night. None enter there: all stand before the dragon-swarming doorway, and cast their offerings into the money chest placed before the threshold, many making contribution of small coin, the very poorest throwing only a handful of rice into the box. Then they clap their hands and bow their heads before the threshold, and reverently gaze through the hall of prayer at the loftier edifice, the holy of holies, beyond it. Each pilgrim remains but a little while, and claps his hands but four times, yet so many are coming and going that the sound of the clapping is like the sound of a cataract.

Passing by the multitude of worshippers to the other side of the *haiden*, we find ourselves at the foot of a broad flight of iron-bound steps leading to the great sanctuary—steps which I am told no European before me was ever permitted to approach. On the lower steps the priests of the temple, in full ceremonial costume, are waiting to receive us. Tall men they are, robed in violet and purple silks shot through with dragon-patterns in gold. Their lofty fantastic headdresses, their voluminous and beautiful costume, and the solemn immobility of their hierophantic attitudes make them at first sight seem marvellous statues only. Somehow or other there comes suddenly back to me the memory of a strange French print I used to wonder at when a child, representing a group of Assyrian astrologers. Only their eyes move as we approach. But as I reach the steps all simultaneously salute me with a most gracious bow, for I am the first foreign pilgrim to be honoured by the privilege of an interview in the holy shrine itself with the princely hierophant, their master, descendant of the goddess of the sun— he who is still called by myriads of humble worshippers in the remoter districts of this ancient province Ikigami, 'the living deity.' Then all become absolutely statuesque again.

I remove my shoes, and am about to ascend the steps, when the tall priest who first received us before the outer gate indicates, by a single significant gesture, that religion and ancient custom require me, before ascending to the shrine of the god, to perform the ceremonial ablution. I hold out my hands. The priest pours the pure water over them thrice from a ladle-shaped vessel of bamboo with a long handle, and then gives me a little blue towel to wipe them on, a votive towel with mysterious white characters on it. Then we all ascend, I feeling very much like a clumsy barbarian in my ungraceful foreign garb.

Pausing at the head of the steps, the priest inquires my rank in society. For at the Izumo Ōyashiro hierarchy and hierarchical forms are maintained with a rigidity as precise as in the period of the gods. There are special forms and regulations for the reception of visitors of every social grade. I do not know what flattering statements Akira may have made about me to the good priest, but the result is that I can rank only as a common person—which veracious fact doubtless saves me from some formalities that would have proved embarrassing, all ignorant as I still am of that finer and more complex etiquette in which the Japanese are the world's masters.

The Guji

The priest leads the way into a vast and lofty apartment opening for its entire length on the broad gallery to which the stairway ascends. I have barely time to notice, while following him, that the chamber contains three immense shrines, forming alcoves on two sides of it. Of these, two are veiled by white curtains reaching from ceiling to matting—curtains decorated with perpendicular rows of black disks about four inches in diameter, each disk having in its centre a golden blossom. But from before the third shrine, in the farther angle of the chamber, the curtains have been withdrawn. These are of gold brocade, and the shrine before which they hang is the chief shrine, that of Ōkuninushi no Kami. Within are visible only some of the ordinary emblems of Shintō, and the exterior of that Holy of Holies into which none may look. Before it a long low bench, covered with strange objects, has been placed, with one end toward the gallery and one toward the alcove. At the end of this bench, near the gallery, I see a majestic bearded figure, strangely coifed and robed all in white, seated on the matted floor in hierophantic attitude. Our priestly guide motions us to take our places in front of him and to bow down before him. For this is Senke Takanori, the *guji* of the Izumo Ōyashiro, to whom even in his own dwelling none may speak save on bended knee, descendant of the goddess of the sun, and still by multitudes revered in thought as a being superhuman. Prostrating myself before him, according to the customary code of Japanese politeness, I am saluted in return with that exquisite courtesy which puts a stranger immediately at ease. The priest who acted as our guide now sits down on the floor at the *guji*'s left hand, while the other priests, who followed us to the entrance of the sanctuary only, take their places on the gallery without.

The Trees that Came Floating
Senke Takanori is a youthful and powerful man. As he sits there before me in his immobile hieratic pose, with his strange lofty head-dress, his heavy curling beard, and his ample snowy sacerdotal robe broadly spreading about him in statuesque undulations, he realises for me all that I had imagined, from the suggestion of old Japanese pictures, about the personal majesty of the ancient princes and heroes. The dignity alone of the man would irresistibly compel respect, but with that feeling of respect there also flashes through me at once the thought of the profound reverence paid him by the population of the most ancient province of Japan, the idea of the immense spiritual power in his hands, the tradition of his divine descent, the sense of the immemorial nobility of his race—and my respect deepens into a feeling closely akin to awe. So motionless he is that he seems a sacred statue only—the temple image of one of his own deified ancestors. But the solemnity of the first few moments is agreeably broken by his first words, uttered in a low rich basso, while his dark, kindly eyes remain motionlessly fixed upon my face. Then my interpreter translates his greeting—large fine phrases of courtesy—to which I reply as I best know how, expressing my gratitude for the exceptional favour accorded me.

'You are, indeed,' he responds through Akira, 'the first European ever permitted to enter into the Izumo Ōyashiro. Other Europeans have visited the Izumo Ōyashiro and a few have been allowed to enter the temple court, but only you have been admitted into the dwelling of the god. In past years, some strangers who desired to visit the temple out of common curiosity only were not allowed to approach even the court, but the letter of Mr. Nishida, explaining the object of your visit, has made it a pleasure for us to receive you thus.'

Again I express my thanks, and after a second exchange of courtesies the conversation continues through the medium of Akira.

'Is not this great temple of Izumo Ōyashiro,' I inquire, 'older than the temples of Ise?'

'Older by far,' replies the *guji*. 'So old that we do not well know its age. For it was first built by order of the goddess of the sun, in the time when deities alone existed. Then it was exceedingly magnificent; it was three hundred and twenty feet high. The beams and the pillars were larger than any existing timber could furnish, and the framework was bound together firmly with a rope made of mulberry fibre, one thousand fathoms long.

'It was first rebuilt in the time of Emperor Suinin. The temple so rebuilt by order of the Emperor was called the Structure of the Iron Rings, because the pieces of the pillars, which were composed of the wood of many great trees, had been bound fast together with huge rings of iron. This temple was also splendid, but far less splendid than the first, which had been built by the gods, for its height was only one hundred and sixty feet.

'A third time the temple was rebuilt, in the reign of Empress Saimei, but this third edifice was only eighty feet high. Since then the structure of the temple has never varied, and the plan then followed has been strictly preserved to the least detail in the construction of the present temple.

'The Izumo Ōyashiro has been rebuilt twenty-eight times, and it has been the custom to rebuild it every sixty-one years. But in the long period of civil war it was not even repaired for more than a hundred years. In the fourth year of Taiei, one Amako Tsunehisa, becoming Lord of Izumo, committed the great temple to the charge of a Buddhist priest, and even built pagodas about it, to the outrage of the holy traditions. But when the Amako family were succeeded by Moro Mototsugo, the latter purified the temple and restored the ancient festivals and ceremonies which before had been neglected.'

'In the period when the temple was built on a larger scale,' I ask, 'were the timbers for its construction obtained from the forests of Izumo?'

The priest Sasa, who guided us into the shrine, answers, 'It is recorded that on the fourth day of the seventh month of the third year of Tenin one hundred large trees came floating to the sea coast of Izumo, and were stranded there by the tide. With these timbers the temple was rebuilt in the third year of Eikyū, and that structure was called the Building of the Trees that came floating. Also in the same third year of Tennin, a great tree trunk, one hundred and fifty feet long, was stranded on the seashore near a shrine called Ube no Yashiro, at Miyanoshita-mura, which is in Inaba. Some people wanted to cut the tree, but they found a great serpent coiled around it, which looked so terrible that they became frightened, and prayed to the deity of Ube no Yashiro to protect them, and the deity revealed himself, and said: "Whensoever the great temple in Izumo is to be rebuilt, one of the gods of each province sends timber for the building of it, and this time it is my turn. Build quickly, therefore, with that great tree which is mine." And therewith the god disappeared. From these and from other records we learn that the deities have always superintended or aided the building of the great temple of Izumo Ōyashiro.'

'In what part of the Izumo Ōyashiro,' I ask, 'do the august deities assemble during the *kamiarizuki*?'

'On the east and west sides of the inner court,' replies the priest Sasa, 'there are two long buildings called *jukusha*. These contain nineteen shrines, no one of which is dedicated to any particular god, and we believe it is in the *jukusha* that the gods assemble.'

'And how many pilgrims from other provinces visit the great shrine yearly?' I inquire.

'About two hundred and fifty thousand,' the *guji* answers. 'But the number increases or diminishes according to the condition of the agricultural classes; the more prosperous the season, the larger the number of pilgrims. It rarely falls below two hundred thousand.'

Nomi no Sukune

Many other curious things the *guji* and his chief priest then related to me; telling me the sacred name of each of the courts, and of the fences and holy groves and the multitudinous shrines and their divinities; even the names of the great pillars of the temple, which are nine in number, the central pillar being called the August Heart Pillar of the Middle. All things within the temple grounds have sacred names, even the *torii* and the bridges.

The priest Sasa called my attention to the fact that the great shrine of Ōkuninushi no Kami faces west, though the great temple faces east, like all Shintō temples. In the other two shrines of the same apartment, both facing east, are the first divine governor of Izumo, his seventeenth descendant, and the father of Nomi no Sukune, wise prince and famous wrestler. For in the reign of the Emperor Suinin one Kehaya of Taima had boasted that no man alive was equal to himself in strength. Nomi no Sukune, by the emperor's command, wrestled with Kehaya, and threw him down so mightily that Kehaya's ghost departed from him. This was the beginning of wrestling in Japan, and wrestlers still pray to Sukune for power and skill.

There are so many other shrines that I could not enumerate the names of all their deities without wearying those readers unfamiliar with the traditions and legends of Shintō. But nearly all those divinities who appear in the legend of the Master of the Great Land are still believed to dwell here with him, and here their shrines are: the beautiful one, magically born from the jewel worn in the tresses of the Sun Goddess, and called by men the Torrent Mist Princess—and the daughter of the Lord of the World of Shadows, she who loved the Master of the Great Land, and followed him out of the place of ghosts to become his wife—and the deity called 'Wondrous Eight Spirits,' grandson of the 'Deity of Water Gates,' who first made a fire drill and platters of red clay for the august banquet of the god at Izumo Ōyashiro—and many of the heavenly kindred of these.

Awabi

The priest Sasa also tells me this:

When Naomasa, grandson of the great Tokugawa Iyeyasu, and first *daimyō* of that mighty Matsudaira family who ruled Izumo for two hundred and fifty years, came to this province, he paid a visit to the Izumo Ōyashiro, and demanded that the *miya* of the shrine within the shrine should be opened that he might look upon the sacred objects—upon the *shintai*, or body of the deity. This being an impious desire, both of the governors unitedly protested against it. But despite their remonstrances and their pleadings, he persisted angrily in his demand, so that the priests found themselves compelled to open the shrine. And the *miya* being opened, Naomasa saw within it a great *awabi* (abalone) of nine holes—so large that it concealed everything behind it. And when he drew still nearer to look, suddenly the *awabi* changed itself into a huge serpent more than fifty feet in length—it massed its black coils before the opening of the shrine, hissed like the sound of raging fire, and looked so terrible, that Naomasa and those with him fled away having been able to see naught else. And ever thereafter Naomasa feared and reverenced the god.

Kotoita

The *guji* then calls my attention to the quaint relics lying on the long low bench between us, which is covered with white silk: a metal mirror, found in preparing the foundation of the temple when rebuilt many hundred years ago; magatama jewels of onyx and jasper; a Chinese flute made of jade; a few superb swords, the gifts of shoguns and emperors; helmets of splendid antique workmanship; and a bundle of enormous arrows with double-pointed heads of brass, fork-shaped and keenly edged.

After I have looked at these relics and learned something of their history, the *guji* rises and says to me, 'Now we will show you the ancient fire drill of the Izumo Ōyashiro, with which the sacred fire is kindled.'

Descending the steps, we pass again before the *haiden*, and enter a spacious edifice on one side of the court, of nearly equal size with the hall of prayer. Here I am agreeably surprised to find a long handsome mahogany table at one end of the main apartment into which we are ushered, and mahogany chairs placed all about it for the reception of guests. I am motioned to one chair, my interpreter to another, and the *guji* and his priests take their seats also at the table. Then an attendant sets before me a handsome bronze stand about three feet long, on which rests an oblong something carefully wrapped in snow-white cloths. The *guji* removes the wrappings, and I behold the most primitive form of fire drill known to exist in the Orient. It is simply a very thick piece of solid white plank, about two and a half feet long, with a line of holes drilled along its upper edge, so that the upper part of each hole breaks through the sides of the plank. The sticks which produce the fire, when fixed in the holes and rapidly rubbed between the palms of the hands, are made of a lighter kind of white wood. They are about two feet long, and as thick as a common lead pencil.

While I am yet examining this curious simple utensil, the invention of which tradition ascribes to the gods, and modern science to the earliest childhood of the human race, a priest places on the table a light, large wooden box, about three feet long, eighteen inches wide, and four inches high at the sides, but higher in the middle, as the top is arched like the shell of a tortoise. This object is made of the same *hinoki* wood as the drill, and two long slender sticks are laid beside it. I at first suppose it to be another fire drill. But no human being could guess what it really is. It is called the *kotoita*, and is one of the most primitive of musical instruments. The little sticks are used to strike it. At a sign from the *guji* two priests place the box on the floor, seat themselves on either side of it, and taking up the little sticks begin to strike the lid with them, alternately and slowly, at the same time uttering a most singular and monotonous chant. One intones only the sounds, '*Ang! ang!*' and the other responds, '*Ong! ong!*' The *kotoita* gives out a sharp, dead, hollow sound as the sticks fall on it in time to each utterance of '*Ang! ang!*' '*Ong! ong!*'

U no Himatsuri

These things I learn:

Each year the temple receives a new fire drill; never at the Izumo Ōyashiro, but in Kumano, where the traditional regulations as to the manner of making it have been preserved from the time of the gods. For the first governor of Izumo, on becoming pontiff, received the fire drill for the great temple from the hands of the deity who was the younger brother of the Sun Goddess, and is now enshrined at Kumano. From his time the fire drills for the Izumo Ōyashiro have been made only at Kumano.

Until very recent times the ceremony of delivering the new fire drill to the *guji* of the Izumo Ōyashiro always took place at the great temple of Oba, on the occasion of the festival called U no Himatsuri. This ancient festival, which used to be held in the eleventh month, became obsolete after the Revolution everywhere except at Oba in Izumo, where Izanami no Kami, the mother of gods and men, is enshrined.

Once a year, on this festival, the governor always went to Oba, taking with him a gift of double rice cakes. At Oba he was met by a personage called the *kamedayū*, who brought the fire drill from Kumano and delivered it to the priests at Oba. According to tradition, the *kamedayū* had to act a somewhat ludicrous role so that no Shintō priest ever cared to perform the part, and a man was hired for it. The duty of the *kamedayū* was to find fault with the gift presented to the temple by the governor, and in this district of Japan there is still a proverbial saying about one who is prone to find fault without reason, 'He is like the Kamedayu.'

The *kamedayū* would inspect the rice cakes and begin to criticise them. 'They are much smaller this year,' he would observe, 'than they were last year.' The priests would reply, 'Oh, you are honourably mistaken, they are in truth much larger.' 'The colour is not so white this year as it was last year, and the rice flour is not finely ground.' For all these imaginary faults of the *mochi* the priests would offer elaborate explanations or apologies.

At the conclusion of the ceremony, the *sakaki* branches used in it were eagerly bid for, and sold at high prices, being believed to possess talismanic virtues.

Storms

It nearly always happened that there was a great storm either on the day the governor went to Oba, or on the day he returned therefrom. The journey had to be made during what is in Izumo the most stormy season (December by the new calendar). But in popular belief these storms were in some tremendous way connected with the divine personality of the governor whose attributes would thus appear to present some curious analogy with those of the dragon god. Be that as it may, the great periodical storms of the season are still in this province called *kokuzō-are*, 'governor's tempest.' It is still the custom in Izumo to say merrily to the guest who arrives or departs in a time of tempest, 'Why, you are like the governor!'

Dance of the Miko

The *guji* waves his hand, and from the farther end of the huge apartment there comes a sudden burst of strange music—a sound of drums and bamboo flutes.

Turning to look, I see the musicians, three men, seated on the matting, and a young girl with them. At another sign from the *guji* the girl rises. She is barefooted and robed in snowy white, a virgin priestess. But below the hem of the white robe I see the gleam of *hakama* of crimson silk. She advances to a little table in the middle of the apartment, on which a queer instrument is lying, shaped somewhat like a branch with twigs bent downward, from each of which hangs a little bell.

Taking this curious object in both hands, she begins a sacred dance, unlike anything I ever saw before. Her every movement is a poem, because she is very graceful, and yet her performance could scarcely be called a dance, as we understand the word. It is rather a light swift walk within a circle, during which she shakes the instrument at regular intervals, making all the little bells ring. Her face remains impassive as a beautiful mask, placid and sweet as the face of a dreaming Kannon. Her white feet are pure of line as the feet of a marble nymph. Altogether, with her snowy raiment and white flesh and passionless face, she seems rather a beautiful living statue than a Japanese maiden. And all the while the weird flutes sob and shrill, and the muttering of the drums is like an incantation.

What I have seen is called the dance of the *miko*, the divineress.

Ofuda

We visit the other edifices belonging to the temple: the storehouse, the library, and the hall of assembly, a massive structure two stories high, where may be seen the portraits of the *Thirty-Six Great Poets*, painted by Tosano Mitsuoki more than a thousand years ago, and still in an excellent state of preservation. Here we are also shown a curious magazine, published monthly by the temple—a record of Shintō news, and a medium for the discussion of questions relating to the archaic texts.

After we have seen all the curiosities of the temple, the *guji* invites us to his private residence near the temple to show us other treasures—letters of Minamoto Yoritomo, of Toyotomi Hideyoshi, of Tokugawa Iyeyasu; documents in the handwriting of the ancient emperors and the great shoguns, hundreds of which precious manuscripts he keeps in a cedar chest. In case of fire the immediate removal of this chest to a place of safety would be the first duty of the servants of the household.

Within his own house the *guji*, attired in ordinary Japanese full dress only, appears no less dignified as a private gentleman than he first seemed as pontiff in his voluminous snowy robe. But no host could be more kindly or more courteous or more generous. I am also much impressed by the fine appearance of his suite of young priests, now dressed, like himself, in the national costume. I am impressed by the handsome, aquiline, aristocratic faces, totally different from those of ordinary Japanese—faces suggesting the soldier rather than the priest. One young man has a superb pair of thick black moustaches, which is something rarely to be seen in Japan.

At parting our kind host presents me with the *ofuda*, or sacred charms given to pilgrimsh—two pretty images of the chief deities of the Izumo Ōyashiro—and a number of documents relating to the history of the temple and of its treasures.

Trial of Strength

Having taken our leave of the kind *guji* and his suite, we are guided to Inasa no Hama, a little sea bay at the rear of the town, by the priest Sasa, and another *kannushi*. This priest Sasa is a skilled poet and a man of deep learning in Shintō history and the archaic texts of the sacred books. He relates to us many curious legends as we stroll along the shore.

This shore, now a popular bathing resort—bordered with airy little inns and pretty teahouses—is called Inasa because of a Shintō tradition that here the god Ōkuninushi no Kami, the Master of the Great Land, was first asked to resign his dominion over the land of Izumo in favour of Masaka Akatsukachi Hayabi Ame no Oshio Mimi no Mikoto, the word Inasa signifying 'Will you consent or not?'

The legend is recorded in the thirty-second section of the first volume of the *Kojiki*. I cite a part thereof.

> The two deities (Toribune no Kami and Takemikadzuchi no O no Kami), descending to the little shore of Inasa in the land of Izumo, drew their swords ten handbreadths long, and stuck them upside down on the crest of a wave, and seated themselves cross-legged on the points of the swords, and asked the Deity Master of the Great Land, saying, 'The Heaven-Shining Great August Deity and

the High-Integrating Deity have charged us and sent us to ask, saying, 'We have deigned to charge our august child with thy dominion, as the land which he should govern. So how is thy heart?'

He replied, saying: 'I am unable to say. My son Yahe Kotoshironushi no Kami will be the one to tell you.'

So they asked the deity again, saying: 'Thy son Kotoshironushi no Kami has now spoken thus. Hast thou other sons who should speak?'

He spoke again, saying: "There is my other son, Takeminagata no Kami.'

While he was thus speaking, Takeminagata no Kami came up from the sea, bearing on the tips of his fingers a rock which it would take a thousand men to lift, and said, 'I should like to have a trial of strength.'

Close to the beach stands a little *miya* called Inasa no Kami no Yashiro, or, the Temple of the God of Inasa. Enshrined inside is Takemikazuchi no Kami, who conquered in the trial of strength. Near the shore the great rock which Takeminagata no Kami lifted on the tips of his fingers, may be seen rising from the water. And it is called Chihiki no Iwa.

We invite the priests to dine with us at one of the little inns facing the breezy sea, and there we talk about many things, but particularly about the Izumo Ōyashiro and the governor.

Kokuzō

Only a generation ago the religious power of the governor (*kokuzō*) extended over the whole of the province of the gods. He was in fact as well as in name the spiritual governor of Izumo. Now, his jurisdiction does not extend beyond the limits of Izumo, and his correct title is no longer *kokuzō* but *guji*. Yet to the simple-hearted people of remoter districts he is still a divine or semi-divine being, and is mentioned by his ancient title, the inheritance of his race from the epoch of the gods. How profound a reverence was paid to him in former ages can scarcely be imagined by any who have not long lived among the country folk of Izumo. Outside of Japan perhaps no human being, except the Dalai Lama of Tibet, was so humbly venerated and so religiously beloved. Within Japan itself only the Son of Heaven, the 'Tenshi-

sama,' standing as mediator 'between his people and the sun,' received like homage, but the worshipful reverence paid to the Mikado was paid to a dream rather than to a person, to a name rather than to a reality, for the Tenshi *sama* was ever invisible as a deity 'divinely retired,' and in popular belief no man could look upon his face and live.

Invisibility and mystery vastly enhanced the divine legend of the Mikado. But the governor, within his own province, though visible to the multitude and often journeying among the people, received almost equal devotion, so that his material power, though rarely, if ever, exercised, was scarcely less than that of the *daimyō* of Izumo himself. It was indeed large enough to render him a person with whom the shogunate would have deemed it wise policy to remain on good terms. An ancestor of the present *guji* even defied the great *taikō* Toyotomi Hideyoshi, refusing to obey his command to furnish troops with the haughty answer that he would receive no order from a man of common birth. This defiance cost the family the loss of a large part of its estates by confiscation, but the real power of the governor remained unchanged until the period of the new civilisation.

Out of many hundreds of stories of a similar nature, two little traditions may be cited as illustrations of the reverence in which the governor was formerly held.

It is related that there was a man who, believing himself to have become rich by favour of the *kokuzō* of the Izumo Ōyashiro, desired to express his gratitude by a gift of robes to the *kokuzō*.

The *kokuzō* courteously declined the proffer, but the pious worshipper persisted in his purpose, and ordered a tailor to make the robes. The tailor, having made them, demanded a price that almost took his patron's breath away. Being asked to give his reason for demanding such a price, he made answer: Having made robes for the *kokuzō*, I cannot hereafter make garments for any other person. Therefore I must have money enough to support me for the rest of my life.'

The second story dates back to about one hundred and seventy years ago.

Among the samurai of the Matsue clan in the time of Nobukori, fifth *daimyō* of the Matsudaira family, there was one Sugihara Kitoji, who was stationed in some military capacity at Izumo. He was a great favourite with the *kokuzō*, and used often to play at chess with him. During a game, one evening, this officer suddenly became as one paralysed, unable to move or speak. For a moment all was anxiety and confusion, but the *kokuzō* said, 'I know the cause. My friend was smoking, and although smoking disagrees with me, I did not wish to spoil his pleasure by telling him so. But the *kami*, seeing that I felt ill, became angry with him. Now I shall make him well.' Whereupon the *kokuzō* uttered some magical word, and the officer was immediately as well as before.

Shintō

Once more we are journeying through the silence of this holy land of mists and of legends, wending our way between green leagues of ripening rice white-sprinkled with arrows of prayer between the far processions of blue and verdant peaks whose names are the names of gods. We have left Izumo far behind. But as in a dream I still see the mighty avenue, the long succession of *torii* with their colossal *shimenawa*, the majestic face of the *guji*, the kindly smile of the priest Sasa, and the girl priestess in her snowy robes dancing her beautiful ghostly dance. It seems to me that I can still hear the sound of the clapping of hands, like the crashing of a torrent. I cannot suppress some slight exultation at the thought that I have been allowed to see what no other foreigner has been privileged to see—the interior of Japan's most ancient shrine, and those sacred utensils and quaint rites of primitive worship so well worthy the study of the anthropologist and the evolutionist.

But to have seen the Izumo Ōyashiro as I saw it is also to have seen something much more than a single wonderful temple. To see the Izumo Ōyashiro is to see the living centre of Shintō, and to feel the life pulse of the ancient faith, throbbing as mightily in this nineteenth century as ever in that unknown past whereof the *Kojiki* itself, though written in a tongue no longer spoken, is but a modern record. Buddhism, changing form or slowly decaying through the centuries, might seem doomed to pass away at last from this Japan to which it came only as an alien faith.

Shintō, unchanging and vitally unchanged, still remains all dominant in the land of its birth, and only seems to gain in power and dignity with time. In certain provinces of Japan Buddhism practically absorbed Shintō in other centuries, but in Izumo Shintō absorbed Buddhism. Now that Shintō is supported by the state there is a visible tendency to eliminate from its cult certain elements of Buddhist origin. Buddhism has a voluminous theology, a profound philosophy, a literature vast as the sea. Shintō has no philosophy, no code of ethics, no metaphysics. And yet, by its very immateriality, it can resist the invasion of Occidental religious thought as no other Orient faith can. Shintō extends a welcome to Western science, but remains the irresistible opponent of Western religion.

The foreign zealots who would strive against it are astounded to find the power that foils their uttermost efforts indefinable as magnetism and invulnerable as air. Indeed the best of our scholars have never been able to tell us what Shintō is. To some it appears to be merely ancestor worship, to others ancestor-worship combined with nature-worship. To others, again, it seems to be no religion at all. To the missionary of the more ignorant class it is the worst form of heathenism. Doubtless the difficulty of explaining Shintō has been due simply to the fact that the sinologists have sought for the source of it in books: in the *Kojiki* and the *Nihongi*, which are its histories; in the Norito, which are its prayers; in the commentaries of Motoori Norinaga and Hirata Atsutane, who were its greatest scholars.

But the reality of Shintō lives not in books, nor in rites, nor in commandments, but in the national heart, of which it is the highest emotional religious expression, immortal and ever young. Far underlying all the surface crop of quaint superstitions and artless myths and fantastic magic there thrills a mighty spiritual force, the whole soul of a race with all its impulses and powers and intuitions. He who would know what Shintō is must learn to know that mysterious soul in which the sense of beauty and the power of art and the fire of heroism and magnetism of loyalty and the emotion of faith have become inherent, immanent, unconscious, instinctive.

Trusting to know something of that Oriental soul in whose joyous love of nature and of life even the unlearned may discern a strange likeness to the soul of the old Greek race, I trust also that I may presume some day to speak of the great living power of that faith now called Shintō, but more anciently Kami no Michi, or 'The Way of the Gods.'

The Kukedo of Kaka

Kaka

It is forbidden to go to Kaka if there be wind enough 'to move three hairs.' Now an absolutely windless day is rare on this wild western coast. Over the Japanese Sea, from Korea, or China, or boreal Siberia, some west or northwest breeze is nearly always blowing. So that I have had to wait many long months for a good chance to visit Kaka.

Taking the shortest route, one goes first to Mitsuura from Matsue, either by *kuruma* or on foot. By *kuruma* this little journey occupies nearly two hours and a half, though the distance is scarcely seven miles, the road being one of the worst in all Izumo. You leave Matsue to enter at once into a broad plain, level as a lake, all occupied by rice fields and walled in by wooded hills. The path, barely wide enough for a single vehicle, traverses this green desolation, climbs the heights beyond it, and descends again into another and a larger level of rice fields, surrounded also by hills. The path over the second line of hills is much steeper. Then a third rice-plain must be crossed and a third chain of green altitudes, lofty enough to merit the name of mountains. Of course one must make the ascent on foot: it is no small labour for a *kurumaya* to pull even an empty *kuruma* up to the top. How he manages to do so without breaking the little vehicle is a mystery, for the path is stony and rough as the bed of a torrent. A tiresome climb I find it, but the landscape view from the summit is more than compensation.

Then descending, there remains a fourth and last wide level of rice fields to traverse. The absolute flatness of the great plains between the ranges, and the singular way in which these latter 'fence off' the country into sections, are matters for surprise even in a land of surprises like Japan. Beyond the fourth rice valley there is a fourth hill-chain, lower and richly wooded, on reaching the base of which the traveller must finally abandon his *kuruma*, and proceed over the hills on foot. Behind them lies the sea. But the very worst bit of the journey now begins. The path makes an easy winding ascent between bamboo growths and young pine and other vegetation for a shaded quarter of a mile, passing before various little shrines and pretty homesteads surrounded by high-hedged gardens. Then it suddenly breaks into steps, or rather ruins of steps—partly hewn in the rock, partly built, everywhere breached and worn which descend, all edgeless, in a manner amazingly precipitous, to the village of Mitsuura. With straw sandals, which never slip, the country folk can nimbly hurry up or down such a path, but with foreign footgear one slips at nearly every step. When you reach the bottom at last, the wonder of how you managed to get there, even with the assistance of your faithful *kurumaya*, keeps you for a moment quite unconscious of the fact that you are already in Mitsuura.

Mitsuura

Mitsuura stands with its back to the mountains, at the end of a small deep bay hemmed in by very high cliffs. There is only one narrow strip of beach at the foot of the heights, and the village owes its existence to that fact, for beaches are rare on this part of the coast. Crowded between the cliffs and the sea, the houses have a painfully compressed aspect. Somehow the greater number give one the impression of things created out of wrecks of junks. The little streets, or rather alleys, are full of boats and skeletons of boats and boat timbers. Everywhere, suspended from bamboo poles much taller than the houses, immense bright brown fishing nets are drying in the sun. The whole curve of the beach is also lined with boats, lying side by side so that I wonder how it will be possible to get to the water's edge without climbing over them. There is no hotel, but I find hospitality in a fisherman's dwelling, while my *kurumaya* goes somewhere to hire a boat for Kaka.

In less than ten minutes there is a crowd of several hundred people about the house, half-clad adults and perfectly naked boys. They blockade the building; they obscure the light by filling up the doorways and climbing into the windows to look at the foreigner. The aged proprietor of the cottage protests in vain, says harsh things; the crowd only thickens. Then all the sliding screens are closed. But in the paper panes there are holes. At all the lower holes the curious take regular turns at peeping. At a higher hole I do some peeping myself. The crowd is not prepossessing: it is squalid, dull-featured, remarkably ugly. But it is gentle and silent, and there are one or two pretty faces in it which seem extraordinary by reason of the general homeliness of the rest.

At last my *kurumaya* has succeeded in making arrangements for a boat, and I effect a sortie to the beach, followed by the *kurumaya* and by all my besiegers. Boats have been moved to make a passage for us, and we embark without trouble of any sort. Our crew consists of two scullers—an old man at the stem, wearing only a *rokushaku* about his loins, and an old woman at the bow, fully robed and wearing an immense straw hat shaped like a mushroom. Both of course stand to their work and it would be hard to say which is the stronger or more skilful sculler. We passengers squat Oriental fashion on a mat in the centre of the boat, where a *hibachi*, well stocked with glowing charcoal, invites us to smoke.

The Goblin Coast

The day is clear blue to the end of the world, with a faint wind from the east, barely enough to wrinkle the sea, certainly more than enough to 'move three hairs.' Nevertheless the boatwoman and the boatman do not seem anxious, and I begin to wonder whether the famous prohibition is not a myth. So delightful the transparent water looks, that before we have left the bay I have to yield to its temptation by plunging in and swimming after the boat. When I climb back on board we are rounding the promontory on the right, and the little vessel begins to rock. Even under this thin wind the sea is moving in long swells. And as we pass into the open, following the westward trend of the land, we find ourselves gliding over an ink-black depth, in front of one of the very grimmest coasts I ever saw.

A tremendous line of dark iron-coloured cliffs, towering sheer from the sea without a beach, and with never a speck of green below their summits. Here and there along this terrible front, monstrous beetlings, breaches, fissures, earthquake rendings, and topplings-down. Enormous fractures show lines of strata pitched up skyward, or plunging down into the ocean with the long fall of cubic miles of cliff. Before fantastic gaps, prodigious masses of rock, of all nightmarish shapes, rise from profundities unfathomed. And though the wind today seems trying to hold its breath, white breakers are reaching far up the cliffs, and dashing their foam into the faces of the splintered crags. We are too far to hear the thunder of them, but their ominous sheet-lightning fully explains to me the story of the three hairs. Along this goblin coast on a wild day there would be no possible chance for the strongest swimmer, or the stoutest boat. There is no place for the foot, no hold for the hand, nothing but the sea raving against a precipice of iron. Even today, under the feeblest breath imaginable, great swells deluge us with spray as they splash past. And for two long hours this jagged frowning coast towers by. As we toil on, rocks rise around us like black teeth. And always, far away, the foam bursts gleam at the feet of the implacable cliffs. But there are no sounds save the lapping and plashing of passing swells, and the monotonous creaking of the sculls on their pegs of wood.

At last, at last, a bay—a beautiful large bay, with a demilune of soft green hills about it, overtopped by far blue mountains—and in the very farthest point of the bay a miniature village, in front of which many junks are riding at anchor: Kaka.

But we do not go to Kaka yet; the caves, or Kukedo, are not there. We cross the broad opening of the bay, journey along another half-mile of ghastly sea-precipice, and finally make for a lofty promontory of naked Plutonic rock. We pass by its menacing foot, slip along its side, and lo! at an angle opens the arched mouth of a wonderful cavern, broad, lofty, and full of light, with no floor but the sea. Beneath us, as we slip into it, I can see rocks fully twenty feet down. The water is clear as air. This is the Shin-Kukedo, called the New Cavern, though assuredly older than human record by a hundred thousand years.

Shin-Kukedo

A more beautiful sea cave could scarcely be imagined. The sea, tunnelling the tall promontory through and through, has also, like a great architect, ribbed and groined and polished its mighty work. The arch of the entrance is certainly twenty feet above the deep water, and fifteen wide. Trillions of wave tongues have licked the vault and walls into wondrous smoothness.

As we proceed, the rock-roof steadily heightens and the way widens. Then we unexpectedly glide under a heavy shower of fresh water, dripping from overhead. This spring is called the *o-chozubachi* or *mitarashi* of Shin-Kukedo-san. From the high vault at this point it is believed that a great stone will detach itself and fall on any evil-hearted person who should attempt to enter the cave. I safely pass through the ordeal!

Suddenly as we advance the boatwoman takes a stone from the bottom of the boat, and with it begins to rap heavily on the bow. The hollow echoing is reiterated with thundering repercussions through all the cave. And in another instant we pass into a great burst of light, coming from the mouth of a magnificent and lofty archway on the left, opening into the cavern at right angles. This explains the singular illumination of the long vault, which at first seemed to come from beneath. For while the opening was still invisible all the water appeared to be suffused with light. Through this grand arch, between outlying rocks, a strip of beautiful green undulating coast appears, over miles of azure water. We glide on toward the third entrance to the Kukedo, opposite to that by which we came in, and enter the dwelling-place of the *kami* and the Hotoke, for this grotto is sacred both to Shintō and to Buddhist faith. Here the Kukedo reaches its greatest altitude and breadth. Its vault is fully forty feet above the water, and its walls thirty feet apart. Far up on the right, near the roof, is a projecting white rock, and above the rock an orifice wherefrom a slow stream drips, seeming white as the rock itself.

This is the legendary fountain of Jizō, the fountain of milk at which the souls of dead children drink. Sometimes it flows more swiftly, sometimes more slowly, but it never ceases by night or day. And mothers suffering from want of milk come hither to pray that milk may be given to them, and their prayer is heard. Mothers having more milk than their infants need come hither also, and pray to Jizō that so much as they can give may be taken for the dead children. And their prayer is heard, and their milk diminishes.

At least thus the peasants of Izumo say.

And the echoing of the swells leaping against the rocks without, the rushing and rippling of the tide against the walls, the heavy rain of percolating water, sounds of lapping and gurgling and plashing, and sounds of mysterious origin coming from no visible where, make it difficult for us to hear each other speak. The cavern seems full of voices, as if a host of invisible beings were holding tumultuous converse.

Below us all the deeply lying rocks are naked to view as if seen through glass. It seems to me that nothing could be more delightful than to swim through this cave and let one's self drift with the sea-currents through all its cool shadows. But as I am on the point of jumping in, all the other occupants of the boat utter wild cries of protest. It is certain death! Men who jumped in here only six months ago were never heard of again! This is sacred water, Kami no Umi! And as if to conjure away my temptation, the boatwoman again seizes her little stone and raps fearfully on the bow. On finding, however, that I am not sufficiently deterred by these stories of sudden death and disappearance, she suddenly screams into my ear the magical word: '*same!*'

Sharks! I have no longer any desire whatever to swim through the many-sounding halls of Shin-Kukedo-*san*. I have lived in the tropics!

And we start forthwith for Kyū-Kukedo-san, the Ancient Cavern.

Goblins

For the ghastly fancies about the Kami no Umi, the word 'same' afforded a satisfactory explanation. But why that long, loud, weird rapping on the bow with a stone evidently kept on board for no other purpose? There was an exaggerated earnestness about the action which gave me an uncanny sensation—something like that which moves a man while walking at night on a lonesome road, full of queer shadows, to sing at the top of his voice. The boatwoman at first declares that the rapping was made only for the sake of the singular echo. But after some cautious further questioning, I discover a much more sinister reason for the performance. Moreover, I learn that all the seamen and seawomen of this coast do the same thing when passing through perilous places, or places believed to be haunted by the *ma*. What are the *ma*?

Goblins!

Kyū-Kukedo

From the caves of the *kami* we retrace our course for about a quarter of a mile. Then we make directly for an immense perpendicular wrinkle in the long line of black cliffs. Immediately before it a huge dark rock towers from the sea, whipped by the foam of breaking swells. Rounding it, we glide behind it into still water and shadow, the shadow of a monstrous cleft in the precipice of the coast.

Suddenly, at an unsuspected angle, the mouth of another cavern yawns before us. In another moment our boat touches its threshold of stone with a little shock that sends a long sonorous echo, like the sound of a temple drum, booming through all the abysmal place. A single glance tells me whither we have come. Far within the dusk I see the face of a Jizō, smiling in pale stone, and before him, and all about him, a weird congregation of grey shapes without shape—a host of fantasticalities that strangely suggest the wreck of a cemetery. From the sea the ribbed floor of the cavern slopes high through deepening shadows back to the black mouth of a farther grotto. The whole slope is covered with hundreds and thousands of forms like shattered *haka*. But as the eyes grow accustomed to the gloaming it becomes manifest that these were never *haka*; they are only little towers of stone and pebbles deftly piled up by long and patient labour.

'*Shinda kodomo no shigoto*,' my *kurumaya* murmurs with a compassionate smile. 'All this is the work of the dead children.'

And we disembark. By counsel, I take off my shoes and put on a pair of *zōri*, or straw sandals provided for me, as the rock is extremely slippery. The others land barefoot. But how to proceed soon becomes a puzzle: the countless stone-piles stand so close together that no space for the foot seems to be left between them.

'*Mada michi ga arimasu!*' the boatwoman announces, leading the way. There is a path.

Following after her, we squeeze ourselves between the wall of the cavern on the right and some large rocks, and discover a very, very narrow passage left open between the stone-towers. But we are warned to be careful for the sake of the little ghosts: if any of their work be overturned, they will cry. So we move very cautiously and slowly across the cave to a space bare of stone-heaps, where the rocky floor is covered with a thin layer of sand, detritus of a crumbling ledge above it. And in that sand I see light prints of little feet, children's feet, tiny naked feet, only three or four inches long—the footprints of the infant ghosts.

Had we come earlier, the boatwoman says, we should have seen many more. For 'tis at night, when the soil of the cavern is moist with dews and drippings from the roof, that They leave their footprints on it, but when the heat of the day comes, and the sand and the rocks dry up, the prints of the little feet vanish away.

There are only three footprints visible, but these are singularly distinct. One points toward the wall of the cavern, the others toward the sea. Here and there, on ledges or projections of the rock, all about the cavern, tiny straw sandals—children's *zōri*—are lying: offerings of pilgrims to the little ones, that their feet may not be wounded by the stones. But all the ghostly footprints are prints of naked feet.

Then we advance, picking our way very, very carefully between the stone-towers, toward the mouth of the inner grotto, and reach the statue of Jizō before it. A seated Jizō carven in granite, holding in one hand the mystic jewel by virtue of which all wishes may be fulfilled, in the other his *shakujō*, or pilgrim's staff. Before him (strange condescension of Shintō faith!) a little *torii* has been erected, and a pair of *gohei*! Evidently this gentle divinity has no enemies; at the feet of the lover of children's ghosts, both creeds unite in tender homage.

I said feet. But this subterranean Jizō has only one foot. The carven lotus on which he reposes has been fractured and broken: two great petals are missing. The right foot, which must have rested on one of them, has been knocked off at the ankle. This, I learn upon inquiry, has been done by the waves. In times of great storm the billows rush into the cavern like raging *oni*, and sweep all the little stone towers into shingle as they come, and dash the statues against the rocks. But always during the first still night after the tempest the work is reconstructed as before!

Hotoke ga shinpai shite, naki-naki tsumi naoshimasu.' They despair, the *hotoke*; weeping, they make up for their sins.'

All about the black mouth of the inner grotto the bone-coloured rock bears some resemblance to a vast pair of yawning jaws. Downward from this sinister portal the cavern-floor slopes into a deeper and darker aperture. And within it, as one's eyes become accustomed to the gloom, a still larger vision of stone towers is disclosed. Beyond them, in a nook of the grotto, three other statues of Jizō smile, each one with a *torii* before it. Here I have the misfortune to upset first one stone-pile and then another, while trying to proceed. My *kurumaya*, almost simultaneously, ruins a third. To atone therefore, we must build six new towers, or double the number of those which we have cast down. And while we are thus busied, the boatwoman tells of two fishermen who remained in the cavern through all one night, and heard the humming of the viewless gathering, and sounds of speech, like the speech of children murmuring in multitude.

Only at night do the shadowy children come to build their little stone-heaps at the feet of Jizō. It is said that every night the stones are changed. When I ask why they do not work by day, when there is none to see them, I am answered, 'o-Hi-*san* (August Fire Lady) might see them; the dead exceedingly fear the Lady Sun.'

To the question, 'Why do they come from the sea?' I can get no satisfactory answer. But doubtless in the quaint imagination of this people, as also in that of many another, there lingers still the primitive idea of some communication, mysterious and awful, between the world of waters and the world of the dead. It is always over the sea, after the Feast of Souls, that the spirits pass murmuring back to their dim realm, in those elfish little ships of straw that are launched for them on the sixteenth day of the seventh moon. Even when these are launched on rivers, or when floating lanterns are set adrift on lakes or canals to light the ghosts on their way, or when a mother bereaved drops into some running stream one hundred little prints of Jizō for the sake of her lost darling, the vague idea behind the pious act is that all waters flow to the sea and the sea itself to the 'Nether-distant Land.'

Some time, somewhere, this day will come back to me at night, with its visions and sounds: the dusky cavern, and its grey hosts of stone climbing back into darkness, and the faint prints of little naked feet, and the weirdly smiling images, and the broken syllables of the waters inward-borne, multiplied by husky echoings, blending into one vast ghostly whispering, like the humming of the Sai no Kawara.

And over the black-blue bay we glide to the rocky beach of Kaka.

Kaka

As at Mitsuura, the water's edge is occupied by a serried line of fishing-boats, each with its nose to the sea, Behind these are ranks of others. It is only just barely possible to squeeze one's way between them over the beach to the drowsy, pretty, quaint little streets behind them. Everybody seems to be asleep when we first land: the only living creature visible is a cat, sitting on the stern of a boat. But wven that cat, according to Japanese beliefs, might not be a real cat, but an *o-bake* or a *nekomata*—in short, a goblin cat, for it has a long tail. It is hard work to discover the solitary hotel: there are no signs, and every house seems a private house, either a fisherman's or a farmer's. But the little place is worth wandering about in. A kind of yellow stucco is here employed to cover the exterior of walls, and this light warm tint under the bright blue day gives to the miniature streets a more than cheerful aspect.

When we do finally discover the hotel, we have to wait quite a good while before going in, for nothing is ready; everybody is asleep or away, though all the screens and sliding doors are open. Evidently there are no thieves in Kaka. The hotel is on a little hillock, and is approached from the main street (the rest are only miniature alleys) by two little flights of stone steps. Immediately across the way I see a Zen temple and a Shintō temple, almost side by side.

At last a pretty young woman, naked to the waist, with a bosom like a Naiad, comes running down the street to the hotel at a surprising speed, bowing low with a smile as she hurries by us into the house. This little person is the waiting maid of the inn, o-Kayo-*san*—name signifying 'Years of Bliss.' Presently she reappears at the threshold, fully robed in a nice kimono, and gracefully invites us to enter, which we are only too glad to do. The room is neat and spacious. Shintō *kakemono* from Izumo are suspended in the *tokonoma* and on the walls, and in one corner I see a very handsome Zen *butsudan*, or household shrine. (The form of the shrine, as well as the objects of worship therein, vary according to the sect of the worshippers.) Suddenly I become aware that it is growing strangely dark. Looking about me, I perceive that all the doors and windows and other apertures of the inn are densely blocked up by a silent, smiling crowd which has gathered to look at me. I could not have believed there were so many people in Kaka.

In a Japanese house, during the hot season, everything is thrown open to the breeze. All the *shōji* or sliding paper screens, which serve for windows, and all the opaque paper screens (*fusuma*) used in other seasons to separate apartments, are removed. There is nothing left between floor and roof save the frame or skeleton of the building; the dwelling is literally unwalled, and may be seen through in any direction. The landlord, finding the crowd embarrassing, closes up the building in front. The silent, smiling crowd goes to the rear. The rear is also closed. Then the crowd masses to right and left of the house, and both sides have to be closed, which makes it insufferably hot. And the crowd make gentle protest.

Wherefore our host, being displeased, rebukes the multitude with argument and reason, yet without lifting his voice. (Never do these people lift up their voices in anger.) And what he says I strive to translate, with emphasis, as follows:

'You-as-for! outrageousness doing—what marvellous is? 'Theatre is not! 'Juggler is not! 'Wrestler is not! 'What amusing is? 'Honourable guest this is! 'Now august-to-eat-time is; to-look-at-evil-matter is. Honourable returning-time-in-to-look-at-as-for-is-good.'

But outside, soft laughing voices continue to plead, pleading, shrewdly enough, only with the feminine portion of the family: the landlord's heart is less easily touched. And these, too, have their arguments:

'*Oba-san*! '*O-Kayo-san*! '*Shōji*-to-open-condescend!—want to see! 'Though-we-look-at, Thing-that-by-looking-at-is-worn-out-it-is-not! 'So that not-to-hinder looking-at is good. 'Hasten therefore to open!'

As for myself, I would gladly protest against this sealing-up, for there is nothing offensive nor even embarrassing in the gaze of these innocent, gentle people. But as the landlord seems to be personally annoyed, I do not like to interfere. The crowd, however, does not go away: it continues to increase, waiting for my exit. And there is one high window in the rear, of which the paper panes contain some holes. And I see shadows of little people climbing up to get to the holes. Presently there is an eye at every hole.

When I approach the window, the peepers drop noiselessly to the ground, with little timid bursts of laughter, and run away. But they soon come back again. A more charming crowd could hardly be imagined: nearly all boys and girls, half-naked because of the heat, but fresh and clean as flower-buds. Many of the faces are surprisingly pretty; there are but very few which are not extremely pleasing. But where are the men, and the old women? Truly, this population seems not of Kaka, but rather of the Sai no Kawara. The boys look like little Jizō.

During dinner, I amuse myself by poking pears and little pieces of radish through the holes in the *shōji*. At first there is much hesitation and silvery laughter, but in a little while the silhouette of a tiny hand reaches up cautiously, and a pear vanishes away. Then a second pear is taken, without snatching, as softly as if a ghost had appropriated it. Thereafter hesitation ceases, despite the effort of one elderly woman to create a panic by crying out the word *mahōtsukai*, or wizard. By the time the dinner is over and the *shōji* removed, we have all become good friends. Then the crowd resumes its silent observation from the four cardinal points.

I never saw a more striking difference in the appearance of two village populations than that between the youth of Mitsuura and of Kaka. Yet the villages are but two hours' sailing distance apart. In remoter Japan, as in certain islands of the West Indies, particular physical types are developed apparently among communities but slightly isolated; on one side of a mountain a population may be remarkably attractive, while on the other you may find a hamlet whose inhabitants are decidedly unprepossessing. But nowhere in this country have I seen a prettier *jeunesse* than that of Kaka.

'Returning-time-in-to-look-at-as-for-is-good.' As we descend to the bay, the whole of Kaka, including even the long invisible ancients of the village, accompanies us, making no sound except the pattering of *geta*. Thus we are escorted to our boat. Into all the other craft drawn up on the beach the younger folk clamber lightly, and seat themselves on the prows and the gunwales to gaze at the marvellous Thing-that-by-looking-at-worn-out-is-not. And all smile, but say nothing, even to each other: somehow the experience gives me the sensation of being asleep; it is so soft, so gentle, and so queer withal, just like things seen in dreams. And as we glide away over the blue lucent water I look back to see the people all waiting and gazing still from the great semicircle of boats; all the slender brown child-limbs dangling from the prows; all the velvety-black heads motionless in the sun; all the boy faces smiling Jizō smiles; all the black soft eyes still watching, tirelessly watching, the Thing-that-by-looking-at-worn-out-is-not. And as the scene, too swiftly receding, diminishes to the width of a *kakemono*, I vainly wish that I could buy this last vision of it, to place it in my *tokonoma*, and delight my soul betimes with gazing thereon. Yet another moment, and we round a rocky point, and Kaka vanishes from my sight for ever. So all things pass away.

Assuredly those impressions which longest haunt recollection are the most transitory: we remember many more instants than minutes, more minutes than hours, and who remembers an entire day? The sum of the remembered happiness of a lifetime is the creation of seconds. 'What is more fugitive than a smile? yet when does the memory of a vanished smile expire? or the soft regret which that memory may evoke?

Regret for a single individual smile is something common to normal human nature, but regret for the smile of a population, for a smile considered as an abstract quality, is certainly a rare sensation, and one to be obtained, I fancy, only in this Orient land whose people smile for ever like their own gods of stone. And this precious experience is already mine; I am regretting the smile of Kaka.

Simultaneously there comes the recollection of a strangely grim Buddhist legend. Once the Buddha smiled; and by the wondrous radiance of that smile were countless worlds illuminated. But there came a Voice, saying, 'It is not real! It cannot last!' And the light passed.

Mihonoseki

Seki wa yoi toko,
Asahi wo ukete;
O-yama arashi ga
Soyo-soyoto!

Seki is a goodly place,
facing the morning sun.
There, from the holy mountains,
the winds blow softly,
softly—*soyosoyoto*.

The Pipe

The god of Mihonoseki hates eggs, hen's eggs. Likewise he hates hens and chickens, and abhors the cock above all living creatures. And in Mihonoseki there are no cocks or hens or chickens or eggs. You could not buy a hen's egg in that place even for twenty times its weight in gold.

And no boat or junk or steamer could be hired to convey to Mihonoseki so much as the feather of a chicken, much less an egg. Indeed, it is even held that if you have eaten eggs in the morning you must not dare to visit Mihonoseki until the following day. For the great deity of Mihonoseki is the patron of mariners and the ruler of storms. Woe to the vessel that bears to his shrine even the odour of an egg.

Once the tiny steamer that runs daily from Matsue to Mihonoseki encountered some unexpectedly terrible weather on her outward journey, just after reaching the open sea. The crew insisted that something displeasing to Kotoshironushi no Kami must have been surreptitiously brought on board. All the passengers were questioned in vain. Suddenly the captain discerned on the stem of a little brass pipe which one of the men was smoking, smoking in the face of death, like a true Japanese, the figure of a crowing cock! Needless to say, that pipe was thrown overboard. Then the angry sea began to grow calm, and the little vessel safely steamed into the holy port, and cast anchor before the great *torii* of the shrine of the god!

Kotoshirononushi no Kami

Concerning the reason why the cock is thus detested by the Great Deity of Mihonoseki, and banished from his domain, divers legends are told. But the substance of all of them is about as follows: As we read in the *Kojiki*, Kotoshironushi no Kami, Son of the Great Deity of Kitsuki, was wont to go to Mihonoseki, 'to pursue birds and catch fish.' And for other reasons also he used to absent himself from home at night, but had always to return before dawn. Now, in those days the cock was his trusted servant, charged with the duty of crowing lustily when it was time for the god to return. But one morning the bird failed in its duty. And the god, hurrying back in his boat, lost his oars, and had to paddle with his hands, and his hands were bitten by the wicked fishes.

Now the people of Yasugi, a pretty little town on the lagoon of Nakaumi, through which we pass on our way to Mihonoseki, most devoutly worship the same Kotoshironushi no Kami. Nevertheless, there are multitudes of cocks and hens and chickens in Yasugi, and the eggs of Yasugi cannot be excelled for size and quality. And the people of Yasugi aver that one may better serve the deity by eating eggs than by doing as the people of Mihonoseki do, for whenever one eats a chicken or devours an egg, one destroys an enemy of Kotoshironushi no Kami.

Go-Mihojin

From Matsue to Mihonoseki by steamer is a charming journey in fair weather. After emerging from the beautiful lagoon of Nakaumi into the open sea, the little packet follows the long coast of Izumo to the left. Very lofty this coast is, all cliffs and hills rising from the sea, mostly green to their summits, and many cultivated in terraces, so as to look like green pyramids of steps. The bases of the cliffs are very rocky, and the curious wrinklings and corrugations of the coast suggest the work of ancient volcanic forces. Far away to the right, over blue still leagues of sea, appears the long low shore of Hoki, faint as a mirage, with its far beach like an endless white streak edging the blue level, and beyond it vapoury lines of woods and cloudy hills, and over everything, looming into the high sky, the magnificent ghostly shape of Daisen, snow-streaked at its summit.

So for perhaps an hour we steam on, between Hoki and Izumo. The rugged and broken green coast on our left occasionally revealing some miniature hamlet sheltered in a wrinkle between two hills. The phantom coast on the right always unchanged. Then suddenly the little packet whistles, heads for a grim promontory to port, glides by its rocky foot, and enters one of the prettiest little bays imaginable, previously concealed from view. A shell-shaped gap in the coast—a semicircular basin of clear deep water, framed in by high corrugated green hills, all wood-clad. Around the edge of the bay the quaintest of little Japanese towns, Mihonoseki.

There is no beach, only a semicircle of stone wharves, and above these the houses, and above these the beautiful green of the sacred hills, with a temple roof or two showing an angle through the foliage. From the rear of each house steps descend to deep water, and boats are moored at all the back-doors. We moor in front of the great temple, the Miho shrine. Its great paved avenue slopes to the water's edge, where boats are also moored at steps of stone. Looking up the broad approach, one sees a grand stone *torii*, and colossal stone lanterns, and two magnificent sculptured lions, *karashishi*, seated on lofty pedestals, and looking down upon the people from a height of fifteen feet or more. Beyond all this the walls and gate of the outer temple court appear, and beyond them, the roofs of the great *haiden*, and the pierced projecting cross-beams of the loftier Go-Mihojin, the holy shrine itself, relieved against the green of the wooded hills. Picturesque junks are lying in ranks at anchor. There are two deepsea vessels likewise, of modern build, ships from Osaka. There is a most romantic little breakwater built of hewn stone, with a stone lantern perched at the end of it, and there is a pretty humped bridge connecting it with a tiny island on which I see a shrine of Benten, the Goddess of Waters. I wonder if I shall be able to get any eggs!

Eggs

To the pretty waiting maiden of the inn Shimaya I put this scandalous question, with an innocent face but a remorseful heart:

'Ano ne! tamago wa arimasenka?'

With the smile of a Kannon she makes reply:-'He! Ahiru-no tamago-ga sukoshi gozarimasu.'

Delicious surprise!

There augustly exist eggs—of ducks!

But there exist no ducks. For ducks could not find life worth living in a city where there is only deep-sea water. And all the ducks' eggs come from Sakai.

Miho no Jinja

This pretty little hotel, whose upper chambers overlook the water, is situated at one end, or nearly at one end, of the crescent of Mihonoseki, and the Miho shrine (*jinja*) almost at the other, so that one must walk through the whole town to visit the temple, or else cross the harbour by boat. But the whole town is well worth seeing. It is so tightly pressed between the sea and the bases of the hills that there is only room for one real street. This is so narrow that a man could anywhere jump from the second story of a house on the water-side into the second story of the opposite house on the land-side. And it is as picturesque as it is narrow, with its awnings and polished balconies and fluttering figured draperies. From this main street several little ruelles slope to the water's edge, where they terminate in steps. In all these miniature alleys long boats are lying, with their prows projecting over the edge of the wharves, as if eager to plunge in. The temptation to take to the water I find to be irresistible: before visiting the Miho shrine I jump from the rear of our hotel into twelve feet of limpid sea, and cool myself by a swim across the harbour.

On the way to the Miho shrine, I notice, in multitudes of little shops, fascinating displays of baskets and utensils made of woven bamboo. Fine bamboo-ware is indeed the *meibutsu*, the special product of Mihonoseki, and almost every visitor buys some nice little specimen to carry home with him.

The Miho shrine is not in its architecture more remarkable than ordinary Shintō temples in Izumo, nor are its interior decorations worth describing in detail. Only the approach to it over the broad sloping space of level pavement, under the granite *torii*, and between the great lions and lamps of stone, is noble. Within the courts proper there is not much to be seen except a magnificent tank of solid bronze, weighing tons, which must have cost many thousands of yen. It is a votive offering. Of more humble ex-votos, there is a queer collection in the *shamusho* or business building on the right of the *haiden*: a series of quaintly designed and quaintly coloured pictures, representing ships in great storms, being guided or aided to port by the power of Kotoshironushi no Kami. These are gifts from ships.

The *ofuda* are not so curious as those of other famous Izumo temples, but they are most eagerly sought for. Those strips of white paper, bearing the deity's name, and a few words of promise, which are sold for a few *rin*, are tied to rods of bamboo, and planted in all the fields of the country roundabout. The most curious things sold are tiny packages of rice seeds. It is alleged that whatever you desire will grow from these rice seeds, if you plant them uttering a prayer. If you desire bamboos, cotton plants, peas, lotus plants, or watermelons, it matters not; only plant the seed and believe, and the desired crop will arise.

The Maid-Mother

Much more interesting to me than the *ofuda* of the Miho shrine are the *yōraku*, the pendent ex-votos in the Hōjin-ji, a temple of the Zen sect that stands on the summit of the beautiful hill above the great Shintō shrine. Before an altar on which are ranged the images of the Thirty-three Kannons, the thirty-three forms of that Goddess of Mercy who represents the ideal of all that is sweet and pure in the Japanese maiden, a strange, brightly coloured mass of curious things may be seen, suspended from the carven ceiling. There are hundreds of balls of worsted and balls of cotton thread of all colours; there are skeins of silk and patterns of silk weaving and of cotton weaving; there are broidered purses in the shape of sparrows and other living creatures; there are samples of bamboo plaiting and countless specimens of needlework. All these are the votive offerings of school children, little girls only, to the maid-mother of all grace and sweetness and pity. So soon as a baby girl learns something in the way of woman's work—sewing, or weaving, or knitting, or broidering, she brings her first successful effort to the temple as an offering to the gentle divinity, 'whose eyes are beautiful,' she 'who looketh down above the sound of prayer.' Even the infants of the Japanese kindergarten bring their first work here—pretty paper-cuttings, scissored out and plaited into divers patterns by their own tiny flower-soft hands.

Sailors

Very sleepy and quiet by day is Mihonoseki: only at long intervals one hears laughter of children, or the chant of oarsmen rowing the most extraordinary boats I ever saw outside of the tropics. Boats heavy as barges, which require ten men to move them. These stand naked to the work, wielding oars with cross-handles (imagine a letter T with the lower end lengthened out into an oar-blade). And at every pull they push their feet against the gunwales to give more force to the stroke, intoning in every pause a strange refrain of which the soft melancholy calls back to me certain old Spanish Creole melodies heard in West Indian waters:

A-ra-ho-no-san-no-sa, Iya-ho-en-ya! *Ghi*! *Ghi*!

The chant begins with a long high note, and descends by fractional tones with almost every syllable, and faints away a last into an almost indistinguishable hum. Then comes the stroke, '*Ghi!*—*ghi!*'

But at night Mihonoseki is one of the noisiest and merriest little havens of western Japan. From one horn of its crescent to the other the fires of the *shokudai*, which are the tall light of banquets, mirror themselves in the water, and the whole air palpitates with sounds of revelry. Everywhere one hears the booming of the *tsuzumi*, the little hand drums of the *geisha*, and sweet plaintive chants of girls, and tinkling of samisen, and the measured clapping of hands in the dance, and the wild cries and laughter of the players at ken. And all these are but echoes of the diversions of sailors. Verily, the nature of sailors differs but little the world over. Every good ship which visits Mihonoseki leaves there, so I am assured, from three hundred to five hundred yen for *sake* and for dancing girls. Much do these mariners pray the Great Deity who hates eggs to make calm the waters and favourable the winds, so that Mihonoseki may be reached in good time without harm. But having come hither over an unruffled sea with fair soft breezes all the way, small indeed is the gift which they give to the temple of the god, and marvellously large the sums which they pay to *geisha* and keepers of taverns. But the god is patient and long-suffering—except in the matter of eggs.

These Japanese seamen are very gentle compared with our own Jack Tars, and not without a certain refinement and politeness of their own. I see them sitting naked to the waist at their banquets, for it is very hot. But they use their chopsticks as daintily and pledge each other in *sake* almost as graciously as men of a better class. Likewise they seem to treat their girls very kindly. It is quite pleasant to watch them feasting across the street. Perhaps their laughter is somewhat more boisterous and their gesticulation a little more vehement than those of the common citizens, but there is nothing resembling real roughness—much less rudeness. All become motionless and silent as statues—fifteen fine bronzes ranged along the wall of the *zashiki* (best and largest room of a Japanese dwelling)—when some pretty *geisha* begins one of those histrionic dances which, to the Western stranger, seem at first mysterious as a performance of witchcraft—but which really are charming translations of legend and story into the language of living grace and the poetry of woman's smile. And as the wine flows, the more urbane becomes the merriment—until there falls upon all that pleasant sleepiness which *sake* brings, and the guests, one by one, smilingly depart. Nothing could be happier or gentler than their evening's joviality—yet sailors are considered in Japan an especially rough class. What would be thought of our own roughs in such a country?

Well, I have been fourteen months in Izumo, and I have not yet heard voices raised in anger, or witnessed a quarrel: never have I seen one man strike another, or a woman bullied, or a child slapped. Indeed I have never seen any real roughness anywhere that I have been in Japan, except at the open ports, where the poorer classes seem, through contact with Europeans, to lose their natural politeness, their native morals—even their capacity for simple happiness.

Man of War

Last night I saw the seamen of old Japan: today I shall see those of New Japan. An apparition in the offing has filled all this little port with excitement—an imperial man-of-war. Everybody is going out to look at her, and all the long boats that were lying in the alleys are already hastening, full of curious folk, to the steel colossus. A cruiser of the first class, with a crew of five hundred.

I take passage in one of those astounding craft I mentioned before—a sort of barge propelled by ten exceedingly strong naked men, wielding enormous oars—or rather, sweeps—with cross-handles. But I do not go alone: indeed I can scarcely find room to stand, so crowded the boat is with passengers of all ages, especially women who are nervous about going to sea in an ordinary *sanpan*. And a dancing girl jumps into the crowd at the risk of her life, just as we push off—and burns her arm against my cigar in the jump. I am very sorry for her, but she laughs merrily at my solicitude. And the rowers begin their melancholy somnolent song: *A-ra-ho-no-san-no-sa, Iya-ho-en-ya! Ghi! Ghi!*

It is a long pull to reach her—the beautiful monster, towering motionless there in the summer sea, with scarce a curling of thin smoke from the mighty lungs of her slumbering engines. And that somnolent song of our boatmen must surely have some ancient magic in it, for by the time we glide alongside I feel as if I were looking at a dream. Strange as a vision of sleep, indeed, this spectacle: the host of quaint craft hovering and trembling around that tremendous bulk. And all the long-robed, wide-sleeved multitude of the antique port—men, women, children—the grey and the young together—crawling up those mighty flanks in one ceaseless stream, like a swarming of ants. And all this with a great humming like the humming of a hive—a sound made up of low laughter, and chattering in undertones, and subdued murmurs of amazement. For the colossus overawes them—this ship of the Tenshi-*sama*, the Son of Heaven. They wonder like babies at the walls and the turrets of steel, the giant guns and the mighty chains, the stern bearing of the white-uniformed hundreds looking down upon the scene without a smile, over the iron bulwarks. Japanese those also—yet changed by some mysterious process into the semblance of strangers. Only the experienced eye could readily decide the nationality of those stalwart marines: but for the sight of the Imperial arms in gold, and the glimmering ideographs on the stern, one might well suppose one's self gazing at some Spanish or Italian ship-of-war manned by brown Latin men.

I cannot possibly get on board. The iron steps are occupied by an endless chain of clinging bodies—blue-robed boys from school, and old men with grey queues, and fearless young mothers holding fast to the ropes with over-confident babies strapped to their backs, and peasants, and fishers, and dancing girls. They are now simply sticking there like flies: somebody has told them they must wait fifteen minutes. So they wait with smiling patience, and behind them in the fleet of high-prowed boats hundreds more wait and wonder. But they do not wait for fifteen minutes! All hopes are suddenly shattered by a stentorian announcement from the deck, '*Mō jikan ga nai kara, miseru koto ga dekimasen!*' The monster is getting up steam— going away: nobody else will be allowed to come on board. And from the patient swarm of clingers to the hand-ropes, and the patient waiters in the fleet of boats, there goes up one exceedingly plaintive and prolonged '*Aa!*' of disappointment, followed by artless reproaches in Izumo dialect, '*Gunjin wa uso iwanu ka to omoya!-usotsuki da na!—aa! sō da na!*' (War-people-as-for-lies-never-say-that-we-thought!—Aa-aa-aa!) Apparently the war people are accustomed to such scenes, for they do not even smile.

But we linger near the cruiser to watch the hurried descent of the sightseers into their boats, and the slow ponderous motion of the chain-cables ascending, and the swarming of sailors down over the bows to fasten and unfasten mysterious things. One, bending head-downwards, drops his white cap, and there is a race of boats for the honour of picking it up. A marine leaning over the bulwarks audibly observes to a comrade, '*Aa! Gaikojn da na!—nani ski ni kite iru darō?*'—The other vainly suggests, '*Yasu no senkyōshi darō.*' My Japanese costume does not disguise the fact that I am an alien, but it saves me from the imputation of being a missionary. I remain an enigma. Then there are loud cries of '*Abunai!*'—if the cruiser were to move now there would be 'danger' of swamping and crushing and drowning unspeakable. All the little boats scatter and flee away.

Our ten naked oarsmen once more bend to their cross-handled oars, and recommence their ancient melancholy song. And as we glide back, there comes to me the idea of the prodigious cost of that which we went out to see, the magnificent horror of steel and steam and all the multiple enginery of death—paid for by those humble millions who toil for ever knee-deep in the slime of rice fields, yet can never afford to eat their own rice! Far cheaper must be the food they live on. Nevertheless, merely to protect the little that they own, such nightmares must be called into existence—

monstrous creations of science mathematically applied to the ends of destruction.

How delightful Mihonoseki now seems, drowsing far off there under its blue tiles at the feet of the holy hills!—immemorial Mihonoseki, with its lamps and lions of stone, and its god who hates eggs!—pretty fantastic Mihonoseki, where all things, save the schools, are medieval still: the high-pooped junks, and the long-nosed boats, and the plaintive chants of oarsmen!

A-ra-ho-no-san-no-sa, Iya-ho-en-ya! Ghi! Ghi!

And we touch the mossed and ancient wharves of stone again: over one mile of lucent sea we have floated back a thousand years! I turn to look at the place of that sinister vision—and lo!—there is nothing there! Only the level blue of the flood under the hollow blue of the sky—and, just beyond the promontory, one far, small white speck: the sail of a junk. The horizon is naked. Gone!—but how soundlessly, how swiftly! She makes nineteen knots. And, oh! Kotoshironushi no Kami, there probably existed eggs on board!

Return to Izumo

Hōnen Odori

Akira is no longer with me. He has gone to Kyoto, the holy Buddhist city, to edit a Buddhist magazine. I already feel without him like one who has lost his way—despite his reiterated assurances that he could never be of much service to me in Izumo, as he knew nothing about Shintō.

But for the time being I am to have plenty of company at Izumo, where I am spending the first part of the summer holidays, for the little city is full of students and teachers who know me. Izumo is not only the holiest place in the Sanindō. It is also the most fashionable bathing resort. The beach at Inasa bay is one of the best in all Japan; the beach hotels are spacious, airy, and comfortable; the bathing houses, with hot and cold freshwater baths in which to wash off the brine after a swim, are simply faultless. And in fair weather, the scenery is delightful, as you look out over the summer space of sea. Closing the bay on the right, there reaches out from the hills over-shadowing the town a mighty, rugged, pine-clad spur—the Izumo promontory. On the left a low long range of mountains serrate the horizon beyond the shore-sweep, with one huge vapoury shape towering blue into the blue sky behind them—the truncated silhouette of Sanbeyama. Before you the Japanese Sea touches the sky. And there, on still clear nights, there appears a horizon of fire—the torches of hosts of fishing-boats riding at anchor three and four miles away—so numerous that their lights seem to the naked eye a band of unbroken flame.

The *guji* has invited me and one of my friends to see a great harvest dance at his residence on the evening of the festival of Tenjin. This dance—Hōnen

Odori—is peculiar to Izumo.[1] The opportunity to witness it in this city is a rare one, as it is going to be performed only by order of the *guji*.

The robust pontiff himself loves the sea quite as much as anyone in Izumo, yet he never enters a beach hotel, much less a public bathing house. For his use alone a special bathing house has been built on a ledge of the cliff overhanging the little settlement of Inasa: it is approached by a narrow pathway shadowed by pine trees, and there is a *torii* before it, and *shimenawa*. To this little house the *guji* ascends daily during the bathing season, accompanied by a single attendant, who prepares his bathing dresses, and spreads the clean mats on which he rests after returning from the sea. The *guji* always bathes robed. No one but himself and his servant ever approaches the little house, which commands a charming view of the bay: public reverence for the pontiff's person has made even his resting place holy ground. As for the country folk, they still worship him with hearts and bodies. They have ceased to believe as they did in former times, that anyone on whom the governor fixes his eye at once becomes unable to speak or move, but when he passes among them through the temple court they still prostrate themselves along his way, as before the Ikigami.

Miko

Always, through the memory of my first day at Izumo, there will pass the beautiful white apparition of the *miko*, with her perfect passionless face, and strange, gracious, soundless tread, as of a ghost.

Her name signifies 'maiden of the gods'—*kami no ko*.

The kind *guji*, at my earnest request, procured me—or rather, had taken for me—a photograph of the *miko*, in the attitude of her dance, upholding the mystic *suzu*, and wearing, over her crimson *hakama*, the snowy priestess robe descending to her feet.

The learned priest Sasa told me these things concerning the maid of the Gods, and the *miko-kagura*—which is the name of her sacred dance.

Contrary to the custom at other great Shintō temples like Ise, the office of *miko* at the Izumo Ōyashiro has always been hereditary. Formerly there were more than thirty families whose daughters served the Ōyashiro as

---

1 Hōnen Odori are not peculiar to Izumo but are still held, notably in the prefectures of Kagoshima, Miyazaki in the souther part of Kyushu, as well as the Satsunan Islands and Okinawa.

miko: today there are but two, and the number of virgin priestesses does not exceed six—the one whose portrait I obtained being the chief.

At Ise and elsewhere the daughter of any Shintō priest may become a *miko*. But she cannot serve in that capacity after becoming nubile, so that, except in Izumo, the *miko* of all the greater temples are children from ten to twelve years of age. But at the Izumo Ōyashiro the maiden priestesses are beautiful girls of between sixteen and nineteen years of age. Sometimes a favourite *miko* is allowed to continue to serve the gods even after having been married. The sacred dance is not difficult to learn: the mother or sister teaches it to the child destined to serve in the temple. The *miko* lives at home, and visits the temple only on festival days to perform her duties. She is not placed under any severe discipline or restrictions; she takes no special vows; she risks no dreadful penalties for ceasing to remain a virgin. But her position being one of high honour, and a source of revenue to her family, the ties which bind her to duty are scarcely less cogent than those vows taken by the priestesses of the antique Occident.

Like the priestesses of Delphi, the *miko* was in ancient times also a divineress—a living oracle, uttering the secrets of the future when possessed by the god whom she served. At no temple does the *miko* now act as sibyl, oracular priestess, or divineress. But there still exists a class of divining-women, who claim to hold communication with the dead, and to foretell the future, and who call themselves *miko*—practising their profession secretly, for it has been prohibited by law.

In the various great Shintō shrines of the empire the *miko-kagura* is differently danced. At the Izumo Ōyashiro, most ancient of all, the dance is the most simple and the most primitive. Its purpose being to give pleasure to the gods, religious conservatism has preserved its traditions and steps unchanged since the period of the beginning of the faith. The origin of this dance is to be found in the *Kojiki* legend of the dance of Ame no Uzume no Mikoto—she by whose mirth and song the Sun-goddess was lured from the cavern into which she had retired, and brought back to illuminate the world. And the *suzu*—the strange bronze instrument with its cluster of bells which the *miko* uses in her dance—still preserves the form of that bamboo-spray to which Ame no Uzume no Mikoto fastened small bells with grass, ere beginning her mirthful song.

O-Kuni

Behind the library in the rear of the great shrine, there stands a more ancient structure still called the Miko-*yashiki*, or dwelling place of the *miko*. Here in former times all the maiden-priestesses were obliged to live, under a somewhat stricter discipline than now. By day they could go out where they pleased, but they were under obligation to return at night to the *yashiki* before the gates of the court were closed. For it was feared that the maidens of the gods might so far forget themselves as to condescend to become the darlings of adventurous mortals. Nor was the fear at all unreasonable, for it was the duty of a *miko* to be singularly innocent as well as beautiful. And one of the most beautiful *miko* who belonged to the service of the Izumo Ōyashiro did actually so fall from grace—giving to the Japanese world a romance you can buy in cheap printed form at any large bookstore in Japan.

Her name was O-Kuni, and she was the daughter of one Nakamura Mongoro of Izumo, where her descendants still live at the present day. While serving as dancer in the great temple she fell in love with a *rōnin* named Nagoya Sanza—a desperate, handsome vagabond, with no fortune in the world but his sword. And she left the temple secretly, and fled away with her lover toward Kyoto. All this must have happened not less than three hundred years ago.

On their way to Kyoto they met another *rōnin*, whose real name I have not been able to learn. For a moment only this 'wave man' figures in the story, and immediately vanishes into the eternal night of death and all forgotten things. It is simply recorded that he desired permission to travel with them, that he became enamoured of the beautiful *miko*, and excited the jealousy of her lover to such an extent that a desperate duel was the result, in which Sanza slew his rival.

Thereafter the fugitives pursued their way to Kyoto without interruption. Whether the fair O-Kuni had by this time found ample reason to regret the step she had taken, we cannot know. But from the story of her afterlife it would seem that the face of the handsome *rōnin* who had perished through his passion for her became a haunting memory.

We next hear of her in a strange role at Kyoto. Her lover appears to have been utterly destitute, for, in order to support him, we find her giving exhibitions of the *miko-kagura* in the Shijō Kawara—which is the name given to a portion of the dry bed of the Kamo River—doubtless the same place in which the terrible executions by torture took place.[2] She must have been looked upon by the public of that day as an outcast. But her extraordinary beauty seems to have attracted many spectators, and to have proved more than successful as an exhibition. Sanza's purse became well filled. Yet the dance of O-Kuni at the Shijō Kawara was nothing more than the same dance the *miko* of the Izumo Ōyashiro dance today, in their crimson *hakama* and snowy robes—a graceful gliding walk.

The pair next appear in Tokyo—or Edo, as it was then called—as actors. O-Kuni, indeed, is universally credited by tradition, with having established the modern Japanese stage—the first profane drama. Before her time only religious plays, of Buddhist authorship, seem to have been known. Sanza himself became a popular and successful actor, under his sweetheart's tuition. He had many famous pupils, among them the great Saruwaka, who subsequently founded a theatre in Edo. The theatre called after him Saruwakaza, in the street Saruwakacho, remains even to this day. But since the time of O-Kuni, women have been—at least until very recently—excluded from the Japanese stage; their parts, as among the old Greeks, are taken by men or boys so effeminate in appearance and so skilful in acting that the keenest observer could never detect their sex.

Nagoya Sanza died many years before his companion. O-Kuni then returned to her native place, to ancient Izumo, where she cut off her beautiful hair, and became a Buddhist nun. She was learned for her century, and especially skilful in that art of poetry called *renga*, and this art she continued to teach until her death. With the small fortune she had earned as an actress she built in Izumo the little Buddhist temple called Renga-ji, in the very heart of the quaint town—so called because there she taught the art of *renga*. Now the reason she built the temple was that she might therein always pray for the soul of the man whom the sight of her beauty had ruined, and whose smile, perhaps, had stirred something within her heart whereof Sanza never knew. Her family enjoyed certain privileges for several centuries because she had founded the whole art of the Japanese

2 The execution grounds were at Rokujō Kawara, a kilometer farther south along the easter bank of the Kamo River. Numerous rebels were put to death here throughout Japan's long feudal history, among them Minamoto Tameyoshi (Hōgen Insurrection), Fujiwara Nobuyori (Heiji Insurrection), Saitō Toshimitsu (Honnō-ji Incident), and Ishida Mitsunari (in the wake of the Battle of Sekigahara).

stage Until so recently as the Restoration the chief of the descendants of Nakamura Mongoro was always entitled to a share in the profits of the Izumo theatre, and enjoyed the title of Zamoto. The family is now very poor.

I went to see the little temple of Renga-*ji*, and found that it had disappeared. Until within a few years it used to stand at the foot of the great flight of stone steps leading to the second Kannondera, the most imposing temple of Kannon in Izumo. Nothing now remains of the Renga-*ji* but a broken statue of Jizō, before which the people still pray. The former court of the little temple has been turned into a vegetable garden, and the material of the ancient building utilised, irreverently enough, for the construction of some petty cottages now occupying its site. A peasant told me that the *kakemono* and other sacred objects had been given to the neighbouring temple, where they might be seen.

Renga-ji

Not far from the site of the Renga-*ji*, in the grounds of the great *hakaba* of the Kannon-*dera*, there stands a most curious pine. The trunk of the tree is supported, not on the ground, but upon four colossal roots which lift it up at such an angle that it looks like a thing walking on four legs. Trees of singular shape are often considered to be the dwelling places of *kami*, and the pine in question affords an example of this belief. A fence has been built around it, and a small shrine placed before it, prefaced by several small *torii*. And many poor people may be seen, at almost any hour of the day, praying to the *kami* of the place.

Before the little shrine I notice, besides the usual Izumo *ex-voto* of seaweed, several little effigies of horses made of straw. Why these offerings of horses of straw? It appears that the shrine is dedicated to Koshin, the Lord of Roads. Those who are anxious about the health of their horses pray to the Road-God to preserve their animals from sickness and death, at the same time bringing these straw effigies in token of their desire. But this role of veterinarian is not commonly attributed to Koshin, and it appears that something in the fantastic form of the tree suggested the idea.

Bekka

Within the first court of the Izumo Ōyashiro, and to the left of the chief gate, stands a small timber structure, ashen-coloured with age, shaped like a common *miya* or shrine. To the wooden gratings of its closed doors are knotted many of those white papers on which are usually written vows or prayers to the gods. But on peering through the grating one sees no Shintō symbols in the dimness within. It is a stable! And there, in the central stall, is a superb horse—looking at you. Japanese horseshoes of straw are suspended to the wall behind him. He does not move. He is made of bronze!

Upon inquiring of the learned priest Sasa the story of this horse, I was told the following curious things:

On the eleventh day of the seventh month, by the ancient calendar, falls the strange festival called Minige, or 'the body-escaping.' Upon that day, 'tis said that the great deity of the Izumo Ōyashiro leaves his shrine to pass through all the streets of the city, and along the seashore, after which he enters into the house of the governor (*kokuzō*). Wherefore on that day the governor was always wont to leave his house. At the present time, though he does not actually abandon his home, he and his family retire into certain apartments, so as to leave the larger part of the dwelling free for the use of the god. This retreat of the governor is still called the Minige.

Now while the great deity Ōkuninushi no Kami is passing through the streets, he is followed by the highest Shintō priest of the shrine—this *kannushi* having been formerly called *bekka*. The word '*bekka*' means 'special' or 'sacred fire.' The chief *kannushi* was so called because for a week before the festival he had been nourished only with special food cooked with the sacred fire, so that he might be pure in the presence of the God. The office of *bekka* was hereditary, and the appellation at last became a family name. But he who performs the rite today is no longer called *bekka*.

If the *bekka* met anyone on the street while performing his function, he ordered them to stand aside with the words, 'Dog, give way!' The common people still believe that anybody thus spoken to by the officiating *kannushi* would be changed into a dog. So on that day of the Minige nobody used to go out into the streets after a certain hour, and even now very few of the people of the little city leave their homes during the festival.

After having followed the deity through all the city, the *bekka* used to perform, between two and three o'clock in the darkness of the morning, some secret rite by the seaside. (I am told this rite is still annually performed at the same hour.) But, except the *bekka* himself, no man might be present. It was believed, and is still believed by the common people, that were any man, by mischance, to see the rite he would instantly fall dead, or become transformed into an animal.

So sacred was the secret of that rite, that the *bekka* could not even utter it until after he was dead, to his successor in office.

Therefore, when he died, the body was laid on the matting of a certain inner chamber of the temple, and the son was left alone with the corpse, after all the doors had been carefully closed. Then, at a certain hour of the night, the soul returned into the body of the dead priest, and he lifted himself up, and whispered the awful secret into the ear of his son—and fell back dead again.

But what, you may ask, has all this to do with the horse of bronze?

Only this:

Upon the festival of the Minige, the great deity of the Izumo Ōyashiro rides through the streets of his city on the horse of bronze.

Tomb

The horse of bronze is far from being the only statue in Izumo which is believed to run about occasionally at night: at least a score of other artistic things are, or have been, credited with similar ghastly inclinations. The great carven dragon which writhes above the entrance of the Izumo Ōyashiro *haiden* used, I am told, to crawl about the roofs at night—until a carpenter was summoned to cut its wooden throat with a chisel, after which it ceased its perambulations. You can see for yourself the mark of the chisel on its throat!

At the splendid Shintō temple of Kasuga, in Matsue, there are two pretty life-size bronze deer—stag and doe—the heads of which seemed to me to have been separately cast, and subsequently riveted very deftly to the bodies. Nevertheless I have been assured by some good country folk that each figure was originally a single casting, but that it was afterwards found necessary to cut off the heads of the deer to make them keep quiet at night.

The most unpleasant customer of all this uncanny fraternity to have encountered after dark was certainly the monster tortoise of Gesshō-*ji* temple in Matsue, where the tombs of the Matsudairas are. This stone colossus is almost seventeen feet in length and lifts its head six feet from the ground. On its now broken back stands a prodigious cubic monolith about nine feet high, bearing a half-obliterated inscription. Fancy—as Izumo folks did—this mortuary incubus staggering abroad at midnight, and its hideous attempts to swim in the neighbouring lotus pond! Well, the legend runs that its neck had to be broken in consequence of this awful misbehaviour. But really the thing looks as if it could only have been broken by an earthquake.

Tenjin

At the Izumo Ōyashiro it is the annual festival of the god of scholarship, the god of calligraphy—Tenjin. Here in Izumo, the festival of the Divine Scribe, the Tenjin Matsuri, is still observed according to the beautiful old custom which is being forgotten elsewhere. Long ranges of temporary booths have been erected within the outer court of the temple. In these are suspended hundreds of long white tablets, bearing specimens of calligraphy. Every schoolboy in Izumo has a sample of his best writing on exhibition. The texts are written only in Chinese characters—not in *hiragana* or *katakana*—and are mostly drawn from the works of Confucius or Mencius.

To me this display of ideographs seems a marvellous thing of beauty—almost a miracle, indeed, since it is all the work of very, very young boys. Rightly enough, the word 'to write' (*kaku*) in Japanese signifies also to 'paint' in the best artistic sense. I once had an opportunity of studying the result of an attempt to teach English children the art of writing Japanese. These children were instructed by a Japanese writing master; they sat on the same bench with Japanese pupils of their own age, beginners likewise. But they could never learn like the Japanese children. The ancestral tendencies within them rendered vain the efforts of the instructor to teach them the secret of a shapely stroke with the brush. It is not the Japanese boy alone who writes; the fingers of the dead move his brush, guide his strokes.

Beautiful as this writing seems to me, it is far from winning the commendation of my Japanese companion, himself a much experienced teacher. 'The greater part of this work,' he declares, 'is very bad.' While I am still bewildered by this sweeping criticism, he points out to me one tablet inscribed with rather small characters, adding, 'Only that is tolerably good.'

'Why,' I venture to observe, 'that one would seem to have cost much less trouble; the characters are so small.'

'Oh, the size of the characters has nothing to do with the matter,' interrupts the master, 'it is a question of form.'

'Then I cannot understand. What you call very bad seems to me exquisitely beautiful.'

'Of course you cannot understand,' the critic replies. 'It would take you many years of study to understand. And even then—

'And even then?'

'Well, even then you could only partly understand.'

Thereafter I hold my peace on the topic of calligraphy.

Toys

Vast as the courts of the Izumo Ōyashiro are, the crowd within them is now so dense that one must move very slowly, for the whole population of Izumo and its environs has been attracted here by the *matsuri*. All are making their way very gently toward a little shrine built upon an island in the middle of an artificial lake and approached by a narrow causeway. This little shrine, which I see now for the first time (the Izumo Ōyashiro being far too large a place to be all seen and known in a single visit), is the Shrine of Tenjin.

As the sound of a waterfall is the sound of the clapping of hands before it, and myriads of *nin*, and bushels of handfuls of rice, are being dropped into the enormous wooden chest there placed to receive the offerings. Fortunately this crowd, like all Japanese crowds, is so sympathetically yielding that it is possible to traverse it slowly in any direction, and thus to see all there is to be seen. After contributing my mite to the coffer of Tenjin, I devote my attention to the wonderful display of toys in the outer courts.

At almost every temple festival in Japan there is a great sale of toys, usually within the court itself—a miniature street of small booths being temporarily erected for this charming commence. Every *matsuri* is a children's holiday. No mother would think of attending a temple festival without buying her child a toy: even the poorest mother can afford it. For the price of the toys sold in a temple court varies from one-fifth of one *sen* or Japanese cent, to three or four *sen*, toys worth so much as five *sen* being rarely displayed at these little shops. But cheap as they are, these frail playthings are full of beauty and suggestiveness, and, to one who knows and loves Japan, infinitely more interesting than the costliest inventions of a Parisian toy manufacturer. Many of them, however, would be utterly incomprehensible to an English child. Suppose we peep at a few of them.

Here is a little wooden mallet, with a loose tiny ball fitted into a socket at the end of the handle. This is for the baby to suck. On either end of the head of the mallet is painted the mystic *tomoe*—that symbol resembling two huge commas so united as to make a perfect circle, which you may have seen on the title page of Percival Lowell's beautiful *Soul of the Far East*. To you this little wooden mallet would seem in all probability just a little wooden mallet and nothing more. But to the Japanese child it is full of suggestions. It is the mallet of the Great Deity of the Izumo Ōyashiro, Ōkuninushi no Kami—vulgarly called Daikoku—the God of Wealth, who, by one stroke of his hammer, gives fortune to his worshippers.

Perhaps this tiny drum, of a form never seen in the Occident (tsudzumi), or this larger drum with a *mitsudomoe*, or triple comma symbol, painted on each end, might seem to you without religious signification. Both are models of drums used in the Shintō and the Buddhist temples. This queer tiny table is a miniature *sanbō*: it is on such a table that offerings are presented to the gods. This curious cap is a model of the cap of a Shintō priest. Here is a toy *miya*, or Shintō shrine, four inches high. This bunch of tiny tin bells attached to a wooden handle might seem to you something corresponding to our Occidental tin rattles, but it is a model of the sacred *suzu* used by the virgin priestess in her dance before the gods. This face of a smiling chubby girl, with two spots on her forehead—a mask of baked clay—is the traditional image of Ame no Uzume no Mikoto, commonly called Otafuku, whose merry laughter lured the goddess of the sun out of the cavern of darkness. And here is a little Shintō priest in full hieratic garb: when this little string between his feet is pulled, he claps his hands as if in prayer.

Hosts of other toys are here—mysterious to the uninitiated European, but to the Japanese child full of delightful religious meaning. In these faiths of the Far East there is little of sternness or grimness—the *kami* are but the spirits of the fathers of the people; the Buddhas and the Bosatsu were men. Happily the missionaries have not succeeded as yet in teaching the

Japanese to make religion a dismal thing. These gods smile for ever: if you find one who frowns, like Fudo, the frown seems but half in earnest; it is only Enma, the Lord of Death, who somewhat appals. Why religion should be considered too awful a subject for children to amuse themselves decently with never occurs to the common Japanese mind. So here we have images of the gods and saints for toys—Tenjin, the Deity of Beautiful Writing—and Uzume, the laughter-loving—and Fukusuke, like a happy schoolboy—and the Seven Divinities of Good Luck, in a group—and Fukurojin, the God of Longevity, with head so elongated that only by the aid of a ladder can his barber shave the top of it—and Hotei, with a belly round and huge as a balloon—and Ebisu, the Deity of Markets and of fishermen, with a tai-fish under his arm—and Daruma, ancient disciple of Buddha, whose legs were worn off by uninterrupted meditation.

Here likewise are many toys which a foreigner could scarcely guess the meaning of, although they have no religious signification. Such is this little badger, represented as drumming on its own belly with both forepaws. The badger is believed to be able to use its belly like a drum, and is credited by popular superstition with various supernatural powers. This toy illustrates a pretty fairy-tale about some hunter who spared a badger's life and was rewarded by the creature with a wonderful dinner and a musical performance. Here is a hare sitting on the end of the handle of a wooden pestle which is set horizontally on a pivot. By pulling a little string, the pestle is made to rise and fall as if moved by the hare. If you have been even a week in Japan you will recognise the pestle as the pestle of a *kometsuki*, or rice cleaner, who works it by treading on the handle. But what is the hare? This hare is the 'hare in the moon,' called *usagi no kometsuki*: if you look up at the moon on a clear night you can see him cleaning his rice.

Now let us see what we can discover in the way of cheap ingenuities.

Tonbo, 'the dragonfly.' Merely two bits of wood joined together in the form of a T. The lower part is a little round stick, about as thick as a match, but twice as long; the upper piece is flat, and streaked with paint. Unless you are accustomed to look for secrets, you would scarcely be able to notice that the flat piece is trimmed along two edges at a particular angle. Twirl the lower piece rapidly between the palms of both hands, and suddenly let it go. At once the strange toy rises revolving in the air, and then sails away slowly to quite a distance, performing extraordinary gyrations, and imitating exactly—to the eye at least—the hovering motion of a dragonfly. Those little streaks of paint you noticed on the top-piece now reveal their purpose, as the *tonbo* darts hither and thither, even the tints appear to be those of a real dragonfly. Even the sound of the flitting toy imitates the dragonfly's hum. The principle of this pretty invention is much like that of the boomerang; an expert can make his *tonbo*, after flying across a large room, return into his hand. All the *tonbo* sold, however, are not as good as this one; we have been lucky. Price, one-tenth of one cent!

Here is a toy that looks like a bow of bamboo strung with wire. The wire is twisted into a corkscrew spiral. On this spiral a pair of tiny birds are suspended by a metal loop. When the bow is held perpendicularly with the birds at the upper end of the string, they descend whirling by their own weight, as if circling round one another. The twittering of two birds is imitated by the sharp grating of the metal loop on the spiral wire. One bird flies head upward, and the other tail upward. As soon as they have reached the bottom, reverse the bow, and they will recommence their wheeling flight. Price, two cents—because the wire is dear.

O-saru, the 'honourable monkey.' A little cotton monkey, with a blue head and scarlet body, hugging a bamboo rod. Under him is a bamboo spring. When you press it, he runs up to the top of the rod. Price, one-eighth of one cent.

0-Saru. Another honourable monkey. This one is somewhat more complex in his movements, and costs a cent. He runs up a string, hand over hand, when you pull his tail.

Tori-kago. A tiny gilded cage, with a bird in it, and plum flowers. Press the edges of the bottom of the cage, and a minuscule wind instrument imitates the chirping of the bird. Price, one cent.

Karuwazashi, 'the acrobat.' A loose-jointed wooden boy clinging with both hands to a string stretched between two bamboo sticks, which are curiously rigged together in the shape of an open pair of scissors. Press the ends of the sticks at the bottom, and the acrobat tosses his legs over the string, seats himself on it, and finally turns a somersault. Price, one-sixth of one cent.

Kobiki, the 'sawyer.' A figure of a Japanese workman, wearing only a *fundoshi* about his loins, and standing on a plank, with a long saw in his hands. If you pull a string below his feet, he will go to work in good earnest, sawing the plank. Notice that he pulls the saw towards him, like a true Japanese, instead of pushing it from him, as our own carpenters do. Price, one-tenth of one cent.

Chie no ita, the 'intelligent boards,' or better, perhaps, 'the planks of intelligence.' A sort of chain composed of about a dozen flat square pieces of white wood, linked together by ribbons. Hold the thing perpendicularly by one end piece, turn the piece at right angles to the chain, and immediately all the other pieces tumble over each other in the most marvellous way without unlinking. Even an adult can amuse himself for half an hour with this: it is a perfect *trompe-l'oeil* in mechanical adjustment. Price, one cent.

Kitsune tanuki. A funny flat paper mask with closed eyes. If you pull a pasteboard slip behind it, it will open its eyes and put out a tongue of surprising length. Price, one-sixth of one cent.

Chin. A little white dog, with a collar round its neck. It is in the attitude of barking. From a Buddhist point of view, I should think this toy somewhat immoral. For when you slap the dog's head, it utters a sharp yelp, as of pain. Price, one *sen* and five rin. Rather dear.

Fuki-agari koboshi, the 'wrestler invincible.' This is still dearer, for it is made of porcelain, and very nicely coloured The wrestler squats on his hams. Push him down in any direction, he always returns of his own accord to an erect position. Price, two sen.

Oroga heika kodomo, the 'child reverencing His Majesty the Emperor.' A Japanese schoolboy with an accordion in his hands, singing and playing the national anthem, or Kimiga. There is a little wind bellows at the bottom of the toy. When you operate it, the boy's arms move as if playing the instrument, and a shrill small voice is heard. Price, one cent and a half.

Jishaku. This, like the preceding, is quite a modern toy. A small wooden box containing a magnet and a tiny top made of a red wooden button with a steel nail driven through it. Set the top spinning with a twirl of the fingers; then hold the magnet over the nail, and the top will leap up to the magnet and there continue to spin, suspended in air. Price, one cent.

It would require at least a week to examine them all. Here is a model spinning wheel, absolutely perfect, for one-fifth of one cent. Here are little clay tortoises which swim about when you put them into water—one *rin* for two. Here is a box of toy-soldiers—samurai in full armour—nine *rin* only. Here is a *kaze-kuruma*, or wind wheel—a wooden whistle with a paper wheel mounted before the orifice by which the breath is expelled, so that the wheel turns furiously when the whistle is blown—three *rin*. Here is an *ogi*, a sort of tiny quadruple fan sliding in a sheath. When expanded it takes the shape of a beautiful flower—one *rin*.

The most charming of all these things to me, however, is a tiny doll—*o*-Hina-*san* (honourable Miss Hina)—or *beppin* (beautiful woman). The body is a phantom, only—a flat stick covered with a paper *kimono*—but the head is really a work of art. A pretty oval face with softly shadowed oblique eyes—looking shyly downward—and a wonderful maiden coiffure, in which the hair is arranged in bands and volutes and ellipses and convolutions and foliole curlings most beautiful and extraordinary. In some respects this toy is a costume model, for it imitates exactly the real coiffure of Japanese maidens and brides. But the expression of the face of the beppin is, I think, the great attraction of the toy; there is a shy, plaintive sweetness about it impossible to describe, but deliciously suggestive of a real Japanese type of girl-beauty. Yet the whole thing is made out of a little crumpled paper, coloured with a few dashes of the brush by an expert hand. There are no two *o*-Hina-*san* exactly alike out of millions; when you have become familiar by long residence with Japanese types, any such doll will recall to you some pretty face that you have seen. These are for little girls. Price, five *rin*.

Living Doll

Here let me tell you something you certainly never heard of before in relation to Japanese dolls—not the tiny *o*-Hina-*san* I was just speaking about, but the beautiful life-sized dolls representing children of two or three years old; real toy-babes which, although far more cheaply and simply constructed than our finer kinds of Western dolls, become, under the handling of a Japanese girl, infinitely more interesting. Such dolls are well dressed, and look so life-like—little slanting eyes, shaven pates, smiles, and all!—that as seen from a short distance the best eyes might be deceived by them. Therefore in those stock photographs of Japanese life, of which so many thousands are sold in the open ports, the conventional baby on the mother's back is most successfully represented by a doll. Even the camera does not betray the substitution. And if you see such a doll, though held quite close to you, being made by a Japanese mother to reach out his hands, to move its little bare feet, and to turn its head, you would be almost afraid to venture a heavy wager that it was only a doll. Even after having closely examined the thing, you would still, I fancy, feel a little nervous at being left alone with it, so perfect the delusion of that expert handling.

Now there is a belief that some dolls do actually become alive.

Formerly the belief was less rare than it is now. Certain dolls were spoken of with a reverence worthy of the *kami*, and their owners were envied folk. Such a doll was treated like a real son or daughter: it was regularly served with food; it had a bed, and plenty of nice clothes, and a name. If in the semblance of a girl, it was *o*-Toku-*san*; if in that of a boy, Tokutarō-*san*. It was thought that the doll would become angry and cry if neglected, and that any ill-treatment of it would bring ill fortune to the house. Moreover, it was believed to possess supernatural powers of a very high order.

In the family of one Sengoku, a samurai of Matsue, there was a Tokutarō-*san* that had a local reputation scarcely inferior to that of Kishimojin—she to whom Japanese wives pray for offspring. Childless couples used to borrow the doll and keep it for a time—ministering to it—and furnish it with new clothes before gratefully returning it to its owners. And all who did so, I am assured, became parents, according to their heart's desire.

'Sengoku's doll had a soul.'

There is even a legend that once, when the house caught fire, Tokutarō-*san* ran out safely into the garden of its own accord!

The idea about such a doll seems to be this: The new doll is only a doll. But a doll that is preserved for a great many years in one family, and is loved and played with by generations of children, gradually acquires a soul. I asked a charming Japanese girl, 'How can a doll live?'

'Why,' she answered, 'if you love it enough, it will live!'

What is this but Renan's thought of a deity *in process of evolution*, uttered by the heart of a child?

Memento

But even the most beloved dolls are worn out at last, or get broken in the course of centuries. And when a doll must be considered quite dead, its remains are still entitled to respect. Never is the corpse of a doll irreverently thrown away. Neither is it burned or cast into pure running water, as all sacred objects of the *miya* must be when they have ceased to be serviceable. And it is not buried. You could not possibly imagine what is done with it.

It is dedicated to the god Kojin, (not to be confused with Koshi, the god of the roads)—a somewhat mysterious divinity, half Buddhist, half Shintō. The ancient Buddhist images of Kojin represented a deity with many arms; the Shintō Kojin of Izumo has, I believe, no artistic representation whatever. But in almost every Shintō, and also in many Buddhist, temple grounds, is planted the tree called *enoki*, which is sacred to him, and in which he is supposed by the peasantry to dwell, for they pray before the *enoki* always to Kojin. And there is usually a small shrine placed before the tree, and a little *torii* also. Now you may often see laid on such a shrine of Kojin, or at the foot of his sacred tree, or in a hollow thereof—if there be any hollow—pathetic remains of dolls. But a doll is seldom given to Kojin during the lifetime of its possessor. When you see one thus exposed, you may be almost certain that it was found among the effects of some poor dead woman—the innocent memento of her girlhood, perhaps even also of the girlhood of her mother and of her mother's mother.

Odori

And now we are to see the Hōnen Odori—which begins at eight o'clock. There is no moon; the night is pitch-black overhead: but there is plenty of light in the broad court of the *guji*'s residence, for a hundred lanterns have been kindled and hung out. I and my friend have been provided with comfortable places in the great pavilion which opens onto the court, and the pontiff has had prepared for us a delicious little supper.

Already thousands have assembled before the pavilion—young men of Izumo and young peasants from the environs, and women and children in multitude, and hundreds of young girls. The court is so thronged that it is difficult to assume the possibility of any dance. Illuminated by the lantern-light, the scene is more than picturesque: it is a carnivalesque display of gala-costume. Of course the peasants come in their ancient attire: some in rain coats (*mino*), or overcoats of yellow straw; others with blue towels tied round their heads; many with enormous mushroom hats—all with their blue robes well tucked up. But the young townsmen come in all guises and disguises. Many have dressed themselves in female attire; some are all in white duck, like police; some have mantles on; others wear shawls exactly as a Mexican wears his *zarape*; numbers of young artisans appear almost as lightly clad as in working-hours, barelegged to the hips, and barearmed to the shoulders. Among the girls some wonderful dressing is to be seen— ruby-coloured robes, and rich greys and browns and purples, confined with exquisite *obi*, or girdles of figured satin; but the best taste is shown in the simple and very graceful black and white costumes worn by some maidens of the better classes—dresses especially made for dancing, and not to be worn at any other time. A few shy damsels have completely masked themselves by tying down over their cheeks the flexible brims of very broad straw hats. I cannot attempt to talk about the delicious costumes of the children: as well try to describe without paint the variegated loveliness of moths and butterflies.

In the centre of this multitude I see a huge rice-mortar turned upside down; and presently a sandalled peasant leaps on it lightly, and stands there—with an open paper umbrella above his head. Nevertheless it is not raining. That is the *ondo-tori*, the leader of the dance, who is celebrated through all Izumo as a singer. According to ancient custom, the leader of the Hōnen Odori, or Dance of the Fruitful Year, always holds an open umbrella above his head while he sings.

Suddenly, at a signal from the *guji*, who has just taken his place in the pavilion, the voice of the *ondo-tori*, intoning the song of thanksgiving, rings out over all the murmuring of the multitude like a silver cornet. A wondrous voice, and a wondrous song, full of trills and quaverings indescribable, but full also of sweetness and true musical swing. And as he sings, he turns slowly round on his high pedestal, with the umbrella always above his head, never halting in his rotation from right to left, but pausing for a regular interval in his singing, at the close of each two verses, when the people respond with a joyous outcry, '*Ya-ha-to-nai!*-ya-ha-to-nai!'

Simultaneously, an astonishingly rapid movement of segregation takes place in the crowd; two enormous rings of dancers form, one within the other, the rest of the people pressing back to make room for the *odori*. And then this great double-round, formed by fully five hundred dancers, begins also to revolve from right to left—lightly, fantastically—all the tossing of arms and white twinkling of feet keeping faultless time to the measured syllabification of the chant. An immense wheel the dance is, with the *ondo-tori* for its axis—always turning slowly on his rice mortar, under his open umbrella, as he sings the song of harvest thanksgiving:

> *Ichi wa—Izumo no taisha-sama e,*
> *Ni ni wa—Niigata no Irokami-sama e,*
> *San wa—Sanuki no Kompira-sama e,*
> *Shi ni wa—Shinano no Zenkō-ji-sama e,*
> *Itsutsu—Ichibata o-Yakushi-sama e,*
> *Roku ni wa—Rokkakudo no o-Jizō-sama e,*
> *Nanatsu—Nanaura no o-Ebisu sama e,*
> *Yattsu—Yawata no Hachiman-sama e,*
> *Kokonotsu—koya no o-teradera e,*
> *To niwa—tokoro no Ujigami-sama e.*

> First—to the Taisha-*sama* of Izunio,
> Second—to Irokami-*sama* of Niigata,
> Third—to Kompira-*sama* of Sanuki,
> Fourth—to *Zenkō-ji-sama* of Shinano,
> Fifth—to O-Yakushi-*san* of Ichibata,
> Sixth—to O-Jizō-*sama* of Rokkakudo,
> Seventh—to O-Ebisu-*sama* of Nana-ura,
> Eighth—to Hachiman-*sama* of Yawata,
> Ninth—to everyholy shrine of Koya,
> Tenth—to the Ujigami-*sama* of our village.

And the voices of all the dancers in unison roll out the chorus: *Ya-ha-to-nai! Ya-ha-to-nai!*

Utterly different this whirling joyous Honen-odori from the Bon Odori which I witnessed last year at Shimoichi, and which seemed to me a very dance of ghosts. But it is also much more difficult to describe. Each dancer makes a half-wheel alternately to left and right, with a peculiar bending of the knees and tossing up of the hands at the same time—as in the act of lifting a weight above the head. There are other curious movements—jerky with the men, undulatory with the women—as impossible to describe as water in motion. These are decidedly complex, yet so regular that five hundred pairs of feet and hands mark the measure of the song as truly as if they were under the control of a single nervous system.

It is strangely difficult to memorise the melody of a Japanese popular song, or the movements of a Japanese dance; for the song and the dance have been evolved through an aesthetic sense of rhythm in sound and in motion as different from the corresponding Occidental sense as English is different from Chinese. We have no ancestral sympathies with these exotic rhythms, no inherited aptitudes for their instant comprehension, no racial impulses whatever in harmony with them. But when they have become familiar through study, after a long residence in the Orient, how nervously fascinant the oscillation of the dance, and the singular swing of the song!

This dance, I know, began at eight o'clock; and the *ondo-tori*, after having sung without a falter in his voice for an extraordinary time, has been relieved by a second. But the great round never breaks, never slackens its whirl; it only enlarges as the night wears on. And the second *ondo-tori* is relieved by a third; yet I would like to watch that dance for ever.

'What time do you think it is?' my friend asks, looking at his watch.

'Nearly eleven o'clock,' I make answer.

'Eleven o'clock! It is exactly eight minutes to three o'clock. And our host will have little time for sleep before the rising of the sun.'

Hinomisaki

My Japanese friends urge me to visit Hinomisaki, where no European has ever been, and where there is a far-famed double temple dedicated to Amaterasu Ōmikami, the Lady of Light, and to her divine brother Takehaya Susanoo no Mikoto. Hinomisaki is a little village on the Izumo coast about five miles from Izumo. It may be reached by a mountain path, but the way is extremely steep, rough, and fatiguing. By boat, when the weather is fair, the trip is very agreeable. So, with a friend, I start for Hinomisaki in a very cozy *ryōsen* (fishing boat), skilfully sculled by two young fishermen.

Leaving the pretty bay of Inasa, we follow the coast to the right—a very lofty and grim coast without a beach. Below us the clear water gradually darkens to inky blackness, as the depth increases, but at intervals pale jagged rocks rise up from this nether darkness to catch the light fifty feet under the surface. We keep tolerably close to the cliffs, which vary in height from three hundred to six hundred feet—their bases rising from the water all dull iron-grey, their sides and summits green with young pines and dark grasses that toughen in sea-wind. All the coast is abrupt, ravined, irregular—curiously breached and fissured. Vast masses of it have toppled into the sea, and the black ruins project from the deep in a hundred shapes of menace. Sometimes our boat glides between a double line of these; or takes a zigzag course through labyrinths of reef channels.

So swiftly and deftly is the little craft impelled to right and left, that one could almost believe it sees its own way and moves by its own intelligence. And again we pass by extraordinary islets of prismatic rock whose sides, just below the waterline, are heavily mossed with seaweed. The polygonal masses composing these shapes are called by the fishermen 'tortoise shell stones.' There is a legend that once Ōkuninushi no Kami, to try his strength, came here, and, lifting up one of these masses of basalt, flung it across the sea to Mount Sanbe. At its foot mount the mighty rock can still be seen, it is alleged, even to this day.

More and more bare and rugged and ghastly the coast becomes as we journey on, and the sunken ledges more numerous, and the protruding rocks more dangerous, splinters of strata piercing the sea-surface from a depth of thirty fathoms. Then suddenly our boat makes a dash for the black cliff, and shoots into a tremendous cleft of it—an earthquake fissure with sides lofty and perpendicular as the walls of a canyon—and lo! there is daylight ahead. This is a miniature strait, a shortcut to the bay. We glide through it in ten minutes, reach open water again, and Hinomisaki is before us—a semicircle of houses clustering about a bay curve, with an opening in their centre, prefaced by a *torii*.

Of all bays I have ever seen, this is the most extraordinary. Imagine an enormous seacliff torn out and broken down level with the sea, so as to leave a great scoop-shaped hollow in the land, with one original fragment of the ancient cliff still standing in the middle of the gap—a monstrous square tower of rock, bearing trees on its summit. And a thousand yards out from the shore rises another colossal rock, fully one hundred feet high. This is known by the name of Fumishima or Okyogashima, and the temple of the sun goddess, which we are now about to see, formerly stood on that islet. The same appalling forces which formed the bay of Hinomisaki doubtless also detached the gigantic mass of Fumishima from this iron coast.

We land at the right end of the bay. Here also there is no beach; the water is black-deep close to the shore, which slopes up rapidly. As we mount the slope, an extraordinary spectacle is before us. On thousands and thousands of bamboo frames—shaped somewhat like our clothes horses—dangle countless pale yellowish things, the nature of which I cannot discern at first. A closer inspection reveals the mystery. Millions of cuttlefish drying in the sun! I could never have believed that so many cuttlefish existed in these waters. And there is scarcely any variation in the dimensions of them: out of ten thousand there is not the difference of half an inch in length.

Hinomisaki-jinja

The great *torii* which forms the sea-gate of Hinomisaki is of white granite, and severely beautiful. Through it we pass up the main street of the village—surprisingly wide for about a thousand yards, after which it narrows into a common highway that slopes up a wooded hill and disappears under the shadow of trees. On the right, as you enter the street, is a long vision of grey wooden houses with awnings and balconies—little shops, little two-story dwellings of fishermen—and ranging away in front of these other hosts of bamboo frames from which other millions of freshly caught cuttlefish are hanging. On the other side of the street rises a cyclopean retaining wall, massive as the wall of a *daimyō*'s castle, and topped by a lofty wooden parapet pierced with gates. Above it tower the roofs of majestic buildings, whose architecture strongly resembles that of the structures of the Izumo Ōyashiro; behind all appears a beautiful green background of hills. This is the Hinomisaki-*jinja*, the Hinomisaki shrine. But one must walk some considerable distance up the road to reach the main entrance of the court, which is at the farther end of the inclosure, and is approached by an imposing broad flight of granite steps.

The great court is a surprise. It is almost as deep as the outer court of the Izumo Ōyashiro, though not nearly so wide, and a paved cloister forms two sides of it. From the court gate a broad paved walk leads to the *haiden* and *shamusho* at the opposite end of the court—spacious and dignified structures above whose roofs appears the quaint and massive gable of the main temple, with its fantastic cross-beams. This temple, standing with its back to the sea, is the shrine of the goddess of the sun. On the right side of the main court, as you enter, another broad flight of steps leads up to a loftier court, where another fine group of Shintō buildings stands—a *haiden* and a *miya*, but these are much smaller, like miniatures of those below. Their woodwork also appears to be quite new. The upper *miya* is the shrine of the god Susanoo, brother of Amaterasu Ōmikami.

Hinomisaki-Jinja

To me the great marvel of the Hinomisaki-*jinja* is that structures so vast, and so costly to maintain, can exist in a mere fishing hamlet, in an obscure nook of the most desolate coast of Japan. Assuredly the contributions of peasant pilgrims alone could not suffice to pay the salary of a single *kannushi*, for Hinomisaki, unlike the Izumo Ōyashiro, is not a place possible to visit in all weathers. My friend confirms me in this opinion, but I learn from him that the temples have three large sources of revenue. They are partly supported by the government; they receive yearly large gifts of money from pious merchants; and the revenues from lands attached to them also represent a considerable sum. Certainly a great amount of money must have been very recently expended here, for the smaller of the two *miya* seems to have just been wholly rebuilt. The beautiful joinery is all white with freshness, and even the carpenters' odorous chips have not yet been all removed.

At the *shamusho* we make the acquaintance of the *guji* of Hinomisaki, a noble-looking man in the prime of life, with one of those fine aquiline faces rarely to be met with except among the high aristocracy of Japan. He wears a heavy black moustache, which gives him, in spite of his priestly robes, the look of a retired army officer. We are kindly permitted by him to visit the sacred shrines, and a *kannushi* is detailed to conduct us through the buildings.

Something resembling the severe simplicity of the Izumo Ōyashiro was what I expected to see. But this shrine of the goddess of the sun is a spectacle of such splendour that for the first moment I almost doubt whether I am really in a Shintō temple. In very truth there is nothing of pure Shintō here. These shrines belong to the famous period of Ryōbu Shintō, when the ancient faith, interpenetrated and allied with Buddhism, adopted the ceremonial magnificence and the marvellous decorative art of the alien creed. Since visiting the great Buddhist shrines of the capital, I have seen no temple interior to be compared with this. Daintily beautiful as a casket is the chamber of the shrine. All its elaborated woodwork is lacquered in scarlet and gold; the altar piece is a delight of carving and colour; the ceiling swarms with dreams of clouds and dragons. And yet the exquisite taste of the decorators—buried, doubtless, five hundred years ago—has so justly proportioned the decoration to the needs of surface, so admirably blended the colours, that there is no gaudiness, no glare, only an opulent repose.

This shrine is surrounded by a light outer gallery which is not visible from the lower court, and from this gallery one can study some remarkable friezes occupying the spaces above the doorways and below the eaves—

friezes surrounding the walls of the *miya*. These, although exposed for many centuries to the terrific weather of the western coast, still remain masterpieces of quaint carving. There are apes and hares peeping through wonderfully chiselled leaves, and doves and demons, and dragons writhing in storms. And while looking up at these, my eye is attracted by a peculiar velvety appearance of the woodwork forming the immense projecting eaves of the roof. Under the tiling it is more than a foot thick. By standing on tiptoe I can touch it, and I discover that it is even more velvety to the touch than to the sight. Further examination reveals that this colossal roofing is not solid timber, only the beams are solid. The enormous pieces they support are formed of countless broad slices thin as the thinnest shingles, superimposed and cemented together into one solid-seeming mass. I am told that this composite woodwork is more enduring than any hewn timber could be. The edges, where exposed to wind and sun, feel to the touch just like the edges of the leaves of some huge thumb-worn volume; their stained velvety yellowish aspect so perfectly mocks the appearance of a book, that while trying to separate them a little with my fingers, I find myself involuntarily peering for a running-title and the number of a folio!

We then visit the smaller temple. The interior of the sacred chamber is equally rich in lacquered decoration and gilding, and below the *miya* itself there are strange paintings of weird foxes—foxes wandering in the foreground of a mountain landscape. But here the colours have been damaged somewhat by time; the paintings have a faded look. Without the shrine are other wonderful carvings, doubtless executed by the same chisel that created the friezes of the larger temple.

I learn that only the shrine chambers of both temples are very old; all the rest has been more than once rebuilt. The entire structure of the smaller temple and its *haiden*, with the exception of the shrine room, has just been rebuilt—in fact, the work is not yet quite done—so that the emblem of the deity is not at present in the sanctuary. The shrines proper are never repaired, but simply reinclosed in the new buildings when reconstruction becomes a necessity. To repair them or restore them today would be impossible: the art that created them is dead. But so excellent their material and its lacquer envelope that they have suffered little in the lapse of many centuries from the attacks of time.

One more surprise awaits me—the homestead of the high pontiff, who most kindly invites us to dine with him; which hospitality is all the more acceptable from the fact that there is no hotel in Hinomisaki, but only a *kichinyado* for pilgrims. The ancestral residence of the high pontiffs of Hinomisaki occupies, with the beautiful gardens about it, a space fully equal to that of the great temple courts themselves. Like most of the old-fashioned homes of the nobility and of the samurai, it is but one story high—an immense elevated cottage, one might call it. But the apartments are lofty, spacious, and very handsome—and there is a room of one hundred tatami. A very nice little repast, with abundance of good wine, is served up to us, and I shall always remember one curious dish, which I at first mistake for spinach. It is seaweed, deliciously prepared—not the common edible seaweed, but a rare sort, fine like moss.

After bidding farewell to our generous host, we take an uphill stroll to the farther end of the village. We leave the cuttlefish behind, but before us the greater part of the road is covered with matting, upon which indigo is drying in the sun. The village terminates abruptly at the top of the hill, where there is another grand granite *torii*—a structure so ponderous that it is almost as difficult to imagine how it was ever brought up the hill as to understand the methods of the builders of Stonehenge. From this *torii* the road descends to the pretty little seaport of Uryo, on the other side of the cape, for Hinomisaki is situated on one side of a great promontory, as its name implies—a mountain range projecting into the Sea of Japan.

The Karō's Daughter

The family of the *guji* of Hinomisaki is one of the oldest of the *kazoku* or noble families of Izumo, and the daughters are still addressed by the antique title of Princess—*o*-Hime-*san*. The ancient official designation of the pontiff himself was *kengyō*, as that of the Izumo Ōyashiro pontiff was *kokuzō*, and the families of the Hinomisaki and Izumo Ōyashiro *guji* are closely related.

There is one touching and terrible tradition in the long history of the *kengyō* of Hinomisaki, which throws a strange light on the social condition of this province in feudal days.

Seven generations ago, a Matsudaira, *daimyō* of Izumo, made with great pomp his first official visit to the temples of Hinomisaki, and was nobly entertained by the *kengyō*—doubtless in the same chamber of a hundred mats which we today were privileged to see. According to custom, the young wife of the host waited on the regal visitor, and served him with dainties and with wine. She was singularly beautiful, and her beauty, unfortunately, bewitched the *daimyō*. With kingly insolence he demanded that she should leave her husband and become his concubine. Although astounded and terrified, she answered bravely, like the true daughter of a samurai, that she was a loving wife and mother, and that, sooner than desert her husband and her child, she would put an end to her life with her own hand. The great Lord of Izumo sullenly departed without further speech, leaving the little household plunged in uttermost grief and anxiety, for it was too well known that the prince would suffer no obstacle to remain in the way of his lust or his hate.

The anxiety, indeed, proved to be well founded. Scarcely had the *daimyō* returned to his domains when he began to devise means for the ruin of the *kengyō*. Soon afterward, the latter was suddenly and forcibly separated from his family, hastily tried for some imaginary offence, and banished to the islands of Oki. Some say the ship on which he sailed went down at sea with all on board. Others say that he was conveyed to Oki, but only to die there of misery and cold. At all events, the old Izumo records state that, in the year corresponding to A.D. 1661 'the *kengyō* Takatoshi died in the land of Oki.'

On receiving news of the *kengyō*'s death, Matsudaira scarcely concealed his exultation. The object of his passion was the daughter of his own *karō*, or minister, one of the noblest samurai of Matsue, by name Kamiya. Kamiya was at once summoned before the *daimyō*, who said to him, 'Thy daughter's husband being dead, there exists no longer any reason that she should not enter into my household. Do thou bring her hither.' The *karō* touched the floor with his forehead, and departed on his errand.

Upon the following day he reentered the prince's apartment, and, performing the customary prostration, announced that his lord's commands had been obeyed—that the victim had arrived.

Smiling for pleasure, the Matsudaira ordered that she should be brought at once into his presence. The *karō* prostrated himself, retired and presently returning, placed before his master a *kubioke* (head rest) on which lay the freshly severed head of a beautiful woman—the head of the young wife of the dead *kengyō*—with the simple utterance:

'This is my daughter.'

Dead by her own brave will—but never dishonoured.

Seven generations have been buried since the Matsudaira strove to appease his remorse by the building of temples and the erection of monuments to the memory of his victim. His own race died with him: those who now bear the illustrious name of that long line of *daimyōs* are not of the same blood, and the grim ruin of his castle, devoured by vegetation, is tenanted only by lizards and bats. But the Kamiya family endures, no longer wealthy, as in feudal times, but still highly honoured in their native city. And each high pontiff of Hinomisakei chooses always his bride from among the daughters of that valiant race.

It should be noted that the *kengyō* of the above tradition was enshrined by Matsudaira in the temple of Shiyekei-*jinja*, at Oyama, near Matsue. This *miya* was built for an atonement, and the people still pray to the spirit of the *kengyō*. Near this temple formerly stood a very popular theatre, also erected by the *daimyō* in his earnest desire to appease the soul of his victim, for he had heard that the *kengyō* was very fond of theatrical performances. The temple is still in excellent preservation, but the theatre has long since disappeared, and its site is occupied by a farmer's vegetable garden.

Shinjū

Innen

Sometimes they simply put their arms round each other, and lie down together on the iron rails, just in front of an express train. (They cannot do it in Izumo because there are no railroads there yet.) Sometimes they make a little banquet for themselves, write very strange letters to parents and friends, mix something bitter with their rice-wine, and go to sleep for ever. Sometimes they select a more ancient and more honoured method: the lover first slays his beloved with a single sword stroke, and then pierces his own throat. Sometimes with the girl's long crape-silk under girdle (*koshiobi*) they bind themselves fast together, face to face, and so embracing leap into some deep lake or stream. Many are the modes by which they make their way to the Meido, when tortured by that world-old sorrow about which Schopenhauer wrote so marvellous a theory.

Their own theory is much simpler.

None love life more than the Japanese; none fear death less. Of a future world they have no dread; they regret to leave this one only because it seems to them a world of beauty and of happiness, but the mystery of the future, so long oppressive to Western minds, causes them little concern. As for the young lovers of whom I speak, they have a strange faith that effaces mysteries for them. They turn to the darkness with infinite trust. If they are too unhappy to endure existence, the fault is not another's, nor yet the world's; it is their own; it is *innen*, the result of errors in a previous life. If they can never hope to be united in this world, it is only because in some former birth they broke their promise to wed, or were otherwise cruel to each other. All this is not heterodox. But they believe likewise that by dying together they will find themselves at once united in another world, though Buddhism proclaims that self-destruction is a deadly sin. Now this idea of winning union through death is incalculably older than the faith of Shaka, but it has somehow borrowed in modern time from Buddhism a particular ecstatic colouring, a mystical glow. *Hasu no hana no ue ni oite mattan.* On the lotus-blossoms of paradise they shall rest together. Buddhism teaches of transmigrations countless, prolonged through millions of millions of years, before the soul can acquire the infinite vision, the infinite memory, and melt into the bliss of Nirvana, as a white cloud melts into the summer 's blue. But these suffering ones think never of Nirvana; love's union, their supremest wish, may be reached, they fancy, through the pang of a single death. The fancies of all, indeed—as their poor letters show—are not the same. Some think themselves about to enter Amida's paradise of light; some see in their visional hope the *saki no yo* only, the future rebirth, when beloved shall meet beloved again, in the all-joyous freshness of another youth. While the idea of many, indeed of the majority, is vaguer far—only a shadowy drifting together through vapoury silences, as in the faint bliss of dreams.

They always pray to be buried together. Often this prayer is refused by the parents or the guardians, and the people deem this refusal a cruel thing, for 'tis believed that those who die for love of each other will find no rest, if denied the same tomb. But when the prayer is granted the ceremony of burial is beautiful and touching. From the two homes the two funeral processions issue to meet in the temple court, by light of lanterns. There, after the recitation of the *kyō* and the accustomed impressive ceremonies, the chief priest utters an address to the souls of the dead. Compassionately he speaks of the error and the sin, of the youth of the victims, brief and comely as the flowers that blossom and fall in the first burst of spring. He speaks of the illusion—*mayoi*—that so wrought upon them; he recites the warning of the Teacher. But sometimes he will even predict the future reunion of the lovers in some happier and higher life, re-echoing the popular heart-thought with a simple eloquence that makes his hearers weep. Then the two processions form into one, which takes its way to the cemetery where the grave has already been prepared. The two coffins are lowered together, so that their sides touch as they rest at the bottom of the excavation. Then the *yama no mono* (mountain folk) remove the planks that separate the pair—making the two coffins into one. Above the reunited dead the earth is heaped, and a *haka*, bearing in chiselled letters the story of their fate. Perhaps a little poem is placed above the mingling of their dust.

Meido

These suicides of lovers are termed *jōshi* or *shinjū*—(both written with the same Chinese characters)—signifying 'heart-death,' 'passion death,' or 'love death.' They most commonly occur, in the case of women, among the *jorō* (courtesan) class, but occasionally also among young girls of a more respectable class. There is a fatalistic belief that if one *shinjū* occurs among the inmates of a *jorōya*, two more are sure to follow. Doubtless the belief itself is the cause that cases of *shinjū* do commonly occur in series of three.

The poor girls who voluntarily sell themselves to a life of shame for the sake of their families in time of uttermost distress do not, in Japan (except, perhaps, in those open ports where European vice and brutality have become demoralising influences), ever reach that depth of degradation to which their Western sisters descend. Many indeed retain, through all the period of their terrible servitude, a refinement of manner, a delicacy of sentiment, and a natural modesty that seem, under such conditions, as extraordinary as they are touching.

Only yesterday a case of *shinjū* startled this quiet city. The servant of a physician in the street called Nadamachi, entering the chamber of his master's son a little after sunrise, found the young man lying dead with a dead girl in his arms. The son had been disinherited. The girl was a *jorō*. Last night they were buried, but not together, for the father was not less angered than grieved that such a thing should have been.

Her name was Kane. She was remarkably pretty and very gentle, and from all accounts it would seem that her master had treated her with a kindness unusual in men of his infamous class. She had sold herself for the sake of her mother and a child sister. The father was dead, and they had lost everything. She was then seventeen. She had been in the house scarcely a year when she met the youth. They fell seriously in love with each other at once. Nothing more terrible could have befallen them, for they could never hope to become man and wife. The young man, though still allowed the privileges of a son, had been disinherited in favour of an adopted brother of steadier habits. The unhappy pair spent all they had for the privilege of seeing each other: she sold even her dresses to pay for it. Then for the last time they met by stealth, late at night, in the physician's house, drank death, and laid down to sleep for ever.

I saw the funeral procession of the girl winding its way by the light of paper lanterns—the wan dead glow that is like a shimmer of phosphorescence—to the street of the temples, followed by a long train of women, white-hooded, white-robed, white-girdled, passing all soundlessly—a troop of ghosts.

So through blackness to the Meido the white shapes flit—the eternal procession of souls—in painted Buddhist dreams of the underworld.

Love Song

My friend who writes for the *Sanin Shimbun*, which tomorrow will print the whole sad story, tells me that compassionate folk have already decked the new-made graves with flowers and with sprays of *shikimi*. Then drawing from a long native envelope a long, light, thin roll of paper covered with beautiful Japanese writing, and unfolding it before me, he adds:—'She left this letter to the keeper of the house in which she lived: it has been given to us for publication. It is very prettily written. But I cannot translate it well, for it is written in woman's language. The language of letters written by women is not the same as that of letters written by men. Women use particular words and expressions. For instance, in men's language "I" is *watakushi*, or *ware*, or *yo*, or *boku*, according to rank or circumstance, but in the language of woman, it is *warawa*. And women's language is very soft and gentle, and I do not think it is possible to translate such softness and amiability of words into any other language. So I can only give you an imperfect idea of the letter.'

And he interprets, slowly, thus:

I leave this letter:

As you know, from last spring I began to love Tashiro-San, and he also fell in love with me. And now, alas!—the influence of our relation in some previous birth having come upon us—and the promise we made each other in that former life to become wife and husband having been broken—even today I must travel to the Meido.

You not only treated me very kindly, though you found me so stupid and without influence, but you likewise aided in many ways for my worthless sake my mother and sister. And now, since I have not been able to repay you even the one myriadth part of that kindness and pity in which you enveloped me—pity great as the mountains and the sea—it would not be without just reason that you should hate me as a great criminal.

But though I doubt not this which I am about to do will seem a wicked folly, I am forced to it by conditions and by my own heart. Wherefore I still may pray you to pardon my past faults. And though I go to the Meido, never shall I forget your mercy to me—great as the mountains and the sea. From under the shadow of the grasses, I shall still try to recompense you—to send back my gratitude to you and to your house. Again, with all my heart I pray you: do not be angry with me.

Many more things I would like to write. But now my heart is not a heart, and I must quickly go. And so I shall lay down my writing-brush.

It is written so clumsily, this.

Kane thrice prostrates herself before you.

From Kane
To—Sama

'Well, it is a characteristic *shinjū* letter,' my friend comments, after a moment's silence, replacing the frail white paper in its envelope. 'So I thought it would interest you. And now, although it is growing dark, I am going to the cemetery to see what has been done at the grave. Would you like to come with me?'

We take our way over the long white bridge, up the shadowy Street of the Temples, toward the ancient *hakaba* of the Myōko-ji—and the darkness grows as we walk. A thin moon hangs just above the roofs of the great temples.

Suddenly a distant voice, sonorous and sweet—a man's voice—breaks into song under the starred night: a song full of strange charm and tones like warblings—those Japanese tones of popular emotion that seem to have been learned from the songs of birds. Some happy workman returning home. So clear the thin frosty air that each syllable quivers to us, but I cannot understand the words: *Saite yuke to ya, ano ya o saite, yukeba chikayoru nushi no soba.*

'What is that?' I ask my friend.

He answers, 'A love song. "Go forward, straight forward that way, to the house that you see before you—the nearer you go, the nearer to her you shal be."'

Yaegaki-jinja

The Manifold Fence

To Yaegaki-*jinja*, which is in the village of Sakusa in Iu, in the land of Izumo, all youths and maidens go who are in love, and who can make the pilgrimage. For in the temple of Yaegaki at Sakusa, Takehaya Susanoo no Mikoto and his wife Inada-*hime* and their son Sakusa no Mikoto are enshrined. And these are the deities of wedlock and of love—and they set the solitary in families—and by their doing are destinies coupled even from the hour of birth. Wherefore one should suppose that to make pilgrimage to their temple to pray about things long since irrevocably settled were simple waste of time. But in what land did ever religious practice and theology agree? Scholiasts and priests create or promulgate doctrine and dogma, but the good people always insist on making the gods according to their own heart—and these are by far the better class of gods. Moreover, the history of Susanoo the impetuous male deity, does not indicate that destiny had anything to do with his particular case: he fell in love with the wondrous Inada at first sight—as it is written in the *Kojiki*:

> Then Takehaya Susanoo no Mikoto descended to a place called *Torikami* at the headwaters of the River Hi in the land of Izumo. At this time a chopstick came floating down the stream. So Takehaya Susanoo no Mikoto, thinking that there must be people at the headwaters of the river, went up it in quest of them.
>
> And he came upon an old man and an old woman who had a young girl between them, and were weeping. Then he asked: "Who are you?"

The old man replied, saying: "I am an earthly deity, son of the deity Ōyamatsumi no Kami. I am called by the name of Ashinazuchi; my wife is called by the name of Tenazuchi; and my daughter is called by the name of Kushi Inada-*hime*."

Again he asked: "What is the cause of your crying?"

The old man answered, saying: "I had originally eight young daughters. But the eight-forked serpent of Koshi has come every year, and devoured one, and it is now its time to come, wherefore we weep."

Then he asked him: "What is its form like?"

The old man answered, saying: "Its eyes are like *akaka-gachi*; it has one body with eight heads and eight tails. Moreover, on its body grow moss and *sugi* and *hinoki* trees. Its length extends over eight valleys and eight hills, and if one look at its belly, it is all constantly bloody and inflamed."

Then Takehaya Susanoo no Mikoto said to the old man: "If this be thy daughter, wilt thou offer her to me?"

He replied: "With reverence, but I know not thine august name." Then he replied, saying: "I am elder brother to Amaterasu Ōmikami. So now I have descended from heaven."

Then the Deities Ashinazuchi and Tenazuchi said: "If that be so, with reverence will we offer her to thee."

Takehaya Susanoo no Mikoto, taking and changing the young girl into a close-toothed comb, which he stuck into his august hair, said to the Deities Ashinazuchi and Tenazuchi: "Distil some eightfold refined liquor. Also make a fence round about; in that fence make eight gates; at each gate tie a platform; on each platform put a liquor-vat; and into each vat pour the eightfold refined liquor, and wait."

As they waited after having prepared everything in accordance with his bidding, the eight-forked serpent came and put a head into each vat and drank the liquor. Intoxicated, all the heads lay down and slept. Then Takehaya Susanoo no Mikoto drew the ten-grasp sabre that was augustly girded upon him, and cut the serpent in pieces, so that the River Hi flowed on changed into a river of blood.

Then Takehaya Susanoo no Mikoto sought in the Land of Izumo where he might build a palace.

When this great Deity built the palace, clouds rose up thence. Then he made an august song:

> *Ya kumo tatsu:*
> *Izumo yaegaki,*
> *Tsumagomi ni yahegaki tsukuru,*
> *Sono yaegaki o!*

> Eight clouds arise.
> The manifold fence of Izumo
> makes a manifold fence for the spouses to retire within.
> Oh! that manifold fence.

The temple of Yaegaki takes its name from the words of the august song Yaegaki, and therefore signifies the Temple of the Manifold Fence. Ancient commentators on the sacred books have said that the name of Izumo (which is now Izumo), as signifying the Land of the Issuing of Clouds, was also taken from that song of the god.

Wagtails

Sakusa, the hamlet where the Yaegaki-*jinja* stands, is scarcely more than one *ri* south from Matsue. But to go there one must follow tortuous paths too rough and steep for a *kuruma*. Of three ways, the longest and roughest happens to be the most interesting. It slopes up and down through bamboo groves and primitive woods, and again serpentines through fields of rice and barley, and plantations of indigo and of ginseng, where the scenery is always beautiful or odd.

Tere are many famed Shintō temples to be visited on the road, such as Takeuchi-*jinja*, dedicated to the venerable minister of Empress Jingo, Take-uchi, to whom men now pray for health and for length of years; and Okusa no Miya, or Rokusho-*jinja*, of the five greatest shrines in Izumo; and Manai-*jinja*, sacred to Izanagi, the Mother of Gods, where strange pictures may be obtained of the Parents of the World; and Oba no Miya, where Izanami is enshrined, also called Kamoshi-*jinja*, which means, 'The Soul of the God.'

At the temple of the Soul of the God, where the sacred fire drill used to be delivered each year with solemn rites to the great governor of the Izumo Ōyashiro, there are curious things to be seen—a colossal grain of rice, more than an inch long, preserved from that period of the *kamiyo* when the rice grew tall as the tallest tree and bore grains worthy of the gods; and a cauldron of iron in which the peasants say that the first governor came down from heaven; and a cyclopean *tōrō* formed of rocks so huge that one cannot imagine how they were ever balanced upon each other; and the Musical Stones of Oba, which chime like bells when smitten. There is a tradition that these cannot be carried away beyond a certain distance, for 'tis recorded that when a *daimyō* named Matsudaira ordered one of them to be conveyed to his castle at Matsue, the stone made itself so heavy that a thousand men could not move it farther than the Ohashi bridge. So it was abandoned before the bridge, and it lies there imbedded in the soil even to this day.

All about Oba you may see many *sekirei* or wagtails—birds sacred to Izanami and Izanagi—for a legend says that from the *sekirei* the gods first learned the art of love. And none, not even the most avaricious farmer, ever hurts or terrifies these birds. So that they do not fear the people of Oba, nor the scarecrows in the fields.

The God of Scarecrows is Sukuna Bikona no Kami.

Tama-Tsubaki

The path to Sakusa, for the last mile of the journey, at least, is extremely narrow, and has been paved by piety with large flat rocks laid on the soil at intervals of about a foot, like an interminable line of stepping-stones. You cannot walk between them nor beside them, and you soon tire of walking on them, but they have the merit of indicating the way, a matter of no small importance where fifty rice field paths branch off from your own at all bewildering angles. After having been safely guided by these stepping-stones through all kinds of labyrinths in rice valleys and bamboo groves, one feels grateful to the peasantry for that clue-line of rocks. There are some quaint little shrines in the groves along this path—shrines with curious carvings of dragons and of lion-heads and flowing water—all wrought ages ago in good *keyaki* wood, which has become the colour of stone. But the eyes of the dragons and the lions have been stolen because they were made of fine crystal quartz, and there was none to guard them, and because neither the laws nor the gods are quite so much feared now as they were before the period of Meiji.

Sakusa is a very small cluster of farmers' cottages before a temple at the verge of a wood—the temple of Yaegaki. The stepping-stones of the path vanish into the pavement of the court, just before its lofty unpainted wooden *torii* between the *torii* and the inner court, entered by a Chinese gate, some grand old trees are growing, and there are queer monuments to see. On either side of the great gateway is a shrine compartment, inclosed by heavy wooden gratings on two sides, and in these compartments are two grim figures in complete armour, with bows in their hands and quivers of arrows on their backs—the *zuijin*, or ghostly retainers of the gods, and guardians of the gate. Before nearly all the Shintō temples of Izumo, except the Izumo Ōyashiro, these *zuijin* keep grim watch. They are probably of Buddhist origin, but they have acquired a Shintō history and Shintō names. Originally, I am told, there was but one *zuijin-kami*, whose name was Toyokushi Iwamato no Mikoto. But at a certain period both the god and his name were cut in two—perhaps for decorative purposes. And now he who sits on the left is called Toyo Iwamato no Mikoto, and his companion on the right, Kushi Iwamato no Mikoto.

Before the gate, on the left side, there is a stone monument on which is graven, in Chinese characters, a *hokku*, the first seventeen syllable line of a *renga*, composed by Chōun:

> Ko-ka-ra-shi-ya
> Ka-mi-no-mi-yu-ki-no
> Ya-ma-no-a-to.

My companion translates the characters thus:

> Where high heap the dead leaves,
> there is the holy place on the hills,
> where dwell the gods.

Nearby are stone lanterns and stone lions, and another monument—a great five-cornered slab set up and chiselled—bearing the names in Chinese characters of the Ji-jin, or Earth-Gods—the Deities who protect the soil: Uga no Mitama no Mikoto (whose name signifies the August Spirit of Food), Amaterasu Ōmikami, Ona Muji no Kami, Kakiyasuhime no Kami, Sukuna Hikona no Kami (who is the Scarecrow God). And the figure of a fox in stone sits before the Name of the August Spirit of Food.

The *miya* or Shintō temple itself is quite small—smaller than most of the temples in the neighbourhood, and dingy, and begrimed with age. Yet, next to the Izumo Ōyashiro, this is the most famous of Izumo shrines. The main shrine, dedicated to Susanoo and Inada-hime and their son, whose name is the name of the hamlet of Sakusa, is flanked by various lesser shrines to left and right. In one of these smaller *miya* the spirit of Ashinazuchi, father of Inada-hime, is supposed to dwell, and in another that of Tenazuchi, the mother of Inada-*hime*. There is also a small shrine of the goddess of the sun. But these shrines have no curious features. The main temple offers, on the other hand, some displays of rarest interest.

To the grey weather-worn gratings of the doors of the shrine hundreds and hundreds of strips of soft white paper have been tied in knots: there is nothing written on them, although each represents a heart's wish and a fervent prayer. No prayers, indeed, are so fervent as those of love. Also there are suspended many little sections of bamboo, cut just below joints so as to form water receptacles: these are tied together in pairs with a small straw cord which also serves to hang them up. They contain offerings of sea-water carried here from no small distance. And mingling with the white confusion of knotted papers there dangle from the gratings many tresses of girls' hair—love-sacrifices (*gan-hodoki*)—and numerous offerings of seaweed, so filamentary and so sun-blackened that at some little distance it would not be easy to distinguish them from long shorn tresses. And all the woodwork of the doors and the gratings, both beneath and between the offerings, is covered with a speckling of characters graven or written, which are names of pilgrims.

And my companion reads aloud the well-remembered name of—Akira!

If one dare judge the efficacy of prayer to these kind gods of Shintō from the testimony of their worshippers, I should certainly say that Akira has good reason to hope. Planted in the soil, all round the edge of the foundations of the shrine, are multitudes of tiny paper flags of curious shape (*nobori*), pasted on splinters of bamboo. Each of these little white things is a banner of victory, and a lover's witness of gratitude. A pilgrim whose prayer has been heard usually plants a single *nobori* as a token. Sometimes you may see *nobori* of five colours (*goshiki*)—black, yellow, red, blue, and white—of which one hundred or one thousand have been planted by one person. But this is done only in pursuance of some very special vow. You will find such little flags stuck into the ground about nearly all the great Shintō temples of Izumo. At the Izumo Ōyashiro they cannot even be counted—any more than the flakes of a snowstorm.

And here is something else that you will find at most of the famous *miya* in Izumo—a box of little bamboo sticks, fastened to a post before the doors. If you were to count the sticks, you would find their number to be exactly one thousand. They are counters for pilgrims who make a vow to the gods to perform a *sendo-mairi*. To perform a *sendo-mairi* means to visit the temple one thousand times. This, however, is so hard to do that busy pious men make a sort of compromise with the gods, thus: they walk from the shrine one foot beyond the gate, and back again to the shrine, one thousand times—all in one day, keeping count with the little splints of bamboo.

There is one more famous thing to be seen before visiting the holy grove behind the temple, and that is the Sacred Tama-tsubaki, or Precious Camellia of Yaegaki. It stands on a little knoll, fortified by a projection wall, in a rice field near the house of the priest. A fence has been built around it, and votive lamps of stone placed before it. It is of vast age, and has two heads and two feet, but the twin trunks grow together at the middle. Its unique shape, and the quality of longevity it is believed to possess, cause it to be revered as a symbol of undying wedded love, and as tenanted by the *kami* who hearken to lovers' prayers—*en-musubi no kami*.

There is a strange superstition, about *tsubaki* trees, and this sacred tree of Yaegaki, in the opinion of some folk, is a rare exception to the general ghastliness of its species. For *tsubaki* trees are goblin trees, they say, and walk about at night. There was one in the garden of a Matsue samurai which did this so much that it had to be cut down. Then it writhed its arms and groaned, and blood spurted at every stroke of the axe.

Hina

At the spacious residence of the *kannushi* some very curious *ofuda* and *o-mamori*—*the* holy talismans and charms of Yaegaki—are sold, together with pictures representing Takehaya Susanoo no Mikoto and his bride Inada-*hime* surrounded by the manifold fence of clouds. On the pictures is also printed the august song whence the temple derives its name of Yaegaki-*jinja*—*Yakumo tatsu Izumo yaegaki*.

Of the *o-mamori* there is quite a variety, but by far the most interesting is that labelled, *Izumo Yaegaki-jinja en-musubi onhina* (August wedlock-producing *hina* of the temple of Yaegaki of Izumo). This oblong, folded paper, with Chinese characters and the temple seal upon it, is purchased only by those in love, and is believed to assure nothing more than the desired union. Within the paper are two of the smallest conceivable doll-figures (*hina*), representing a married couple in antique costume—the tiny wife folded to the breast of the tiny husband by one long-sleeved arm. It is the duty of whoever purchases this *mamori* to return it to the temple if he or she succeed in marrying the person beloved. As already stated, the charm is not supposed to assure anything more than the union: it cannot be accounted responsible for any consequences thereof. He who desires perpetual love must purchase another *mamori* labelled, *Renritama tsubaki aikyō goki to on-mamori* (August amulet of august prayer-for-kindling-love of the jewel-precious *tsubaki* tree of union). This charm should maintain at constant temperature the warmth of affection; it contains only a leaf of the singular double-bodied camellia tree before mentioned. There are also small amulets for exciting love, and amulets for the expelling of diseases, but these have no special characteristics worth dwelling on.

Then we take our way to the sacred grove—the Okuno-in, or Mystic Shades of Yaegaki.

Grove

This ancient grove—so dense that when you first pass into its shadows out of the sun all seems black—is composed of colossal cedars and pines, mingled with bamboo, *tsubaki*, and *sakaki*, the sacred and mystic tree of Shintō. The dimness is chiefly made by the huge bamboos. In nearly all sacred groves bamboos are thickly set between the trees, and their feathery foliage, filling every lofty opening between the heavier crests, entirely cuts off the sun. Even in a bamboo grove where no other trees are, there is always a deep twilight.

As the eyes become accustomed to this green gloaming, a pathway outlines itself between the trees—a pathway wholly covered with moss, velvety, soft, and beautifully verdant. In former years, when all pilgrims were required to remove their footgear before entering the sacred grove, this natural carpet was a boon to the weary. The next detail one observes is that the trunks of many of the great trees have been covered with thick rush matting to a height of seven or eight feet, and that holes have been torn through some of the mats. All the giants of the grove are sacred, and the matting was bound about them to prevent pilgrims from stripping off their bark, which is believed to possess miraculous virtues. But many, more zealous than honest, do not hesitate to tear away the matting in order to get at the bark. And the third curious fact which you notice is that the trunks of the great bamboos are covered with ideographs—with the wishes of lovers and the names of girls. There is nothing in the world of vegetation so nice to write a sweetheart's name upon as the polished bark of a bamboo: each letter, however lightly traced at first, enlarges and blackens with the growth of the bark, and never fades away.

The deeply mossed path slopes down to a little pond in the very heart of the grove—a pond famous in the land of Izumo. Here there are many *imori*, or water newts, about five inches long, which have red bellies. Here the shade is deepest, and the stems of the bamboos most thickly tattooed with the names of girls. It is believed that the flesh of the newts in the sacred pond of Yaegaki possesses aphrodisiac qualities, and the body of the creature, reduced to ashes, by burning, was formerly converted into love powders. There is a little Japanese song referring to the practice:

> *Hore-gusuri*
> *koka niwa naika*
> *to imori ni toeba,*
> *yubi o marumete*
> *kore bakari.*

On being asked
if there were any other love charm,
the newt replied,
making a ring with two of his toes, 'Only this.'

The water is very clear, and there are many of these newts to be seen. And it is the custom for lovers to make a little boat of paper, and put into it one *rin*, and set it afloat and watch it. So soon as the paper becomes wet through, and allows the water to enter it, the weight of the copper coin soon sends it to the bottom, where, owing to the purity of the water, it can be still seen distinctly as before. If the newts then approach and touch it, the lovers believe their happiness assured by the will of the gods, but if the newts do not come near it, the omen is evil. One poor little paper boat, I observe, could not sink at all; it simply floated to the inaccessible side of the pond, where the trees rise like a solid wall of trunks from the water's edge, and there became caught in some drooping branches. The lover who launched it must have departed sorrowing at heart.

Close to the pond, near the pathway, there are many camellia bushes, of which the tips of the branches have been tied together, by pairs, with strips of white paper. These are shrubs of presage. The true lover must be able to bend two branches together, and to keep them united by tying a paper tightly about them—all with the fingers of one hand. To do this well is good luck. Nothing is written on the strips of paper.

But there is enough writing on the bamboos to occupy curiosity for many an hour, in spite of the mosquitoes. Most of the names are *yobina*—that is to say, pretty names of women, but there are likewise names of men—*jitsumyō*. Oddly enough, a girl's name and a man's are in no instance written together. To judge by all this ideographic testimony, lovers in Japan—or at least in Izumo—are even more secretive than in our Occident. The enamoured youth never writes his own *jitsumyō* and his sweetheart's *yobina* together, and the family name, or *myōji*, he seldom ventures to inscribe. If he writes his *jitsumyō*, then he contents himself with whispering the *yobina* of his sweetheart to the gods and to the bamboos. If he cuts her *yobina* into the bark, then he substitutes for his own name a mention of his existence and his age only, as in this touching instance:

Takata Toki to
en-musubi negaimasu.
Jūhassai no otoko.

That I may be wedded
to Takaki Toki, I humbly pray.
—A youth of eighteen.'

This lover presumes to write his girl's whole name, but the example, so far as I am able to discover, is unique. Other enamoured ones write only the *yobina* of their bewitchers, and the honourable prefix, 'O,' and the honourable suffix, 'San,' find no place in the familiarity of love. There is no O-Haru-San, O-Kin San, O-Take-San, O-Kiku-San, but there are hosts of Haru, and Kin, and Take, and Kiku.

Girls, of course, never dream of writing their lovers' names. But there are many *geimyō* here, artistic names—names of mischievous *geisha* who worship the Golden Kitten, written by their saucy selves: Rakue and Asa and Wakai, Aikichi and Kotabuki and Kohachi, Kohana and Tamakichi and Katsuko, and Asakichi and Hanakichi and Katsukichi, and Chiyoe and Chiyotsuru. Fortunate Pleasure, Happy Dawn, and Youth (such are their appellations), Blest Love and Length of Days, and Blossom Child and Jewel of Fortune and Child of Luck, and Joyous Sunrise and Flower of Bliss and Glorious Victory, and Life-as-the-Stork's for a Thousand Years. Often shall he curse the day the man who was born who falls in love with Happy Dawn; thrice unlucky the wight bewitched by the Child-of-Luck; woe to him who hopes to cherish the Flower of Bliss; and more than once shall he wish himself dead whose heart is snared by Life-as-the-Stork's for a Thousand Years.

I see that somebody who inscribes his age as twenty-three has become enamoured of young Wakagusa, whose name signifies the tender grass of spring. Now there is but one possible misfortune for you, dear boy, worse than falling in love with Wakagusa—and that is that she should happen to fall in love with you. Because then you would, both of you, write some beautiful letters to your friends, drink death, and pass away in each other's arms, murmuring your trust to rest together on the same lotus flower in paradise, '*Hasu no ha no ue ni oite matsu.*' Nay! Pray the deities rather to dissipate the bewitchment that is upon you:

> *Te ni toruna,*
> *Yahari no ni*
> *oke gengebana.*

> Take it not into your hand:
> the flowers of the *gengebana*
> are fair to view
> only when left all together in the field.

The *gengebana* (also called *renge-so*, and in Izumo *miakobana*) is a herb planted only for fertilizing purposes. Its flowers are extremely small, but so numerous that in their blossoming season miles of fields are coloured by them a beautiful lilaceous blue. A gentleman who wished to marry a *jorō* despite the advice of his friends, was gently chided by them with the above little verse.

And here is a lover's inscription—in English! Who presumes to suppose that the gods know English? Some student, no doubt, who for pure shyness engraved his soul's secret in this foreign tongue of mine—never dreaming that a foreign eye would look upon it. 'I wish you, Haru!' Not once, but four—no, five times!—each time omitting the preposition. Praying—in this ancient grove—in this ancient Land of Izumo—to the most ancient gods in English! Verily, the shyest love presumes much upon the forbearance of the gods. And great indeed must be, either the patience of Takehaya Susanoo no Mikoto, or the rustiness of the ten-grasp sabre that was augustly girded upon him.

Kitsune

Broken Noses

By every shady wayside and in every ancient grove, on almost every hilltop and in the outskirts of every village, you may see, while travelling through the Hondo country, some little Shintō shrine, before which, or at either side of which, are images of seated foxes in stone. Usually there is a pair of these, facing each other. But there may be a dozen, or a score, or several hundred, in which case most of the images are very small. And in more than one of the larger towns you may see in the court of some great *miya* a countless host of stone foxes, of all dimensions, from toy-figures but a few inches high to the colossi whose pedestals tower above your head, all squatting around the temple in tiered ranks of thousands. Such shrines and temples, everybody knows, are dedicated to Inari the God of Rice. After having travelled much in Japan, you will find that whenever you try to recall any country place you have visited, there will appear in some nook or corner of that remembrance a pair of green-and-grey foxes of stone, with broken noses. In my own memories of Japanese travel, these shapes have become de rigueur, as picturesque detail.

In the neighbourhood of the capital and in Tokyo itself—sometimes in the cemeteries—very beautiful idealised figures of foxes may be seen, elegant as greyhounds. They have long green or grey eyes of crystal quartz or some other diaphanous substance, and they create a strong impression as mythological conceptions. But throughout the interior, fox-images are much less artistically fashioned. In Izumo, particularly, such stone-carving has a decidedly primitive appearance. There is an astonishing multiplicity and variety of fox-images in the Province of the Gods—images comical, quaint, grotesque, or monstrous, but, for the most part, very rudely chiselled. I cannot declare them less interesting on that account. The work of the Tōkaidō sculptor copies the conventional artistic notion of light grace and ghostliness. The rustic foxes of Izumo have no grace: they are uncouth, but they betray in countless queer ways the personal fancies of their makers. They are of many moods—whimsical, apathetic, inquisitive, saturnine, jocose, ironical; they watch and snooze and squint and wink and sneer; they wait with lurking smiles; they listen with cocked ears most stealthily, keeping their mouths open or closed. There is an amusing individuality about them all, and an air of knowing mockery about most of them, even those whose noses have been broken off. Moreover, these ancient country foxes have certain natural beauties which their modern Tokyo kindred cannot show. Time has bestowed on them divers speckled coats of beautiful soft colours while they have been sitting on their pedestals, listening to the ebbing and flowing of the centuries and snickering weirdly at mankind. Their backs are clad with finest green velvet of old mosses; their limbs are spotted and their tails are tipped with the dead gold or the dead silver of delicate fungi. And the places they most haunt are the loveliest—high shadowy groves where the uguisu sings in green twilight, above some voiceless shrine with its lamps and its lions of stone so mossed as to seem things born of the soil—like mushrooms.

I found it difficult to understand why, out of every thousand foxes, nine hundred should have broken noses. The main street of the city of Matsue might be paved from end to end with the tips of the noses of mutilated Izumo foxes. A friend answered my expression of wonder in this regard by the simple but suggestive word *kodomo*, which means 'children.'

Inari

Inari the name by which the Fox-God is generally known, signifies 'Load-of-Rice.' But the antique name of the Deity is the August Spirit of Food: he is the Uka no Mitama no Mikoto of the *Kojiki*. In much more recent times only has he borne the name that indicates his connection with the fox-cult, Miketsu no Kami, or the Three-Fox God. Indeed, the conception of the fox as a supernatural being does not seem to have been introduced into Japan before the tenth or eleventh century, and although a shrine of the deity, with statues of foxes, may be found in the court of most of the large Shintō temples, it is worth noting that in all the vast domains of the oldest Shintō shrine in Japan—the Izumo Ōyashiro—you cannot find the image of a fox. And it is only in modern art—the art of Utagawa Toyokuni and others—that Inari is represented as a bearded man riding a white fox, a favourite subject with Japanese artists.

Inari is not worshipped as the God of Rice only. Indeed, there are many Inari just as in antique Greece there were many deities called Hermes, Zeus, Athena, Poseidon—one in the knowledge of the learned, but essentially different in the imagination of the common people. Inari has been multiplied by reason of his different attributes. For instance, Matsue has a Kamiya-*san* no Inari-*san*, who is the God of Coughs and Bad Colds—afflictions extremely common and remarkably severe in the land of Izumo. He has a temple in the Kamachi at which he is worshipped under the vulgar appellation of Kaze no Kami and the politer one of Kamiya-*san* no Inari. And those who are cured of their coughs and colds after having prayed to him, bring to his temple offerings of *tōfu*.

At Oba, likewise, there is a particular Inari, of great fame. Fastened to the wall of his shrine is a large box full of small clay foxes. The pilgrim who has a prayer to make puts one of these little foxes in his sleeve and carries it home. He must keep it, and pay it all due honour, until such time as his petition has been granted. Then he must take it back to the temple, and restore it to the box, and, if he be able, make some small gift to the shrine.

Inari is often worshipped as a healer, and still more frequently as a deity having power to give wealth. (Perhaps because all the wealth of old Japan was reckoned in *koku* of rice.) Therefore his foxes are sometimes represented holding keys in their mouths. And from being the deity who gives wealth, Inari has also become in some localities the special divinity of the *jorō* class. There is, for example, an Inari temple worth visiting in the neighbourhood of the Yoshiwara at Yokohama. It stands in the same court with a temple of Benten, and is more than usually large for a shrine of Inari. You approach it through a succession of *torii*, one behind the other: they are of different heights, diminishing in size as they are placed nearer to the temple, and planted more and more closely in proportion to their smallness. Before each *torii* sit a pair of weird foxes—one to the right and one to the left. The first pair are large as greyhounds; the second two are much smaller, and the sizes of the rest lessen as the dimensions of the *torii* lessen. At the foot of the wooden steps of the temple there is a pair of very graceful foxes of dark grey stone, wearing pieces of red cloth about their necks. On the steps themselves are white wooden foxes—one at each end of each step—each successive pair being smaller than the pair below, and at the threshold of the doorway are two very little foxes, not more than three inches high, sitting on sky-blue pedestals. These have the tips of their tails gilded. Then, if you look into the temple you will see on the left something like a long low table on which are placed thousands of tiny fox-images, even smaller than those in the doorway, having only plain white tails. There is no image of Inari. Indeed, I have never seen an image of Inari as yet in any Inari temple. On the altar appear the usual emblems of Shintō. Before it, just opposite the doorway, stands a sort of lantern, having glass sides and a wooden bottom studded with nailpoints on which to fix votive candles.

And here, from time to time, if you will watch, you will probably see more than one handsome girl, with brightly painted lips and the beautiful antique attire that no maiden or wife may wear, come to the foot of the steps, toss a coin into the money box at the door, and call out, 'O-rōsoku!' which means 'an honourable candle.' Immediately, from an inner chamber, some old man will enter the shrine room with a lighted candle, stick it on a nailpoint in the lantern, and then retire. Such candle offerings are always accompanied by secret prayers for good fortune. But this Inari is worshipped by many besides members of the *jorō* class.

The pieces of coloured cloth about the necks of the foxes are also votive offerings.

Wild Fox

Fox images in Izumo seem to be more numerous than in other provinces, and they are symbols there, so far as the mass of the peasantry is concerned, of something else besides the worship of the rice deity. Indeed, the old conception of the deity of rice fields has been overshadowed and almost effaced among the lowest classes by a weird cult totally foreign to the spirit of pure Shintō—the fox cult. The worship of the retainer has almost replaced the worship of the god. Originally the fox was sacred to Inari only as the tortoise is still sacred to Kompira; the deer to the great deity of Kasuga; the rat to Daikoku; the sea bream to Ebisu; the white serpent to Benten; or the centipede to Bishamon, God of Battles. But in the course of centuries the fox usurped divinity.

The stone images of him are not the only outward evidences of his cult. At the rear of almost every Inari temple you will generally find in the wall of the shrine building, one or two feet above the ground, an aperture about eight inches in diameter and perfectly circular. It is often made so as to be closed at will by a sliding plank. This circular orifice is a fox hole, and if you find one open, and look within, you will probably see offerings of *tōfu* or other food which foxes are supposed to be fond of. You will also, most likely, find grains of rice scattered on some little projection of woodwork below or near the hole, or placed on the edge of the hole itself, and you may see some peasant clap his hands before the hole, utter some little prayer, and swallow a grain or two of that rice in the belief that it will either cure or prevent sickness. Now the fox for whom such a hole is made is an invisible fox, a phantom fox—the fox respectfully referred to by the peasant as *o-kitsune-san*. If he ever suffers himself to become visible, his colour is said to be snowy white.

According to some, there are various kinds of ghostly foxes. According to others, there are two sorts of foxes only, the Inari fox (*o-kitsune-san*) and the wild fox (*nogitsune*). Some people again class foxes into superior and inferior foxes, and allege the existence of four superior sorts—*byakko*, *kokko*, *jenko*, and *reiko*—all of which possess supernatural powers. Others again count only three kinds of foxes—the field fox, the human fox, and the Inari fox. But many confound the field fox or wild fox with the human fox, and others identify the Inari fox with the human fox. One cannot possibly unravel the confusion of these beliefs, especially among the peasantry. The beliefs vary, moreover, in different districts. I have only been able, after a residence of fourteen months in Izumo, where the superstition is especially strong, and marked by certain unique features, to make the following very loose summary of them:

All foxes have supernatural power. There are good and bad foxes. The Inari fox is good, and the bad foxes are afraid of the Inari fox. The worst fox is the *hito-kitsune* (human fox): this is especially the fox of demoniacal possession. It is no larger than a weasel, and somewhat similar in shape, except for its tail, which is like the tail of any other fox. It is rarely seen, keeping itself invisible, except to those to whom it attaches itself. It likes to live in the houses of men, and to be nourished by them, and to the homes where it is well cared for it will bring prosperity. It will take care that the rice fields shall never want for water, nor the cooking pot for rice. But if offended, it will bring misfortune to the household and ruin to the crops.

The wild fox (*nogitsune*) is also bad. It also sometimes takes possession of people, but it is especially a wizard, and prefers to deceive by enchantment. It has the power of assuming any shape and of making itself invisible, but the dog can always see it, so that it is extremely afraid of the dog. Moreover, while assuming another shape, if its shadow fall on water, the water will only reflect the shadow of a fox. The peasantry kill it, but he who kills a fox incurs the risk of being bewitched by that fox's kindred, or even by the *ki*, or ghost of the fox. Still if one eats the flesh of a fox, one cannot be enchanted afterwards. The *nogitsune* also enters houses. Most families having foxes in their houses have only the small kind, or Ninko, but occasionally both kinds will live together under the same roof. Some people say that if the *nogitsune* lives a hundred years it becomes all white, and then takes rank as an Inari fox.

There are curious contradictions involved in these beliefs, and other contradictions will be found in the following pages of this sketch. To define the fox superstition at all is difficult, not only on account of the confusion of ideas on the subject among the believers themselves, but also on account of the variety of elements out of which it has been shapen. Its origin is Chinese, but in Japan it became oddly blended with the worship of a Shintō deity, and again modified and expanded by the Buddhist concepts of thaumaturgy and magic. So far as the common people are concerned, it is perhaps safe to say that they pay devotion to foxes chiefly because they fear them. The peasant still worships what he fears.

Possessed

It is more than doubtful whether the popular notions about different classes of foxes, and about the distinction between the fox of Inari and the fox of possession, were ever much more clearly established than they are now, except in the books of old literati. Indeed, there exists a letter from Hideyoshi to the fox god which would seem to show that in the time of the great Taiko the Inari-fox and the demon fox were considered identical. This letter is still preserved at Nara, in the Buddhist temple called Todai-*ji*:

Kyoto, the seventeenth day of the third month.

To Inari Daimyōjin:

My Lord—I have the honour to inform you that a fox under your jurisdiction has bewitched one of my servants, causing her and others a great deal of trouble. I have to request that you will make minute inquiries into the matter, and endeavour to find out the reason of your subject misbehaving in this way, and let me know the result.

If it turns out that the fox has no adequate reason to give for his behaviour, you are to arrest and punish him at once. If you hesitate to take action in this matter, I shall issue orders for the destruction of every fox in the land.

Any other particulars that you may wish to be informed of in reference to what has occurred, you can learn from the high priest Yoshida.

Apologising for the imperfections of this letter, I have the honour to be,

Your obedient servant,

Hideyoshi *taikō*

But there certainly were some distinctions established in localities, owing to the worship of Inari by the military caste. With the samurai of Izumo, Inari, for obvious reasons, was a highly popular deity, and you can still find in the garden of almost every old shizoku residence in Matsue, a small shrine of Inari Daimyōjin, with little stone foxes seated before it. And in the imagination of the lower classes, all samurai families possessed foxes.

But the samurai foxes inspired no fear. They were believed to be 'good foxes', and the superstition of the *hito-kitsune* does not seem to have unpleasantly affected any samurai families of Matsue during the feudal era. It is only since the military caste has been abolished, and its name, simply as a body of gentry, changed to *shizoku*, that some families have become victims of the superstition through intermarriage with the *chōnin* or mercantile classes, among whom the belief has always been strong.

By the peasantry the Matsudaira *daimyō* of Izumo were supposed to be the greatest fox-possessors. One of them was believed to use foxes as messengers to Tokyo (be it observed that a fox can travel, according to popular credence, from Yokohama to London in a few hours), and there is some Matsue story about a fox having been caught in a trap near Tokyo, attached to whose neck was a letter written by the prince of Izumo only the same morning. The great Inari temple of Inari in the castle grounds—O-Shiroyama no Inari-*sama*—with its thousands upon thousands of foxes of stone, is considered by the country people a striking proof of the devotion of the Matsudaira, not to Inari, but to foxes.

It is no longer possible to establish distinctions of genera in this ghostly zoology, where each species grows into every other. It is not even possible to disengage the *ki* or soul of the fox and the August Spirit of Food from the confusion in which both have become hopelessly blended, under the name Inari by the vague conception of their peasant worshippers. The old Shintō mythology is indeed quite explicit about the August Spirit of Food, and quite silent on the subject of foxes. But the peasantry in Izumo, like the peasantry of Catholic Europe, make mythology for themselves. If asked whether they pray to Inari as to an evil or a good deity, they will tell you that Inari is good, and that Inari foxes are good. They will tell you of white foxes and dark foxes—of foxes to be reverenced and foxes to be killed—of the good fox which cries 'kon-kon,' and the evil fox which cries *kai-kai*. But the peasant possessed by the fox cries out, 'I am Inari—*Tamabushi no Inari!*'—or some other Inari.

Fox-Women

Goblin foxes are peculiarly dreaded in Izumo for three evil habits attributed to them. The first is that of deceiving people by enchantment, either for revenge or pure mischief. The second is that of quartering themselves as retainers on some family, and thereby making that family a terror to its neighbours. The third and worst is that of entering into people and taking diabolical possession of them and tormenting them into madness. This affliction is called *kitsune-tsuki*.

The favourite shape assumed by the goblin fox for the purpose of deluding mankind is that of a beautiful woman. Much less frequently the form of a young man is taken in order to deceive someone of the other sex. Innumerable are the stories told or written about the wiles of fox-women. And a dangerous woman of that class whose art is to enslave men, and strip them of all they possess, is popularly named by a word of deadly insult— *kitsune*.

Many declare that the fox never really assumes human shape, but that he only deceives people into the belief that he does so by a sort of magnetic power, or by spreading about them a certain magical effluvium.

The fox does not always appear in the guise of a woman for evil purposes. There are several stories, and one really pretty play, about a fox who took the shape of a beautiful woman, and married a man, and bore him children—all out of gratitude for some favour received—the happiness of the family being only disturbed by some odd carnivorous propensities on the part of the offspring. Merely to achieve a diabolical purpose, the form of a woman is not always the best disguise. There are men quite insusceptible to feminine witchcraft. But the fox is never at a loss for a disguise; he can assume more forms than Proteus. Furthermore, he can make you see or hear or imagine whatever he wishes you to see, hear, or imagine. He can make you see out of time and space; he can recall the past and reveal the future. His power has not been destroyed by the introduction of Western ideas, for did he not, only a few years ago, cause phantom trains to run on the Tōkaidō railway, thereby greatly confounding and terrifying the engineers of the company?

Like all goblins, the fox prefers to haunt solitary places. At night he is fond of making queer ghostly lights, in semblance of lantern fires, flit about dangerous places. To protect yourself from this trick of his, it is necessary to learn that by joining your hands in a particular way, so as to leave a diamond-shaped aperture between the crossed fingers, you can extinguish the witch fire at any distance simply by blowing through the aperture in the direction of the light and uttering a certain Buddhist formula.

But it is not only at night that the fox manifests his power for mischief: at high noon he may tempt you to go where you are sure to get killed, or frighten you into going by creating some apparition or making you imagine that you feel an earthquake. Consequently the old-fashioned peasant, on seeing anything extremely queer, is slow to credit the testimony of his own eyes. The most interesting and valuable witness of the stupendous eruption of Bandai-*san* in 1888—which blew the huge volcano to pieces and devastated an area of twenty-seven square miles, levelling forests, turning rivers from their courses, and burying numbers of villages with all their inhabitants—was an old peasant who had watched the whole cataclysm from a neighbouring peak as unconcernedly as if he had been looking at a drama. He saw a black column of ashes and steam rise to the height of twenty thousand feet and spread out at its summit in the shape of an umbrella, blotting out the sun. Then he felt a strange rain pouring on him, hotter than the water of a bath. Then all became black, and he felt the mountain beneath him shaking to its roots, and heard a crash of thunders that seemed like the sound of the breaking of a world. But he remained quite still until everything was over. He had made up his mind not to be afraid—deeming that all he saw and heard was delusion wrought by the witchcraft of a fox.

What Foxes Eat

Strange is the madness of those into whom demon foxes enter. Sometimes they run naked shouting through the streets. Sometimes they lie down and froth at the mouth, and yelp as a fox yelps. And on some part of the body of the possessed a moving lump appears under the skin, which seems to have a life of its own. Prick it with a needle, and it glides instantly to another place. By no grasp can it be so tightly compressed by a strong hand that it will not slip from under the fingers. Possessed folk are also said to speak and write languages of which they were totally ignorant prior to possession. They eat only what foxes are believed to like—*tōfu*, *aburage* (fried bean-curds), *azuki meshi* (red beans boiled with rice)—and they eat a great deal, alleging that not they, but the possessing foxes, are hungry.

220

It not infrequently happens that the victims of fox-possession are cruelly treated by their relatives—being severely burned and beaten in the hope that the fox may be thus driven away. Then the *yamabushi* is sent for—the exorciser. The exorciser argues with the fox, who speaks through the mouth of the possessed. When the fox is reduced to silence by religious argument on the wickedness of possessing people, he usually agrees to go away on condition of being supplied with plenty of *tōfu* or other food. The food promised must be brought immediately to that particular Inari temple of which the fox declares himself a retainer. For the possessing fox, by whomsoever sent, usually confesses himself the servant of a certain Inari though sometimes even calling himself the god.

As soon as the possessed has been freed from the possessor, he falls down senseless, and remains for a long time prostrate. And it is said, also, that he who has once been possessed by a fox will never again be able to eat *tōfu*, *aburage*, *azuki meshi*, or any of those things which foxes like.

Human Foxes

It is believed that the human fox (*hito-kitsune*) cannot be seen. But if he goes close to still water, his shadow can be seen in the water. Those 'having foxes' are therefore supposed to avoid the vicinity of rivers and ponds.

The invisible fox, as already stated, attaches himself to persons. Like a Japanese servant, he belongs to the household. But if a daughter of that household marry, the fox not only goes to that new family, following the bride, but also colonises his kind in all those families related by marriage or kinship with the husband's family. Now every fox is supposed to have a family of seventy-five—neither more, nor less than seventy-five—and all these must be fed. So that although such foxes, like ghosts, eat very little individually, it is expensive to have foxes. The fox-possessors (*kitsune-mochi*) must feed their foxes at regular hours, and the foxes always eat first—all the seventy-five. As soon as the family rice is cooked in the *kama* (a great iron cooking pot), the *kitsune-mochi* taps loudly on the side of the vessel, and uncovers it. Then the foxes rise up through the floor. And although their eating is soundless to the human ear and invisible to the human eye, the rice slowly diminishes. For these reasons it is fearful for a poor man to have foxes.

But the cost of nourishing foxes is the least evil connected with the keeping of them. Foxes have no fixed code of ethics, and have proved themselves untrustworthy servants. They may initiate and long maintain the prosperity of some family. But should some grave misfortune fall upon that family in spite of the efforts of its seventy-five invisible retainers, then these will suddenly flee away, taking all the valuables of the household along with them. And all the fine gifts that foxes bring to their masters have been stolen from somebody else. It is therefore extremely immoral to keep foxes. It is also dangerous for the public peace, inasmuch as a fox, being a goblin, and devoid of human susceptibilities, will not take certain precautions. He may steal the next-door neighbour's purse by night and lay it at his own master's threshold, so that if the next-door neighbour happens to get up first and see it there is sure to be a row.

Another evil habit of foxes is that of making public what they hear said in private, and taking it on themselves to create undesirable scandal. For example, a fox attached to the family of Kobayashi-*san* hears his master complain about his neighbour Nakayama-*san*, whom he secretly dislikes. Therewith the zealous retainer runs to the house of Nakayama-*san*, and enters into his body, and torments him grievously, saying, 'I am the retainer of Kobayashi-*san* to whom you did such-and-such a wrong, and until such time as he command me to depart, I shall continue to torment you.'

And last, but worst of all the risks of possessing foxes, is the danger that they may become wroth with some member of the family. Certainly a fox may be a good friend, and make rich the home in which he is domiciled. But as he is not human, and as his motives and feelings are not those of men, but of goblins, it is difficult to avoid incurring his displeasure. At the most unexpected moment he may take offence without any cause knowingly having been given, and there is no saying what the consequences may be.

Kitsune-mochi

For all these reasons, and, doubtless many more, people believed to have foxes are shunned. Intermarriage with a fox-possessing family is out of the question, and many a beautiful and accomplished girl in Izumo cannot secure a husband because of the popular belief that her family harbours foxes. As a rule, Izumo girls do not like to marry out of their own province, but the daughters of a *kitsune-mochi* must either marry into the family of another *kitsune-mochi*, or find a husband far away from the province of the gods. Rich fox-possessing families have not overmuch difficulty in disposing of their daughters by one of the means above indicated, but many a fine sweet girl of the poorer *kitsune-mochi* is condemned by superstition to remain unwedded. It is not because there are none to love her and desirous of marrying her—young men who have passed through public schools and who do not believe in foxes. It is because popular superstition cannot be yet safely defied in country districts except by the wealthy. The consequences of such defiance would have to be borne, not merely by the husband, but by his whole family, and by all other related families—which are consequences to be thought about!

Among men believed to have foxes there are some who know how to turn the superstition to good account. The country folk, as a general rule, are afraid of giving offence to a *kitsune-mochi*, lest he should send some of his invisible servants to take possession of them. Accordingly, certain *kitsune-mochi* have obtained great ascendancy over the communities in which they live. In the town of Yonago, for example, there is a certain prosperous *chōnin* whose will is almost law, and whose opinions are never opposed. He is practically the ruler of the place, and in a fair way of becoming a very wealthy man. All because he is thought to have foxes.

Wrestlers, as a class, boast of their immunity from fox-possession, and care neither for *kitsune-mochi* nor for their spectral friends. Very strong men are believed to be proof against all such goblinry. Foxes are said to be afraid of them, and instances are cited of a possessing fox declaring, 'I wished to enter into your brother, but he was too strong for me, so I have entered into you, as I am resolved to be revenged upon someone of your family.'

Chinomiya no Wakuri

The belief in foxes does not affect persons only: it affects property. It affects the value of real estate in Izumo to the amount of hundreds of thousands.

The land of a family supposed to have foxes cannot be sold at a fair price. People are afraid to buy it, for it is believed the foxes may ruin the new proprietor. The difficulty of obtaining a purchaser is greatest in the case of land terraced for rice fields, in the mountain districts. The prime necessity of such agriculture is irrigation—irrigation by a hundred ingenious devices, always in the face of difficulties. There are seasons when water becomes terribly scarce, and when the peasants will even fight for water. It is feared that on lands haunted by foxes, the foxes may turn the water away from one field into another, or make holes in the dikes and so destroy the crop.

There is no lack of shrewd men to take advantage of this queer belief. One gentleman of Matsue, a good agriculturist of the modern school, speculated in the fox-terror fifteen years ago, and purchased a vast tract of land in eastern Izumo which no one else would bid for. That land has sextupled in value, besides yielding generously under his system of cultivation, and by selling it now he could realise an immense fortune. His success, and his having been an official of the government, broke the spell: it is no longer believed that his farms are fox-haunted. But success alone could not have freed the soil from the curse of the superstition. The power of the farmer to banish the foxes was due to his official character. With the peasantry, the word 'Government' is talismanic.

Indeed, the richest and the most successful farmer of Izumo, worth more than a hundred thousand yen—Wakuri-*san* of Chinomiya in Kandegori— is almost universally believed by the peasantry to be a *kitsune-mochi*. They tell curious stories about him. Some say that when a very poor man he found in the woods one day a little white fox-cub, and took it home, and petted it, and gave it plenty of *tōfu*, *azuki meshi*, and *aburage*—the three sorts of food which foxes love—and that from that day prosperity came to him. Others say that in his house there is a special *zashiki*, or guest room for foxes, and that there, once in each month, a great banquet is given to hundreds of *hito-kitsune*. But Chinomiya no Wakuri, as they call him, can afford to laugh at all these tales. He is a refined man, highly respected in cultivated circles where superstition never enters.

When a Fox Knocks

When a *hito-kitsune* comes to your house at night and knocks, there is a peculiar muffled sound about the knocking by which you can tell the visitor is a fox—if you have experienced ears. For a fox knocks at doors with its tail. If you open, you will see a man, or perhaps a beautiful girl, who will talk to you only in fragments of words, but nevertheless in such a way that you can perfectly understand. A fox cannot pronounce a whole word, but parts only—as 'Nish... sa...' for 'Nishida-san'; 'de goz...' for 'de gozarimasu, or 'uch... de...?' for 'uchi desu ka?' Then, if you are a friend of foxes, the visitor will present you with a little gift of some sort, and at once vanish away into the darkness. Whatever the gift may be, it will seem much larger that night than in the morning. Only a part of a fox gift is real.

A Matsue *shizoku*, going home one night by way of the street called Horomachi, saw a fox running for its life pursued by dogs. He beat the dogs off with his umbrella, thus giving the fox a chance to escape. On the following evening he heard someone knock at his door, and on opening saw a very pretty girl standing there, who said to him, 'Last night I should have died but for your august kindness. I know not how to thank you enough: this is only a pitiable little present. And she laid a small bundle at his feet and went away. He opened the bundle and found two beautiful ducks and two pieces of silver money—those long, heavy, leaf-shaped pieces of money—each worth ten or twelve dollars—such as are now eagerly sought for by collectors of antique things. After a little while, one of the coins changed before his eyes into a piece of grass; the other was always good.

Sugitean-*san*, a physician of Matsue, was called one evening to attend a case of confinement at a house some distance from the city, on the hill called Shiraga-*yama*. He was guided by a servant carrying a paper lantern painted with an aristocratic crest. He entered into a magnificent house, where he was received with superb samurai courtesy. The mother was safely delivered of a fine boy. The family treated the physician to an excellent dinner, entertained him elegantly, and sent him home, loaded with presents and money. Next day he went, according to Japanese etiquette, to return thanks to his hosts. He could not find the house: there was, in fact, nothing on Shiraga-*yama* except forest. Returning home, he examined again the gold which had been paid to him. All was good except one piece, which had changed into grass.

Tōfuya

Curious advantages have been taken of the superstitions relating to the Fox-God. In Matsue, several years ago, there was a *tōfuya* which enjoyed an unusually large patronage. A *tōfuya* is a shop where *tōfu* is sold—a curd prepared from beans, and much resembling good custard in appearance. Of all eatable things, foxes are most fond of *tōfu* and of *soba*, which is a preparation of buckwheat. There is even a legend that a fox, in the semblance of an elegantly attired man, once visited Nogi no Kuriharaya, a popular *sobaya* on the lake shore, and ate much *soba*. But after the guest was gone, the money he had paid changed into wooden shavings.

The proprietor of the *tōfuya* had a different experience. A man in wretched attire used to come to his shop every evening to buy *tōfu*, which he devoured on the spot with the haste of one long famished. Every evening for weeks he came, and never spoke. But the landlord saw one evening the tip of a bushy white tail protruding from beneath the stranger's rags. The sight aroused strange surmises and weird hopes. From that night he began to treat the mysterious visitor with obsequious kindness. But another month passed before the latter spoke. Then what he said was about as follows:

'Though I seem to you a man, I am not a man; I took the human form only for the purpose of visiting you. I come from Taka-machi, where my temple is, at which you often visit. And being desirous to reward your piety and goodness of heart, I have come tonight to save you from a great danger. For by the power which I possess I know that tomorrow this street will burn, and all the houses in it shall be utterly destroyed except yours. To save it I am going to make a charm. But in order that I may do this, you must open your godown (*kura*) that I may enter, and allow no one to watch me, for should living eye look upon me there, the charm will not avail.'

The shopkeeper, with fervent words of gratitude, opened his storehouse, and reverently admitted the seeming Inari and gave orders that none of his household or servants should keep watch. And these orders were so well obeyed that all the stores within the storehouse, and all the valuables of the family, were removed without hindrance during the night. Next day the *kura* was found to be empty. And there was no fire.

There is also a well-authenticated story about another wealthy shopkeeper of Matsue who easily became the prey of another pretended Inari. This Inari told him that whatever sum of money he should leave at a certain *miya* by night, he would find it doubled in the morning—as the reward of his lifelong piety. The shopkeeper carried several small sums to the *miya*, and found them doubled within twelve hours. Then he deposited larger sums, which were similarly multiplied. He even risked some hundreds of dollars, which were duplicated. Finally he took all his money out of the bank and placed it one evening within the shrine of the god—and never saw it again.

Hiza-kuruge

Vast is the literature of the subject of foxes—ghostly foxes. Some of it is old as the eleventh century. In ancient romances and modern cheap novels, in historical traditions and in popular fairytales, foxes perform wonderful parts. There are very beautiful and very sad and very terrible stories about foxes. There are legends of foxes discussed by great scholars, and legends of foxes known to every child in Japan—such as the history of Tamamonomae, the beautiful favourite of Emperor Toba—Tamamonomae, whose name has passed into a proverb, and who proved at last to be only a demon fox with nine tails and a fur of gold. But the most interesting part of fox literature belongs to the Japanese stage, where the popular beliefs are often most humorously reflected—as in the following excerpts from the comedy of *Hiza-kuruge*, written by Jippensha Ikku:

> Kidahachi and Iyaji are travelling from Edo to Osaka. When within a short distance of Akasaka, Kidahachi hastens on in advance to secure good accommodations at the best inn. Iyaji, travelling along leisurely, stops a little while at a small wayside refreshment house kept by an old woman
>
> OLD WOMAN.—Please take some tea, sir.
>
> IYAJI.—Thank you! How far is it from here to the next town?—Akasaka?
>
> OLD WOMAN.—About one *ri*. But if you have no companion, you had better remain here tonight, because there is a bad fox on the way, who bewitches travellers.
>
> IYAJI.—I am afraid of that sort of thing. But I must go on, for my companion has gone on ahead of me, and will be waiting for me.
>
> [After having paid for his refreshments, Iyaji proceeds on his way. The night is very dark, and he feels quite nervous on account of what the old woman has told him. After having walked a considerable distance, he suddenly hears a fox yelping—*kon-kon*. Feeling still more

afraid, he shouts at the top of his voice:

IYAJI.—Come near me, and I will kill you!

Meanwhile Kidahachi, who has been frightened by the old woman's stories, and has therefore determined to wait for Iyaji, is saying to himself in the dark, 'If I do not wait for him, we shall certainly be deluded.' Suddenly he hears Iyaji's voice, and cries out to him:

KIDAHACHI.—O Iyaji-*san*!

IYAJI.—What are you doing there?

KIDAHACHI.—I did intend to go on ahead, but I became afraid, and so I concluded to stop here and wait for you.

IYAJI (who imagines that the fox has taken the shape of Kidahachi to deceive him).—Do not think that you are going to dupe me!

KIDAHACHI.—That is a queer way to talk! I have some nice *mochi* here which I bought for you.

IYAJI.—Horse dung cannot be eaten!

KIDAHACHI.—Don't be suspicious!—I am really Kidahachi.

IYAJI (springing on him furiously).—Yes! you took the form of Kidahachi just to deceive me!

KIDAHACHI.—What do you mean?—What are you going to do to me?

IYAJI.—I am going to kill you! (Throws him down.)

KIDAHACHI.—Oh! you have hurt me very much—please leave me alone!

IYAJI.—If you are really hurt, then let me see you in your real shape! (They struggle together.)

KIDAHACHI.—What are you doing?—putting your hand there?

IYAJI.—I am feeling for your tail. If you don't put out your tail at once, I shall make you! (Takes his towel, and with it ties Kidahachi's hands behind his back, and then drives him before him.)

KIDAHACHI.—Please untie me—please untie me first!

By this time they have almost reached Akasaka, and Iyaji, seeing a dog, calls the animal, and drags Kidahachi close to it, for a dog is believed to be able to detect a fox through any disguise. But the dog takes no notice of Kidahachi. Iyaji therefore unties him, and apologises, and they both laugh at their previous fears.

Pleasant Fox Gods

But there are some very pleasing forms of the fox god. For example, there stands in a very obscure street of Matsue—one of those streets no stranger is likely to enter unless he loses his way—a temple called Jigyoba no Inari, 'Earthwork's Inari' and also Kodomo no Inari, or 'the Children's Inari.' It is very small, but very famous, and it has been recently presented with a pair of new stone foxes, very large, which have gilded teeth and a peculiarly playful expression of countenance. These sit one on each side of the gate: the male grinning with open jaws, the female demure, with mouth closed. In the court you will find many ancient little foxes with noses, heads, or tails broken, two great *karashishi* before which straw sandals (*waraji*) have been suspended as votive offerings by somebody with sore feet who has prayed to the *karashishi-sama* that they will heal his affliction, and a shrine of Kojin, occupied by the corpses of many children's dolls.

The grated doors of the shrine of Jigyoba no Inari, like those of the shrine of Yaegaki, are white with the multitude of little papers tied to them, which papers signify prayers. But the prayers are special and curious. To right and to left of the doors, and also above them, odd little votive pictures are pasted on the walls, mostly representing children in bathtubs, or children getting their heads shaved. There are also one or two representing children at play. Now the interpretation of these signs and wonders is as follows:

Doubtless you know that Japanese children, as well as Japanese adults, must take a hot bath every day. Also that it is the custom to shave the heads of very small boys and girls. But in spite of hereditary patience and strong ancestral tendency to follow ancient custom, young children find both the razor and the hot bath difficult to endure, with their delicate skins. For the Japanese hot bath is very hot (not less than 110 degs F., as a general rule), and even the adult foreigner must learn slowly to bear it, and to appreciate its hygienic value. Also, the Japanese razor is a much less perfect instrument than ours, and is used without any lather, and is apt to hurt a little unless used by the most skilful hands. And finally, Japanese parents are not tyrannical with their children: they pet and coax, very rarely compel or terrify. So that it is quite a dilemma for them when the baby revolts against the bath or mutinies against the razor.

The parents of the child who refuses to be shaved or bathed have recourse to Jigyoba no Inati. The god is besought to send one of his retainers to amuse the child, and reconcile it to the new order of things, and render it both docile and happy. If a child is naughty, or falls sick, this Inari is appealed to. If the prayer be granted, some small present is made to the temple— sometimes a votive picture, such as those pasted by the door, representing the successful result of the petition. To judge by the number of such pictures, and by the prosperity of the temple, the Kodomo no Inani would seem to deserve his popularity. Even during the few minutes I passed in his court I saw three young mothers with infants on their backs come to the shrine and pray and make offerings. I noticed that one of the children—remarkably pretty—had never been shaved. This was evidently a very obstinate case.

While returning from my visit to the Jigyoba Inani, my Japanese servant, who had guided me there, told me this story:

The son of his next-door neighbour, a boy of seven, went out to play one morning, and disappeared for two days. The parents were not at first uneasy, supposing that the child had gone to the house of a relative, where he was accustomed to pass a day or two from time to time. But on the evening of the second day it was learned that the child had not been at the house in question. Search was at once made, but neither search nor inquiry availed. Late at night, however, a knock was heard at the door of the boy's dwelling, and the mother, hurrying out, found her truant fast asleep on the ground. She could not discover who had knocked. The boy, on being woken, laughed, and said that on the morning of his disappearance he had met a lad of about his own age, with very pretty eyes, who had coaxed him away to the woods, where they had played together all day and night and the next day at very curious funny games. But at last he got sleepy, and his comrade took him home. He was not hungry. The comrade promised 'to come tomorrow.'

But the mysterious comrade never came, and no boy of the description given lived in the neighbourhood. The inference was that the comrade was a fox who wanted to have a little fun. The subject of the fun mourned long in vain for his merry companion.

Tengu

Some thirty years ago there lived in Matsue an ex-wrestler named Tobikawa, who was a relentless enemy of foxes and used to hunt and kill them. He was popularly believed to enjoy immunity from bewitchment because of his immense strength. But there were some old folks who predicted that he would not die a natural death. This prediction was fulfilled:

Tobikawa died in a very curious manner. He was excessively fond of practical jokes. One day he disguised himself as a *tengu*, or sacred goblin, with wings and claws and long nose, and ascended a lofty tree in a sacred grove near Rakusan, whither, after a little while, the innocent peasants thronged to worship him with offerings. While diverting himself with this spectacle, and trying to play his part by springing nimbly from one branch to another, he missed his footing and broke his neck in the fall.

Science

But these strange beliefs are swiftly passing away. Year by year more shrines of Inari crumble down, never to be rebuilt. Year by year the statuaries make fewer images of foxes. Year by year fewer victims of fox-possession are taken to the hospitals to be treated according to the best scientific methods by Japanese physicians who speak German. The cause is not to be found in the decadence of the old faiths: a superstition outlives a religion. Much less is it to be sought for in the efforts of proselytising missionaries from the West—most of whom profess an earnest belief in devils. It is purely educational. The omnipotent enemy of superstition is the public school, where the teaching of modern science is unclogged by sectarianism or prejudice; where the children of the poorest may learn the wisdom of the Occident; where there is not a boy or a girl of fourteen ignorant of the great names of Tyndall, of Darwin, of Huxley, of Herbert Spencer. The little hands that break the Fox-god's nose in mischievous play can also write essays on the evolution of plants and about the geology of Izumo. There is no place for ghostly foxes in the beautiful nature-world revealed by new studies to the new generation. The omnipotent exorciser and reformer is the *kodomo*—the child.

Glossary

abunai:	Dangerous.
amacha:	Herbal tea made from fermented leaves.
amado:	Siding shutter.
amazake:	Sweet rice wine.
ameya:	Candy store.
an:	Straw hat.
andon:	Paper-covered lamp stand.
awabi:	Abalone.
azukimeshi:	Festive meal made with rice and red beans.
baba:	Old woman.
bekka :	Sacred fire.
beppin:	Beautiful woman.
bettō:	Footman.
biwa:	Four- or five-stringed lute.
bokkuri:	Wooden clogs with supports at least five inches high.
bosatsu:	Bodhisattva.
butsudan:	Household Buddhist altar.
butsuma:	Buddhist family altar room.
chaya:	Teahouse.
chōnin:	Mercantile classes.
daikon:	Radish (*Raphanus sativus var. longipinnatus*).
dainagon:	High officer in the ancient imperial court.
dango:	Dumpling made of rice flour.
daimyō:	Feudal lord.

dohyōba:	Wrestling ring.
enoki:	Chinese hackberry (*Celtis sinensis*).
fumibako:	Lacquered box used to keep letters in.
fusuma:	Sliding door covered with thick paper.
gaki:	Dead who, because of their bad conduct in life, are made to suffer from hunger in hell.
gan-hodoki:	Love sacrifice.
geimyō:	Artistic name.
gengebana:	Herb planted only for fertilizing purposes.
geta:	Wooden clogs.
gohei:	Sacred wand.
goshiki:	Five colors.
guji:	Head priest of a shrine.
haiden:	Chapel.
haka:	Grave.
hakaba:	Graveyard.
hakama:	Skirt-like trousers.
hankō:	Woodcut.
haori:	Lightweight silk jacket worn by men.
hashi:	Chopsticks.
hibachi:	Small Japanese charcoal heating appliance somewhat resembling a brazier.
hime:	Princess.
hina:	Doll.
hinoki:	Japanese cypress (*Chamaecyparis obtusa*).
hiragana:	Japanese syllabary consisting of 46 base characters used for words other than *kanji* and grammatical inflections.
hito-kitsune:	Human fox
hokku:	First seventeen syllable line of a *renga*.
hotoke:	Buddha.
imori:	Water newt.
innen:	Fate.
jinja:	Shintō shrine.
jinrikisha:	Rickshaw.
jishaku:	Magnet.

jitsumyō:	One's real name.
jorō:	Prostitute.
joroya:	Brothel.
jōshi:	Love suicide.
jukusha:	School buildings.
kageoni:	Children's game, lit., 'Shadow and the demon.'
kago:	Litter.
kaimyō:	Posthumous (Buddhist) name.
kakemono:	Hanging scroll.
kakitsubata:	Japanese iris (*Iris laevigata*).
kami:	God(s).
kamiarizuki:	The month of the gods.
kamiyo:	Land of the ancient gods.
kannushi:	Shintō priest.
katakana:	Japanese syllabary consisting of 46 base characters used for transcription of foreign language words.
kawarake:	Unglazed earthen sake cup.
karashishi:	Stone lions found at (the entrance) of shrines.
karō:	Councilor to a feudal lord.
kashi:	Cake or confectionery.
kengyō:	Ancient shrine supervisor.
keyaki:	Japanese elm (*Zelkova serrata*).
ki:	Soul or spirit.
kichinyado:	Cheap inn catering to the poor.
kimono:	Traditional female garment.
kitsu:	Good fortune.
kitsune:	Fox.
kitsune-mochi:	Fox-possessor.
kobiki:	Sawyer.
kokuzō:	Shrine supervisor.
koku:	Measure, equal to about 5 bushels, used also as a measure of land assessment
komageta:	Wooden sandals.
kometsuki:	Rice polisher.
koshiobi:	Under-girdle.

kotoita:	Traditional Shintō instrument made of wood.
kubioke:	Head-rest for the display of decapitated heads.
kura:	Storehouse.
kuruma:	Vehicle, drawn by either by man or animal.
kurumaya:	Runner who draws a *kuruma*.
kusunoki:	Camphor tree.
kyō:	Evil.
ma:	Goblin.
machi:	Stiff pasteboard sewn into the waist of the *hakama* at the back, so as to keep the folds of the garment perpendicular and neat-looking.
mahōtsukai:	Wizard.
mamori:	Paper charm.
manji:	Buddhist swastika.
matsuri:	Festival.
mayoi:	Illusion.
meibutsu:	Special (local) product.
mekusangokko:	Children's game; a sort of blindman's buff.
miko:	Shrine maiden.
mikuji:	Portable shrine.
mino:	Rain coat made from straw.
misohagi:	Purple loosestrife (*Lythrum anceps*).
mizuame:	Candy.
miya:	Shintō shrine.
mochi:	Rice cake.
mokugyo:	Wooden drum (in a Buddhist temple).
mukaebi:	Welcome-fire.
mon:	Gate.
myōji:	Family name.
nekomata:	Phantom in the guise of a cat.
niō:	Muscular statues of the Buddha standing at the entrance of Buddhist temples.
nobori:	Streamer.
nogitsune:	Wild fox.
obi:	Broad sash for a *kimono*.

odori:	Dance.
ofuda:	Good luck charm.
ogara:	Peeled hemp sticks.
ogi:	Tiny quadruple fan sliding in a sheath.
oni:	Devil(s).
ondo-tori:	Leader of the dance.
onigokko:	Children's game, lit., 'Game of the devil.'
renga:	Series of poems composed by several poets.
ri:	3.9 km.
rin:	One-thousandth of a yen.
rokushaku(obi):	Simple girdle of roughly six feet long.
rōnin:	Masterless samurai.
rōsoku:	Candle.
ryōgu:	Boiled (temple) food.
ryōsen:	Fishing boat.
sakaki:	Flowering evergreen tree native to warm areas (*Cleyera japonica*).
sake:	Japanese rice wine.
sakura:	Cherry blossom.
sama:	Mr., Miss., or Mrs. More formal than the suffix *san*.
same:	Shark.
sanbō:	Small wooden offering stand.
sando-wara:	Small straw mat.
saru:	Monkey.
sanya-bukuro:	Wallet.
sayōnara:	Good-bye.
segaki:	Offerings for the repose of the soul of the dead.
sekirei:	Wagtail.
sen:	One-hundredth of a yen.
sendo-mairi:	Visit a temple one thousand times.
shaku:	Regal wand.
shakujō:	Crozier.
shamisen:	Three-stringed musical instrument.
shamusho:	Shrine office.
shari:	Relic of Buddha.

shikimi:	Five colors.
shimenawa :	Twisted straw rope with stripes of zigzag-shaped white paper streamers (shide) that are hung around an object to ward off evil spirits.
shinjū:	Love suicide.
shintai:	Body of the deity.
shizoku:	Nobility.
shōgun:	Hereditary military ruler during Japan's feudal era.
shōji:	Lightweight sliding doors covered with paper.
shōjin-gu:	Uncooked food.
shokudai:	Candle stand.
shōryōbune:	Spirit boats.
shu:	(Religious) sect.
sobaya:	*Soba* shop.
sōmen:	Thin white noodles made of wheat flour.
sotoba:	Symbolic *stupa* of a long thin board to be set up behind a tombstone in memory of the dead.
suika:	Watermelon.
suzu:	Hollow Japanese Shinto bell that contains pellets that sound when shaken.
tabi:	Traditional socks with pouches separating the big toe from the four other toes.
taikō:	Retired regent, used specifically for Toyotomi Hideyoshi.
takageta:	Wooden clogs with supports at least five inches high.
tanabiku:	Shelving.
tatami:	Straw mat roughly six by three feet.
ten:	The shortest stroke, or rather a dot, used in writing *kanji*.
tengu:	Bird-like type of legendary creatures found in Japanese folk religion.
tennin:	Heavenly beings.
tera:	Temple.
tōfu:	Bean curd.
tōfuya:	*Tōfu* shop.
tomoe:	Symbol resembling two huge commas so united as to make a perfect circle.

tonbo:	Dragonfly.
torii:	Gateway built at the entrance to a Shintō shrine.
tōrō:	Stone lantern.
tsue:	Walking stick.
tsubaki:	Japanese camellia (*Camellia japonica*).
tsuzumi:	Hand drum of mainland origin.
uguisu:	Japanese bush warbler (*Horornis diphone*).
ujigami:	(Shrine of) a tutelary deity.
ujiko:	People under the protection of the local tutelary deity.
uri:	Melon.
waraji:	Straw sandal.
wasan:	Buddhist psalm.
yadoya:	Inn.
yama:	Mountain.
yamabushi:	Exorciser.
yaneshōbu:	Roof plant.
yashiki:	Samurai mansion.
yobina:	Calling name.
yodarekake:	Infant bib.
yōraku:	Stringed ornaments used to decorate Buddhist effigies.
yukata:	Informal light cotton *kimono*.
zashiki:	Best and largest room of a Japanese dwelling.
zen:	Small lacquered table.
zōri:	Japanese sandals made of rice straw.
zuijin:	Ghostly retainers of the gods.

Index

TOYO REFERENCE SERIES
SAMURAI TRAILS

LUCIAN SWIFT KIRTLAND
EDITED BY WILLIAM DE LANGE

TOYO REFERENCE SERIES
TRAVELING JAPAN'S DEEP INTERIOR

ISABELLA LUCY BIRD
EDITED BY WILLIAM DE LANGE

TOYO REFERENCE SERIES
AN ARTIST'S LETTERS FROM JAPAN

JOHN LA FARGE
EDITED BY WILLIAM DE LANGE

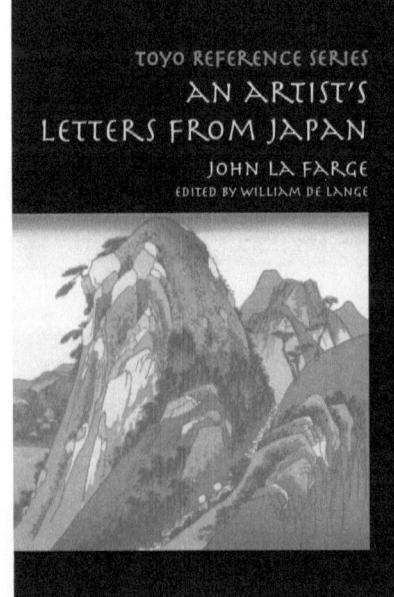

TOYO REFERENCE SERIES
JAPAN'S CRITICAL YEARS

ERNEST SATOW
EDITED BY WILLIAM DE LANGE

TOYO PRess: Explore Dream Discover

Editorial supervision: William de Lange. Book and cover design:
Chōkei Studios. Printing and binding: IngramSpark. The typefaces
used are Perpetua, Prescript, and Herculanum.